Profit Opportunities In Commercial and Industrial Real Estate

Weldon Girard

Prentice-Hall, Inc.
Englewood Cliffs, NJ

Prentice-Hall International, Inc., *London*
Prentice-Hall of Australia, Pty. Ltd., *Sydney*
Prentice-Hall of Canada, Ltd., *Toronto*
Prentice-Hall of India Private Ltd., *New Delhi*
Prentice-Hall of Japan, Inc., *Tokyo*
Prentice-Hall of Southeast Asia Pte. Ltd., *Singapore*
Whitehall Books, Ltd., *Wellington, New Zealand*

Library of Congress Cataloging in Publication Data

Girard, Weldon
  Profit opportunities in commercial and industrial real estate.

  Includes index.
  1. Real estate investment. I. Title.
HD1375.G57   332.6'324   78-23611
ISBN 0-13-726075-X

Printed in the United States of America

Dedication

To my wife, Jean, who is always there when I need her

Also by the author:

How to Make Big Money Selling Commercial and Industrial Property

About the Author

Weldon Girard is the owner of his own successful real estate company in Phoenix, Arizona and has personally sold in excess of one million dollars in commercial and industrial real estate every year since being in the business.

Specializing in the sale and development of prime commercial and industrial property, he is a consultant to large corporations, an advisor to major investors and a lecturer on real estate at universities and colleges. With his vast experience, he has handled many multimillion dollar land transactions, developed shopping centers, apartment projects, office buildings, industrial tracts and even a golf course.

He is a Realtor member of the National Board of Realtors, the Phoenix Board of Realtors and the Arizona Association of Realtors. In addition, he is a member of the prestigious President's Round Table, as a result of his outstanding sales achievements.

His twenty years of practical, down-to-earth real estate experience is very much in evidence in his first book, *How to Make Big Money Selling Commercial and Industrial Property,* Prentice-Hall, Inc. 1977. It is widely accepted by real estate brokers and salesmen, and continues to increase their knowledge, efficiency and commissions.

What This Book Can Do For You

The successful real estate entrepreneur who just made $500,000 on a single commercial real estate transaction was not just lucky; neither was he born with the ability to make money, nor was that ability given to him as a gift. He was smart. Studying and analyzing the commercial and industrial market, he developed the ability to recognize and evaluate a property with high profit potential. Through the application of established procedures, he concluded an advantageous purchase. Then, with a practical knowledge of marketing techniques, he structured the sale of that property, resulting in the amazing profit of $500,000.

The profit opportunities available today in commercial and industrial real estate are limited only by the capabilities of the investor. There are untold millions of dollars of such property just waiting for that astute and knowledgeable person who can recognize and evaluate an investment that can yield the maximum return on his invested dollars.

This book will explain why commercial and industrial income property is not only a good investment but *the best* investment by showing you how to *provide sheltered income* through the use of *applicable tax procedures* allowing *deductions for depreciation, interest, fees,* and other necessary and related operating expenses. *No other investment can provide such flexibility* with an *assured income over a long period of time*—not the stock market, or the commodity market or the currency exchanges.

The ability to recognize, evaluate and structure the purchase of an income producing commercial or industrial property which will provide the security of an assured income over a long period of time is the desire of many. *To the sophisticated investor, such knowledge is essential.* In this book, I'll show you in clear, concise, step-by-step procedures how to accomplish that desire and become that sophisticated investor.

In addition to tax shelters and an assured income, I'll whet your appetite with other advantages that are available to that knowledgeable real estate investor in commercial and industrial income producing properties. A few such advantages are:

1. Tax-free cash flow
2. Gain in equity through amortization
3. Acceptable yield on invested capital
4. Appreciation in value
5. Hedge against inflation.

Also, I'll show you *how profit opportunities are available in other types of commercial and industrial real estate* and *how such investments can be equally as appealing to you as the investor.* In addition, I'll show you how, by proper planning and zoning, the value of a parcel of land can be increased two, five or even ten times its purchase price.

Included in this book are the *procedures, guidelines,* and *practices* that will enable you not only to improve your knowledge and techniques in commercial and industrial investing but also to assist you in *developing your own investment program,* one which will point the way to success and *greater riches.* The following are some examples of the practical ideas you'll find:

A CLOSE LOOK at commercial and industrial real estate investing;

PROVEN METHODS and STRATEGIES in investing for PROFIT—showing not only what to buy and how to find it but how to make the purchase;

The technique of STRUCTURED FINANCING—increasing PROFITS and making money work for you;

BIG PROFITS from LITTLE DOLLARS—providing an insight to commercial and industrial investments;

PROFIT OPPORTUNITIES in APARTMENT INVESTMENT—giving dependable guidelines in analyzing and evaluating an apartment investment;

LAND as a REAL PROFIT MAKER—showing procedures and methods to use in planning a MULTIPLE SALES project;

SHOPPING CENTERS—the highly PROFITABLE and very FLEXIBLE investment, outlining the technique of buying a shopping center giving checklists and proven practices to use;

REDEVELOPMENT—converting PROBLEMS to PROFIT, showing profit opportunities for the creative and innovative investor.

There are many other profit opportunities discussed in this book giving you ideas and concepts on the sophisticated approach to commercial and industrial investments . . . leases and leaseholds for profit and growth . . . medical centers, though costly, can be profitable . . . investing or speculating . . . industrial investments for secured income . . . profitable investments in neighborhood office buildings bringing the building to the tenants . . . proven development procedures for greater profits . . . carefree profit opportunities with stores, shops and service buildings . . . trading strategies that bring big profits . . . the necessity of an appraisal and the importance of comparables . . . an insight on how the IRS views investing in real estate . . . the advantages of the industrial park, proving the concept of profit and beauty . . . plus other timely and important subjects shown in detail. Throughout the book are *actual examples* and *case histories* of the procedures followed by successful investors in making their commercial and industrial investments.

By following the principles and procedures shown in this book, you, too, can become an astute and knowledgeable investor. *You will gain the ability to recognize and evaluate a good investment* and you will know *how to get the most out of your invested dollars*—whether you buy with a pride of ownership or based entirely upon that bottom line.

Just remember, the way to make money investing in commercial and industrial real estate is to structure the purchase for the greatest yield while minimizing its risks. The purpose of this book is to show you how to do just that.

Good luck.

Weldon Girard

ACKNOWLEDGEMENT

I want to thank my daughter, Doris, for her help and assistance in the preparation and writing of this book. I was indeed fortunate to have her working with me.

CONTENTS

1

A Close Look at the Profit Opportunities in Commercial and Industrial Real Estate

Investing in commercial and industrial property can be a most rewarding and exciting phase of real estate. For the knowledgeable and astute investor, profit opportunities are everywhere—in apartments, office buildings, shopping centers, stores, shops, service buildings, medical buildings, industrial warehouses, distribution centers, land, farms, ranches, industrial parks, plus commercial and industrial lots.

In this chapter, we will discuss a broad view of the many profit opportunities in commercial and industrial investments, including how many investors made it big in different types of real estate, with examples of numerous actual transactions. The advantages of a secure income, an explanation of tax shelters in income property, the significance of appreciation in property values, and how the recovery of capital investment is made through depreciation, are all briefly explained. Additional case examples amplify the main thrust of each section. We will give you an insight into the importance of acceptable yields and will outline the principles of real estate investing, whether buying or selling.

A BROAD VIEW OF THE PROFIT OPPORTUNITIES IN COMMERCIAL AND INDUSTRIAL INVESTMENTS

Before showing you specific details of investing in various segments of commercial and industrial real estate, it is beneficial to know the many profit opportunities today in every phase of this profit-producing market.

Investing in commercial and industrial real estate can be divided into two separate and distinct classifications of property, itemized as follows:

1. Income producing properties
2. All other, classified as commercial and industrial

Typical examples of income producing properties are:

1. Apartments
2. Office Buildings
3. Shopping Centers
4. Stores, Shops and Service Buildings
5. Medical Buildings
6. Industrial Warehouses
7. Distribution Centers
8. Manufacturing Complex

Other types of real estate classified as commercial and industrial include:

1. Land
2. Farms
3. Ranches
4. Commercial Lots
5. Industrial Lots
6. Industrial Parks
7. Mobile Home Parks
8. Commercial and Multiple Acreage
9. Industrial Acreage

As you can see, commercial and industrial real estate covers a vast market with unlimited profit opportunities available to the knowledgeable investor. To those who want to invest for a secure, tax-sheltered income, properties are available in different types of income producing real estate. For others who want to develop and sell, make a capital gain profit through buying and selling, or package a property for others to develop, other types of commercial and industrial property offer many profit opportunities.

The old adage "It takes money to make money" is very true in commercial and industrial investments. *The secret of success is in structuring your investment to provide the greatest yield with the minimum risk.*

HOW MANY INVESTORS MADE IT BIG IN DIFFERENT TYPES OF REAL ESTATE TRANSACTIONS

To whet your appetite and to show you how other investors have made big profits in the many opportunities available in commercial and industrial real estate, some actual examples will be explained.

There is an investor/builder who specializes in apartment building. In one complex, recently, he constructed 104 units consisting of studios and one-bedroom apartments. His total cost including land was $984,000. After renting the units he placed the complex on the market for sale at $1,475,000, which would provide another investor with a solid 10 percent yield on his cash invested. The sales price was determined by capitalizing the net rental income before anticipated debt service. He had learned in previous transactions that building, renting and then selling the units provided a far greater profit than if he had added a normal builder's profit to his cost and then sold the complex—a difference in this transaction of nearly $300,000 more to the investor.

How a $20,000 option was converted to more than $5,000,000 in profit

Another very knowledgeable investor converted a $20,000 option on a large ranch into a tremendous multi-million dollar profit. This was accomplished by selling the ranch to one of the largest land development corporations in the country. Instead of selling the ranch at a set price per acre, which would have been the customary method of selling, his sale was a contingent amount based upon a percentage of their gross sales. When their gross sales hit $100,000,000 his percentage was a staggering $5,000,000 and the company had only developed and sold about 75 percent of the ranch.

How an investor increased his equity by "trading up"

Many investors begin their real estate investment career by making a small investment. One such investor began by purchasing a small 2,400 square foot building on an arterial street for $48,000. His down payment was only 10 percent and the rent from the tenant not only serviced the debt but provided a 10 percent yield on his down payment. After a few years, higher rent and appreciation in the value of the property had increased its valuation to $96,000. By using the increase in value and accrued equity, the investor traded the property into a larger, better building valued at $300,000, using his increased equity as the down payment. It was not too long until his original investment of $4,800 had increased in equity value in the new building to an astounding $75,000. In addition, his cash flow had grown from a beginning $480 to nearly $7,000 a year.

There are big profits in small strategically located parcels

A wise investor once told me that he liked to buy land—not large pieces but strategically located smaller parcels in the path of future development. He explained that he would go out beyond where land was valued at a price per square foot, beyond where it sold at a price per front foot, to where it could be purchased on an acre basis. He then showed me his latest transactions wherein he had purchased a five acre corner for $5,000 per acre or a total price of $25,000. As development approached he re-evaluated his property to a price of $150 per front foot and based upon its 660 foot frontage, its new value was $99,000. Then he had sold the five acre corner at its present valuation. Since his initial investment was only $3,750 representing a 15 percent down payment, he was very pleased with the high profit he had made on his capital invested.

Using leverage and tax shelters for tremendous profits

Office buildings present an excellent profit opportunity for the astute investor, not necessarily as a high, single-shot, profit item, but as a solid investment producing an acceptable cash yield and a much needed tax shelter. One such classic example is worth repeating. A group of high-income doctors purchased a large office building which was owned at the time by a tax-exempt organization. The purchase price was $2,500,000 subject to an existing mortgage with an approximate current balance of $1,100,000 amortized at $133,020 per year. They purchased the property with $300,000 down and gave a second mortgage to the selling institution in the amount of $1,100,000 payable annually, interest only at the rate of 8 percent per annum with the principal amount due in 10 years. After allowing for a 10 percent vacancy factor and after deducting current operating expenses, the building showed an operating profit of $251,100. Payment of the debt service including the amortization of the first mortgage and interest on the second mortgage, the cash flow was a little over $30,000, or a respectable yield of 10 percent. In recommending the purchase to the doctors, their accounting firm had calculated that in addition to the cash flow, the building would show a book loss of over $100,000 per year in the early years of ownership, thereby creating a badly needed tax shelter. The $130,000 gain, a combination of book loss and tax-sheltered cash flow, was an excellent return on the $300,000 invested.

An innovative technique for acquiring a farm for future development

There are many profit opportunities to be found in the purchase, development and resale of strategically located farm land. Many investors have referred to farms as the ideal investment. They provide for an income producing holding action while development proceeds by leasing the land for continued farming. About 10 years ago a group of investors, knowing that a certain area in Northwest Phoenix was destined to grow since it was in the path of development, purchased a section of 640 acres about three miles beyond where farm land was currently being purchased at the going price of $1,500 per acre. In negotiating the purchase, the investors offered the land-owning farmer that same price per acre even though it was considered a little high for a section three miles to the north. The terms of their offer made the difference. Their offer included a down payment of $100,000 plus five years prepaid interest calculated at an annual rate of 5 percent with principal and interest payments to begin in five years and extending over the next ten years. They required that the farmer lease the land for those first five years at the rate of $75 per acre per year, totaling $48,000 each year. During the first five years, their investment totaled $315,000 with the $100,000 down payment and $215,000 in prepaid interest. The lease income produced a yield of 15.2 percent, but more importantly, the land appreciated during those five years.

The first sale to a home builder was for 80 acres at a price of $3,750 per acre and succeeding sales were made to other builders at increasing prices until the last 80 acre parcel was sold for $6,250 per acre. In less than two years, they had sold the entire section to builders for a total sales price of $3,200,000 representing a gross profit of $2,240,000 on an investment of $315,000, most of which was in tax deductible prepaid interest. In addition, they received $240,000 in lease income during those first five years.

How to use the purchase/leaseback technique for greater profits

While the situation doesn't present itself too often, the enterprising and innovative investor can find profit opportunities in purchase/leaseback transactions. One astute investor was always interested in industrial and manufacturing plants for his investment portfolio. Finding a manufacturing plant that fabricated items for the construction business, he structured a purchase/leaseback transaction wherein he purchased the facility at its appraised value of $840,000 and then leased the property to the sellers for $7,000 per month, net-net-net, with the tenant paying, in addition to the rent, all real estate taxes, insurance and maintenance. His plan of purchase included a down payment of $240,000 and securing a new mortgage in the amount of $600,000 to be amortized at 8¼ percent for 25 years. After payment of the debt service, he realized a cash flow of $27,230, representing an excellent yield of 11.34 percent on his cash invested. In addition, the investment provided the other advantages of sheltered income. The sellers were satisfied because they still operated their successful business at the same place. Since the depreciation base on the property had been reduced over the years, their income taxes had proportionately increased. By selling the property and leasing it back, they received not only $840,000 in cash but also they were now able to charge off the rent against income—a substitution for the early years of depreciation.

The technique of packaging industrial acreage for developers

Industrial acreage offers additional profit opportunities to the informed investor. Industrial developers are always in the market for well-located parcels of land having access to rail, freeways and truck routes. One investor packages such parcels for those developers. One small transaction last year involved the purchase of 20 acres of land. Since the property was in an area of industrial development near truck routes and the freeway systems, he was able to rezone the property for industrial use. His purchase price was $10,000 per acre but later, after securing industrial zoning, he was able to sell the parcel to an industrial developer for $15,000 per acre on convenient terms which would permit the development of the land into a small industrial park. By selecting a well-located parcel of land and obtaining industrial zoning, the investor was able to make an excellent profit on the transaction of $100,000, less certain costs of selling and attorney fees. Not bad for a short term investment.

How an investor specialized in "build to suit" profit opportunities

There is a demand for free-standing stores and shops that are well located on highly traveled arterial streets. Since it is most difficult to find a suitable building, another investor makes a specialty of providing such facilities for qualified tenants in a "build to suit" program. One transaction required that the investor provide a furniture store for an established chain. After being provided with a financial statement and a current operating statement of their furniture business, the investor was satisfied with the financial stability and operating capability of his future tenant. Following the selection of the location for the store and the preparation of preliminary plans, the architect gave an estimated cost of construction based upon the size of the building, floor plan and other related features required by the tenant.

The investor next met with a mortgage company to determine the availability and cost of a new mortgage. He knew that with the financial statement of the tenant, plus his own financial condition, it would not be difficult to arrange a more than satisfactory mortgage commitment by capitalizing the lease income. The investor knew the costs of the necessary component parts to his transaction—land, construction, financing. After adding a profit to provide the yield he wanted, a monthly rental amount was determined. After the lease was prepared and executed, the property was purchased and construction commenced. The investor was satisfied with this transaction because he was able to practically mortgage out and not have to put up very much of his own cash.

How an investor used the prepaid interest technique for a tremendous profit

There are times when a good property can be purchased on extreme terms if the investor has the "nerve" to submit such an offer. One investor was not bashful in a transaction that was not necessarily unusual but resulted in a big profit on his invested cash. He located a large commercial lot in a "hot" area near the intersection of two major arterials in the heart of this area. The property was owned by an insurance company and was adjacent to their headquarters building. They wanted to sell the lot but mainly wanted to change its status from land owned to a mortgage receivable. Their asking price was more or less consistent with the area. Anticipating an increase in valuation of all lots in the area, this investor made an offer slightly less than their asking price but with extreme terms. The offer was accepted and the escrow closed upon payment of an amount equivalent to one year's prepaid interest, with the total purchase price secured by a $70,000, 20 year, 7 percent amortized mortgage, with payment to begin one year from the close of escrow. Within that next year, the investor sold the lot for $120,000, representing a quick profit of $50,000 on an investment of $4,900 in prepaid interest.

Making it big with a series of real estate transactions—an actual case history

As has been shown in this section, it is interesting to discover how different investors go about their business of making big profits in commercial and industrial real estate—how they explore and exploit the many profit opportunities available to them. Without exception, the successful investors have a definite investment plan which guides their actions and decisions. One such investor could also be called a "developer." His specialty was building shopping centers, not to own and operate but to sell. He always purchased more land than was required for the shopping center, knowing that the value of his adjacent land would appreciate considerably in value following the construction of the shopping center. Instead of reciting his plan in detail, an actual example of how he does it will be described in the following series of transactions.

The investor purchased a 20 acre parcel of land which was situated on a main artery, slated for development into a combination of a shopping center, commercial buildings and apartments. After a master plan of the property had been completed and zoning granted, the escrow was closed at the total purchase price of $800,000.

Following the execution of leases with the major tenants, plans and specifications were completed and construction of the shopping center was commenced on approximately eight acres of the property. During this construction phase, one of the corners of the remaining property was sold to an oil company for a service station at a price of $100,000. Another corner was sold to a bank for $75,000.

Later, before construction of the center had been half completed, 174,240 square feet of commercially zoned lots were sold at a price of $3.00 per square foot. About 60 days before completion of the center, the remaining six acres of land were sold to another developer who planned to construct deluxe apartments on the site. The price was $40,000 per acre. With the sale of the apartment land, the success of the investment was assured. All of the remaining land had been sold for a total value of $937,720. After allocating a proportionate cost of land, the gross profit, before sales and other expenses, was a whopping $457,720.

Following his detailed investment plan, the shopping center was completed and opened for business. After an analysis of its income and an evaluation of its value, the shopping center was sold a short time later for $2,100,000.

The following statement indicates the degree of success enjoyed by this investor:

Income from sales		
Service Station Site	$ 100,000.00	
Bank Site	75,000.00	
Commercial Lots	522,720.00	
Apartment Land	240,000.00	
Shopping Center	2,100,000.00	
Total sales income		$3,037,720.00
Expenses		
Cost of construction	$1,200,000.00	
Land	800,000.00	
Other costs—sales, legal interest, financing, etc.	347,000.00	
Total expenses and costs		2,347,000.00
Profit		$ 690,720.00

Not every venture turns out to be so profitable, but the opportunity is there for those who have the knowledge and financial skill required in commercial and industrial investing.

THE ADVANTAGES OF A SECURE INCOME

The sophisticated and knowledgeable investor whose income is derived from the ownership of commercial or industrial income producing real estate, is convinced that his investment is not only a good investment but also is the best investment. The knowledge that his income is secured by an advantageous lease (providing not only tax, insurance and maintenance increases, but also percentage factors which will increase the income through greater sales and/or a rise in the rate of inflation) permits him to realize one of the advantages of an assured income.

The security of income in one investment, permitting an investment in another commercial or industrial property without fear of jeopardizing one or the other, is another advantage to an astute investor.

The beauty of a secure income

One can also say that "peace of mind" is yet another distinct advantage of a secured income.

One sophisticated investor was interested only in investments which provided an assured income over a long period of time with an acceptable yield and with little or no risks involved. When I asked which he considered his best investment, he told me of the following transaction.

A number of years ago he purchased a large industrial warehouse leased to a national grocery chain on a triple net basis. The purchase was structured to provide a yield of 12 percent, which was an excellent return at the time. Due to the escalation provisions of the lease, the rental income has increased to a point where the yield has also increased to nearly 20 percent, and the value of the building has nearly doubled. A new lease is now being negotiated upon terms which will further increase the yield. This has proven to be an excellent investment and without question is his best investment.

THE BENEFITS OF TAX SHELTERS IN INCOME PROPERTY

An astute real estate investor is familiar with the advantages of tax shelters since they provide the guidelines whereby many of his investments are made. Whether or not an investment is good or bad tax-wise can make the difference in whether that investment is made in a particular property or a sale is made at a specific time.

There are two income figures of interest to every investor. One is *Cash Spendable Income,* more commonly referred to as *Cash Flow,* and the other is *Taxable Income.*

Cash Spendable Income or Cash Flow is determined in a very simple manner. After adding all income, deduct allowable operating expenses including real property taxes and insurance. From that resulting figure, which is called Net Operating Income, further deduct all debt service paid. This bottom line figure is called Cash Spendable Income. It represents the actual cash left after paying all operating and capital expenses.

Taxable income is determined by deducting from Net Operating Income all interest expense on the debt plus the allowance for depreciation. The resulting figure is Taxable Income or Loss. From this figure, the tax liability is calculated.

Since the combination of interest expense and depreciation is usually much larger in the early years of ownership than the amortized payment on the debt, Cash Spendable Income is a much larger amount than the Taxable Income. Many times, Cash Spendable Income can be sizeable, while Taxable Income may be a negative figure, indicating a loss.

Therefore *maximum tax shelters are created when capital losses, resulting from the application of allowable deductions, are used to offset income.* Such tax shelters will diminish as the allowable deductions decrease, until such time as amortization of the debt service is greater than the combined total of interest expense and depreciation. This is the reason why some investors will retain an income property in their portfolio for only seven or eight years, or until the investment no longer creates the desired tax shelter.

Sheltered income is most important to many investors. Each has his own program for investing. Some, with a large ordinary income, can be interested in income producing properties that just break even cash-wise, but show a sizeable operating loss. Such loss can then be used to offset other ordinary income. Others are interested in properties that create a negative cash flow while showing a huge capital loss. To them, adding a little money each year to maintain the investment in a fluid condition is a small amount to pay for such huge capital losses.

Tax laws governing income and taxes are continually changing. Each change plugs another loophole in tax regulations. The 1976 Tax Reform Act closed so many loopholes in tax shelters of other types of investments that real estate is the only desirable tax shelter left. It is, therefore, always advisable and recommended that a tax accountant be consulted regarding the latest and most up-to-date changes in the tax laws before any transaction is considered.

How an investor used a small cash flow and a big tax loss to his advantage

Many investors with large ordinary incomes are interested only in investments which will provide tax shelters. Whether the cash flow is positive or negative or breaks even is of little importance to them as long as the investment can offset a portion of their ordinary income with a book loss on the investment. One such investor considered apartments to be the type of investment most suited for this purpose. Not long ago, he purchased an apartment complex for $570,000, having a current mortgage balance of $340,000 amortized at $3,021 per month. His down payment was $60,000 and he gave a second mortgage to the seller for $170,000, payable in monthly payments of $2,107.80 for the next ten years bearing interest at the rate of 8½ percent per annum. The rental income of the apartments was $95,500, with operating expenses totaling $33,020, leaving an operating profit of $62,480. The combined payment on the two mortgages totaled $61,545.60 resulting in a Cash Flow of only $935.

While the Cash Flow was small, the book loss on the operation of the apartments for the first year was $27,520, which could be used to offset other income. To him this represented a good return on his $60,000 investment, not counting the $16,000 he gained in equity.

THE SIGNIFICANCE OF APPRECIATION IN PROPERTY VALUES

Appreciation is a term used in real estate meaning an increase in value. This is especially true in commercial and industrial property. Such appreciation can be caused by the following conditions:

1. Economic factors
2. Times
3. Change in use
4. Rezoning
5. Other development

Economic factors can directly influence the appreciation of a commercial or industrial property. An increase in the income produced will definitely increase the value of a property. Inflation is another economic factor that keeps driving prices and values up and up. Any change in the tax laws to the advantage of the owner of an income producing property can also make that property more valuable and desirable.

Time is another economic factor. In a rising economy such as our country has been experiencing over the past number of years, time will automatically appreciate the value of all real estate.

A change in use can appreciate the value of an income producing commercial or industrial property, especially if such change increases the income produced by that property. What was a sour lemon as an old theatre building can turn into a sweet orange when it is converted to a junior department store.

Rezoning can probably cause the greatest appreciation in potential commercial and industrial real estate. A given parcel of land, when its zoning is changed from single-family residential to commercial, can appreciate in value from, for example, $5,000 to $6,000 per acre to maybe $3.00 per squre foot—a change in value to $130,000 per acre.

Other developments in an area can most significantly appreciate the value of commercial and industrial real estate. The proximity of a good shopping center can appreciate the value of an apartment complex. Likewise, a shopping center will enhance in value as more apartments are built in its vicinity.

As the owner of commercial or industrial real estate, you should periodically determine the appreciation in your property. It is always wise to know the current market value of your investment. The most reliable and acceptable method to determine value is to have the property appraised by a competent and reliable real estate appraiser. He takes the guesswork out of trying to arrive at a true value, and his appraisal can be used for many purposes.

THE MAGIC OF DEPRECIATION

Depreciation is the magic word to all real estate investors and is much sought after. Being the opposite of appreciation, it means a decrease or fall in value.

By following provisions in our complex tax structure, the owner of improved commercial or industrial real estate may deduct a portion of the value of his investment each year in computing his tax liability. The process can be quite complicated, so we will just discuss the high spots and recommend that a tax accountant be consulted to prepare your final tax return.

To begin, only the improvements placed upon a property may be depreciated. According to the IRS, land does not depreciate, so the value of the land can never be included in the value of the property to be depreciated.

The best method and probably the most beneficial to the taxpayer in determining the percentage factor to use in calculating depreciation is the component method. In this procedure the useful life of each component part of the improvement: building, air conditioning, electrical facilities, plumbing, elevator, paving, etc. is determined and its percentage factor established. A composite percentage rate is then determined. In all cases, this method results in a higher percentage factor than the method whereby the entire improvement is treated as one unit. It is readily understandable that the higher the percentage factor the larger the deduction for depreciation.

In calculating depreciation your accountant will probably use one of the following methods:

1. Straight Line
2. 200% Declining Balance
3. 150% Declining Balance

Each method is designed to accomplish certain results within stipulated limitations imposed by the Internal Revenue Service, and the one to use is that which best suits your purpose. Therefore, it should be readily understandable why depreciation is so important to investors in all types of income producing commercial and industrial real estate. *It is the only method approved by the IRS which permits an investor to recapture the cost of his investment.* That's what makes investing in this type of real estate so attractive and profitable.

One knowledgeable investor always has his accountant determine the depreciable value of a proposed investment and calculate the approximate amount of depreciation which may be deducted each year. It has a direct bearing upon his analysis and evaluation of the property under consideration.

THE IMPORTANCE OF ACCEPTABLE YIELDS FOR ALL TYPES OF COMMERCIAL AND INDUSTRIAL PROPERTY

One of the most widely used words in investment terminology is "yield." The term is expressed as a percentage and represents the rate or amount of return an investor receives on his investment dollars. It can be expressed as a cash on cash yield or an amount including other things which are not tangible such as the gain in equity through amortization.

Astute investors in commercial and industrial real estate have established in their investment programs certain yields or rates of return that are acceptable for various types of property. Their acceptable yields will vary with the type of property, the problems of maintenance and management, the risks of ownership, the amount of personal time required, the economy of the country, the value and cost of money and other timely factors which will help determine the amount of yield each will expect from that particular property. All of their decisions are based upon experience and history. Some will buy with a pride of ownership without regard to the economic factors, but most will make their decision entirely upon that bottom line that indicates to them a sound and secure investment.

A complete list of acceptable yields for all types of commercial and industrial real estate will be given in Chapter 2, along with a short, descriptive analysis of each yield.

THE PRINCIPLES OF REAL ESTATE INVESTING ARE IMPORTANT IN BUYING OR SELLING

Investing in commercial and industrial real estate have proven most successful for many investors. In every instance their investment programs included certain principles by which they made their decisions. Predominant principles are:

1. Have a thorough knowledge of the property under consideration
2. Be cognizant of the market value of the property
3. Be thoroughly familiar with all aspects of financing procedures
4. Structure the purchase to create the maximum yield with the minimum risks
5. Use every tax advantage permitted under current tax laws
6. Employ the services of competent and reliable specialists, such as real estate broker, appraiser, lawyer, and accountant
7. Have the necessary financial capability
8. Know what should be done with the property

Having a thorough knowledge of the property under consideration requires much time and effort. All information relative to the physical property along with detailed income, expense and debt service of the property must be obtained. Such information is available at one or more of the following sources:

1. Public records
2. Title companies
3. Real estate brokers
4. Owner of the property
5. Personal inspection of the property

It will be explained in the following chapter how to use a detailed Checklist in preparing a Fact and Information Profile on the property. From an intelligent study of the information provided in the profile, all pertinent data relative to the property becomes known.

Being thoroughly familiar with all aspects of financing procedures is another important principle—one which requires an understanding of financing techniques and knowledge of how to use such techniques to make additional profits. In Chapter 3, you will be shown 25 ways to finance the purchase or sale of a commercial or industrial property.

Structuring the purchase to create maximum yield with the minimum of risk is the goal and desire of many. This can be accomplished through the use of innovative financing techniques and purchasing procedures that are designed to minimize the risk factor while increasing yield. This very specialized technique is described in subsequent chapters as it applies to various types of commercial and industrial real estate.

Use every tax advantage permitted under current tax laws. An understanding of the tax laws as they apply to your investment future is essential. It has been established over the years that in nearly all investment decisions, taxes play an important role. When to buy or sell—what to buy or sell—how to buy or sell—whether to buy or sell are all decisions that can be influenced by the tax implications of each situation. Every investor should seek the advice and counsel of his accountant or lawyer regarding these and other decisions relative to the taxation which can result from actions taken.

Employ the services of competent and reliable specialists such as: a real estate broker, appraiser, lawyer and/or accountant. There are times when it is advisable and recommended that the services of one or more of these specialists be used. In addition, the services of a professional appraiser may be required to establish a value for many purposes.

Have the necessary financial capability. Whether it is having the available cash necessary to conclude the purchase or the financial stability to secure a mortgage, your financial capability is most important. Never enter into a purchase agreement unless you have the means to fulfull your end of the transaction.

Know what should be done with the property. Your investment technique should include not only procedures necessary in purchasing or selling property, but also, knowledge of what should be done with the property after it has been acquired. Should the property be retained and operated for its tax-sheltered income or resold at a profit? Your investment knowledge should be broad enough in scope to answer these and other important questions.

KEY POINTS

1. Know available profit opportunities
2. Understand how other investors made big profits

3. Realize the many advantages of a secure income
4. Have an understanding of tax shelters in commercial and industrial property
5. Keep abreast of appreciation in real estate
6. Know how to use depreciation
7. Realize the importance of acceptable yields
8. Have a thorough knowledge of the principles of real estate investing

2

How to Recognize and Evaluate a Good Profit Opportunity

In this chapter, we will learn how to recognize and evaluate good profit opportunities in commercial and industrial real estate. Proven methods used in obtaining detailed and factual information on each investment and how to check and utilize public records will be outlined and explained in detail. We will discuss not only what to look for but also how to find properties, with guidelines and procedures to use, followed by dependable techniques and checklists that will explain how to evaluate a potential investment. Positive guidelines in determining the value of an income property are given and a simple method in how to capitalize an income investment is fully explained. Also, a complete checklist of acceptable yields for all types of commercial and industrial property along with a short, descriptive explanation of each yield is given. The technique of evaluating land through the use of comparables and the importance of the professional appraisal are described. Throughout the chapter are case examples of how other investors utilized their techniques and knowledge for bigger profits.

PROVEN METHODS USED IN OBTAINING DETAILED FACTUAL INFORMATION ON EACH INVESTMENT

The first principle of investing in commercial and industrial real estate, *having a thorough knowledge of the property under consideration,* is most important and essential. Detailed, factual information regarding any property can be obtained from a number of different sources. Listed below are several sources and the type of information that can be obtained from each.

Title companies

Title companies can provide a wealth of necessary and essential information on any parcel of real estate situated within the area serviced by that company. They will be cooperative and helpful since their business is built upon escrows and title policies resulting from real estate transactions. The information provided by them includes a plat of the property showing size, shape, and physical dimensions, ownership with names and addresses, and legal description. At a small charge a Condition of Title Report can be provided which will indicate not only most of the aforementioned information, but also will show all indebtedness and to whom owed, easements, restrictions and anything else recorded against the property.

Public records

In addition to the information provided by the title companies, an inspection of public records will show other information regarding the property. The importance of this fact-finding segment of your investment program is more fully described in the following section of this chapter.

Real estate brokers

If the investment has been presented to you by a real estate broker for your consideration, he can be the source of most of the essential information required. The securing of the information from the title company can be delegated to him. Also, in accordance with the provisions of his listing agreement with the owner of the property, he can furnish all required financial, income, expense and debt information needed as well as the conditions of purchase.

Owner of the property

In the event it is your desire not to work with or through a real estate broker, certain information can only be obtained from the owner. He can provide complete financial and operating data to include total (1) income and expense, (2) existing debt with current information as to amount and to whom owed along with amortization payments and rate of interest, (3) real estate taxes, (4) insurance, (5) leases, and other information needed and required. Also, as the owner of the property, he can state the price, terms and conditions under which he will sell the property.

Personal inspection of the property

All physical information must be checked and verified by a personal inspection of the property. All information provided by the owner should be checked and verified pertaining to construction and maintenance of the property, along with the spaces occupied by all tenants in accordance with the terms of their respective leases. Always make your own personal inspection to verify the accuracy of information provided by others.

HOW TO CHECK AND UTILIZE PUBLIC RECORDS

All legal instruments and documents of any importance relating to the proposed investment are recorded against the property. Such documents could include but not necessarily be limited to the following:

1. Deeds
2. Trust Agreement
3. Partnership Agreement
4. Mortgages
5. Liens and other encumbrances
6. Sales and other agreements
7. Easements
8. Restrictions
9. Mineral and other rights
10. Options
11. Assignments
12. Leases

As you can see, a lot of factual information can be gleaned from a study of public information recorded against any property. All you need to know is the legal description of the property, where to look, and how to find it.

Where to look is simple. Such information is recorded in Books of Record at the County Recorder's Office in the county seat of every county. Each recording is entered by number on a daily basis against the legal description of the property.

Ask for the book containing the legal description of the property to be checked. Opening the book to the last and most recent entry, check the legal description column and, each time the legal description of the property appears, make a note of that entry. You can continue to work back in time, making a note of every entry until you have as much information as is needed. If you want copies made of any particular entry, such copies can be made from microfilm data. By the time you leave the Recorder's Office, you will have all of the recorded information available to that very day.

Other public records can provide additional information on the property. The amount of real estate taxes assessed against the property can be provided by the Tax Assessor's Office. Again, by using the legal description of the property, the amount of taxes can be determined by simply asking one of the employees at the information desk in that office. Zoning information can be provided by the Planning and Zoning Department of the city or county in which the property is located.

WHAT TO LOOK FOR AND HOW TO FIND GOOD COMMERCIAL AND INDUSTRIAL PROPERTY

An investment in commercial or industrial property is usually made for one of the following reasons:

1. Income
2. Resale for profit
3. Development for either income or resale for profit

After the reason for the investment has been determined, the type of property most suited must be found and evaluated.

Chapter 1 explained how commercial and industrial real estate is divided into two separate and distinct classifications of property, income producing and all other types. For purposes of analyzing, checking and evaluating such property, a classification system has proven most effective with identifying numbers given to each type of property as shown below:

1. Apartments
2. Office Buildings
3. Shopping Centers
4. Stores, Shops and Service Buildings
5. Medical Buildings
6. Industrial Warehouses
7. Distribution Centers
8. Manufacturing Complexes
9. Land
10. All other types

By a study of the various types of property, a decision can be made as to the type of property most suitable for investment and one that will produce the greatest profit.

Since you have determined the type of property most suitable, how to find that good commercial or industrial property becomes the next step. One of the most expeditious and effective methods in locating a desirable property is to utilize the services of a competent and reliable real estate broker. He is not only knowledgeable about all types of available commercial and industrial property, but can also provide all of the essential information to enable the investor to make the right decision. On the other hand, talking to people in the business, title companies, mortgage people, attorneys, banks, accountants and friends can provide information that will lead to a good investment property. Studying the classified ad section of your local newspaper can also provide information on available property.

Being able to look at a property and see more than appears to the eye is an ability that has to be developed. The property has to be analyzed not only from the standpoint of what can be seen but also from the standpoint of what can be done with it to produce more profit. To develop this capability a continued use and study of reliable methods in determining the suitability of a property is required. Step 1 in this process is to itemize all known information relative to the property being analyzed. This requires a detailed checklist, that includes questions relating to all aspects of the property. Opposite each question are classification numbers representing the various types of commerical and industrial property applicable to that question.

Such a checklist is shown below, using classification numbers as shown in this section.

PROPERTY ANALYSIS CHECKLIST

	Question	Applicable Type of Property
1.	Price	1-2-3-4-5-6-7-8-9-10
2.	Description of Property	1-2-3-4-5-6-7-8-9-10
3.	Location of Property	1-2-3-4-5-6-7-8-9-10
4.	Type of Construction	1-2-3-4-5-6-7-8-x-x
5.	Land Area—Dimensions (sq. ft. or acres)	1-2-3-4-5-6-7-8-9-10
6.	Present Zoning	1-2-3-4-5-6-7-8-9-10
7.	Size of Building—Rentable Area	1-2-3-4-5-6-7-8-x-x
8.	Number of Units—Type	1-2-3-4-5-6-7-8-x-x
9.	Parking Facilities	1-2-3-4-5-6-7-8-x-x
10.	Services Provided	1-2-3-4-5-6-7-8-x-x
11.	Furnishings	1-x-x-x-x-x-x-x-x-x
12.	Income and Operating Expenses	1-2-3-4-5-6-7-8-x-x

	Question	Applicable Type of Property
13.	Taxes and Insurance	1-2-3-4-5-6-7-8-9-10
14.	Encumbrance—Where—How Much	1-2-3-4-5-6-7-8-9-10
15.	Amortization—Term—Rate of Interest	1-2-3-4-5-6-7-8-9-10
16.	Tenants—Leases—Rate—Term	1-2-3-4-5-6-7-8-x-x
17	Location of Existing Water—Sewer—Power	x-x-x-x-x-x-x-x-9-10
18.	Quality of Area—Surrounding Developments	1-2-3-4-5-6-7-8-9-10
19.	Distances to: City Business Area Employment Centers Airport—Rail—Bus Highway—Freeways	1-2-3-4-5-6-7-8-9-10
20.	Public Transportation	1-2-3-4-5-6-7-8-9-10
21.	Nearest Shopping Center—Describe	1-x-3-4-x-x-x-x-9-x
22.	Schools—Nursery—Elementary—High— College—Parochial	1-x-x-x-x-x-x-x-9-10
23.	Churches—Denomination—Distance	1-x-x-x-x-x-x-x-9-10
24.	Existing Easements on Property	x-x-x-x-x-x-x-x-9-x
25.	Population Within 1 Mile 2 Miles 3 Miles	x-2-3-4-5-x-x-x-9-10

A smart investor can recognize the importance of the foregoing questions as they relate to any investment being considered. This checklist should be prepared and analyzed before any decision is made.

Step 2 requires that a Fact and Information Profile be made on each property from information gathered in the checklist. Every question in which the numbered classification of that property appears should be answered. This profile is then used in the process of selecting the desired investment property.

A Fact and Information Profile on a large apartment complex can be prepared by referring to the Property Checklist and answering all questions containing the figure 1.

A sample profile is shown below.

FACT AND INFORMATION PROFILE
INDIAN CASCADES—DATED 7/1/77 OWNER: CASCADES, INC.

1. Price—$825,000.00
2. Description of Property—Lots 1 and 2, Unit 1, Indian Heights
3. Location of Property—21st Lane and Indian Road
4. Type of Construction—Block and Wood Batten
5. Land Area—Approximately 2 acres
6. Present Zoning—R-4
7. Size of Buildings—Rentable Area—Two 24 Unit Buildings
8. Number of Units—Types—12 Studios—24 1-Bedrm—12 2-Bedrm
9. Parking Facilities—1 Space per Unit—Guest parking

10. Services Provided—All utilities paid by Lessor
11. Furnishings—All units furnished
12. Income and Expenses—
    Total Income $131,674.00
    Total Expenses 47,402.00
13. Taxes and Insurance —Taxes— 11,800.00
    Insurance — 900.00
14. Encumbrance — $572,350.00—Western Bank
15. Amortization — 61,662.00 annual—8¾%—25 yrs.
16. Tenants—Leases—Rates—See attached rental schedule
18. Quality of area—Medium income
19. Distances to—City business area—6 miles
    Employment center—3 miles
    Airport—bus—rail—6 miles—9 miles
20. Public Transportation—Indian Road
21. Nearest Shopping Center—2 miles
22. Schools—2 miles College—1 mile Elementary and High
23 Church—1 mile

It is readily understandable how such a Fact and Information Profile can greatly assist every real estate investor in making the right decision.

HOW TO EVALUATE A POTENTIAL INVESTMENT WITH DEPENDABLE TECHNIQUES AND CHECKLISTS TO USE

From an intelligent study of the Fact and Information Profile, a property may be recognized as being a potentially good profit opportunity. However, another step is required before the potentially good property can be recognized as a good commercial or industrial investment. This next step involves a detailed evaluation.

There are different methods used in evaluating the two classifications of commercial and industrial property. This section describes the technique used to evaluate an income producing property.

Step 3 requires the use of an Income Analysis and Evaluation Form to determine the quality and performance of an income property. A sample form is shown below:

INCOME ANALYSIS AND EVALUATION

Type of Property: Dated:
Location:
Owner:
Total Listed Price:

Current Mortgage Balance:		
Amortization:		
Cash Required:		
Total Rental Income		
Operating Expenses:		
Taxes		
Insurance		
Maintenance		
Repair and Replacement		
Management		
Utilities		
Miscellaneous		
Total Operating Expenses		
Operating Profit		
Less Debt Service		
Cash Spendable Income		
Gain in Equity		
Total Gain		
Yield—Gain in Cash		%
Total Yield		%

This Income Analysis and Evaluation Form provides a space to indicate all income from whatever source. Following are spaces to show all operating expenses by type and amount, including real estate taxes and insurance. By the deduction of operating expenses from income, an Operating Profit can be shown.

Using information obtained from the Fact and Information Profile, the Income Analysis can be completed. The debt service amount is then deducted from the Operating Profit, resulting in a cash flow which is referred to as Cash Spendable Income.

The Gain in Equity, which is the amortized payment on the debt less interest, is then added to the Cash Spendable Income. The resulting amount represents the Total Gain in that particular property.

There are now two figures which interest a prospective investor—Cash Spendable Income and Total Gain. These two figures must be further related to the amount of cash the investor is expected to invest in the property. Each result will be described as yield and will be represented as a percentage. To arrive at the percentage figures, the amount of cash invested is divided into the Cash Spendable Income for the Cash on Cash Yield, and into the Total Gain for the Total Yield.

As an example, the following represents an Income Analysis and Evaluation on the apartment complex described in the foregoing Fact and Information Profile:

Total Listed Price	$825,000.00	
Current Mortgage Balance	572,350.00	
8¾%—5,138.50 Mo. P+I		
Cash Required	$252,650.00	
Total Rental Income	131,674.00	
Total Operating Expenses	47,402.00	
Operating Profit		$84,272.00
Less Debt Service		61,662.00
Cash Spendable Income		22,610.00
Gain in Equity		10,620.00
Total Gain		33,230.00
Yield—Cash on Cash		8.94%
Total Yield		13.15%

The following steps have now been used in evaluating an income producing property:

Step 1—Preparation of a Detailed Checklist
Step 2—Fact and Information Profile
Step 3—Income Analysis and Evaluation to determine:

1. Operating Profit
2. Cash Spendable Income
3. Gain in Equity
4. Total Gain
5. Yield—Cash on Cash
6. Total Yield

How a smart investor used the Income Analysis and Evaluation technique to prepare an offer

A smart investor studied the Income Analysis and Evaluation of the apartment complex and made the following offer. The total purchase price was to be $750,000, payable by assuming the existing mortgage balance and paying $177,650 at the close of escrow. By capitalizing the Cash Spendable Income at 13 percent and adding the resulting amount to the current mortgage balance, the investor arrived at a price of $746,273 which he rounded off to $750,000. This was done by dividing the Cash Flow of $22,610 by the desired yield of 13 percent, resulting in the capitalized amount of $173,923 plus the current mortgage balance of $572,350. When the seller was hesitant about accepting the offer, the investor explained that he wanted a yield of 13 percent on his invested capital, and by adding the capitalized cash flow to the current mortgage, the offered price produced the yield he wanted.

The seller agreed that 13 percent would be an excellent yield. However, he countered with another line of reasoning. He also knew that Cash Spendable Income was determined by deducting debt service from Operating Profit. Therefore, since the debt service was predicated upon an original mortgage of $625,000, that amount should be added to the capitalized Cash Flow. Therefore, his counter-offer was $795,000, a little less than his figures indicated. Quickly calculating the effect of this new price, the investor came up with a yield of 10.1 percent. This was still not good enough, so he made one more offer, capitalizing the Cash Flow at 12 percent but again adding the current mortgage balance. His final offer of $760,000 was accepted by the seller.

POSITIVE GUIDELINES IN DETERMINING THE VALUE OF AN INCOME PROPERTY

Many rules of thumb have been applied to an income property to determine its value. One such rule is that if an apartment complex can be purchased at an amount equivalent to 6½ times its annual gross rental, it is a good buy.

Rules of thumb are convenient but not always accurate

This rule is no longer applicable, however, because of the high cost of money, the high cost of operations, and high taxes. For example, an investor was interested in an apartment complex which consisted of one and two-bedroom unfurnished units having an average monthly rental of $225. It was fully rented with an annual income of $97,200. Using the 6½ times gross, its listed price was $630,000. The original mortgage was $470,000, amortized 25 years at 9 percent interest, and with a current mortgage balance of $410,000. The operating expenses totalled $34,992, including real estate taxes and insurance, representing an amount equivalent to 36 percent of gross income. Such a percentage factor was consistent with apartment expenses in the area.

The results of the Income Analysis and Evaluation are shown below:

Total Listed Price		$630,000.00
Current Mortgage Balance		410,000.00
Cash Required		$220,000.00
Total Rental Income	$97,200.00	
Total Operating Exenses	34,992.00	

Operating Profit	62,208.00
Less Debt Service	47,332.00
Cash Spendable Income	$14,876.00
Gain in Equity	5,180.00
Total Gains	$20,056.00
Yield—Cash on Cash	6.76%
Total Yield	9.11%

Since investors in today's market expect a yield—cash on cash—of between 13 percent and 15 percent, this is not a good investment at its listed price. After looking at his Income Analysis, the investor made an offer of $525,000 wanting to make a yield of 13 percent on his cash invested. His offer was determined by using the figures available. The Cash Spendable Income of $14,876 was divided by the yield he wanted—13 percent. This resulted in a total of $114,430 which was added to the mortgage balance of $410,000. The total of $524,430 was adjusted to $525,000, and that was his offer. The owner countered at $535,000, which was acceptable to the investor. By calculation, he determined that he could make 12 percent on his cash at this new price, and since he liked the apartments, the transaction was finalized.

While the owner of these apartments wanted to sell them at a price based upon an out-dated rule of thumb, its ultimate purchase was determined by a more sophisticated method. Rules of thumb are fast and convenient but not always accurate. In the acquisition of any type of income property, whether it be apartments, office buildings, warehouses, shopping centers or a medical complex, the numbers are important. All sophisticated investors want to look at that bottom line on the operating statement.

Through experience, certain guidelines have been established to assist the investor to determine the value of an income property. These guidelines take the guesswork out of establishing the value of an income producing commercial or industrial property.

ACCEPTABLE YIELDS

The following guidelines indicate the range of acceptable yields of cash on cash that investors expect in various types of income property, along with remarks regarding each type.

APARTMENTS 13%–15%

Due to a fluctuating income resulting from vacancies and seasonal rentals, plus rising operational and management costs against a competitive rental market, an investor wants a higher yield on this type of investment.

OFFICE BUILDINGS 10%–13%
Those with a history of high occupancy—well built in a prime location—are in demand. Others are marginal. One that meets the requirements of the investor is expected to yield within this range.

SHOPPING CENTERS 8%—11%
Good shopping centers are in demand today and are acceptable at a lower yield than other types of income property. The quality of the major tenants and the ratio of national to local tenants determine the variance in acceptable yields. Operational and management costs are proportionately low, resulting in a reasonably high operating profit.

STORES, SHOPS and SERVICE BUILDINGS 13%—15%
Those located on arterial streets in populated areas are in demand. However, the quality of the tenants determines the high yield requirement.

MEDICAL BUILDINGS 10%—13%
A special type of building, and costly to construct. Rents are high, as are operational costs. A very good investment when priced within this range.

INDUSTRIAL WAREHOUSES and DISTRIBUTION CENTERS 9%—12%
The quality of the tenant and the terms of the lease determine the high and low yield. A very desirable investment especially with a triple net lease.

MANUFACTURING COMPLEX 10%—13%
Not the usual type of investment. Its single purpose facility requires a higher yield, but with a good tenant on an advantageous lease, the investment could be considered satisfactory to excellent.

The foregoing apartment example explained how to equate a Cash Spendable Income with a property value by dividing an acceptable yield into the income. To some, multiplying is easier than dividing, so listed below are factors that can be used to achieve the same result.

Desired Yield	Multiplying Factor
8%	12.5
8½%	11.764
9%	11.11
9½%	10.526
10%	10
11%	9.09
12%	8.33
13%	7.693
14%	7.142
15%	6.666

To illustrate, the figures used in the apartment analysis will be repeated:

The desired yield of 13 percent was divided into the Cash Spendable Income of $14,876, resulting in a total of $114,430. By using the multiplying factor for 13 percent of 7.693 times $14,876, a total of $114,441 results.

Any multiplying factor can be determined by dividing the desired yield into 100.

A SIMPLE METHOD FOR CAPITALIZING AN INCOME INVESTMENT

Another word frequently used in real estate terminology is CAPITALIZE, meaning to compute the present value of income over an extended period of time. This procedure is used to determine the value of an income producing property as was shown in the previous example. In that instance, the investor divided the desired yield into the Cash Spendable Income and then added the amount of the existing mortgage to that resulting figure to arrive at a valuation of the property.

This method can sometimes result in a distorted value if the existing mortgage balance is disproportionately low. To explain, the same figures, but with a much smaller mortgage balance, will again be used:

Total Listed Price		$630,000.00
Current Mortgage Balance		270,000.00
Cash Required		360,000.00
Total Rental Income	$97,200.00	
Total Operating Expenses	34,992.00	
Operating Profit		62,208.00
Less Debt Service		47,332.00
Cash Spendable Income		14,876.00
Gain in Equity		23,300.00
Total Gain		38,176.00
Yield—Cash on Cash		4.13%
Total Yield		10.60%

Following the same procedure as before, the Cash Spendable Income is divided by the adjusted yield of 12 percent resulting in a figure of $123,966, but this time it is added to a smaller mortgage balance of $270,000. This procedure indicates a value of $393,966, which is obviously a distorted value since the property actually sold for $535,000.

To prevent this from happening, another simple method of capitalization in which financing, amortization or mortgage balances are not considered can be used. This method simply capitalizes the Operating Profit as if no debt existed on the property. To explain this simple method, the same example will again be used. The Operating Profit of $62,208 is divided by the yield of 12 percent, resulting in a valuation of $518,400. As you can readily see, this method produces a value slightly under $535,000 previously computed by the other method. Therefore, it is wise to compute the valuation of an income producing property using both methods.

THE TECHNIQUE OF EVALUATING LAND THROUGH THE USE OF COMPARABLES

An entirely different technique must be used in evaluating land. Since its value is influenced by various factors—location, zoning, size, shape, and topography—the only acceptable method is by Land Valuation through the use of Comparables. This is the method used by all appraisers. *Step 1* and *Step 2* as set forth under the procedure for Income Property are also applicable to the evaluation of land. *Step 3* of this method requires that the sale of a number of comparable properties in the same general area be analyzed. This information is available at the title plant of all title companies and can be found in their Plat Books which are kept up to date, day by day. From these Plat Books and recorded documents, the sales price of each comparable property can be determined. The same information is also available at the County Recorder's Office.

Step 4. The sales price of the comparable should then be reduced to a common denominator, one that can be applied to the property being evaluated. If the property is a commercial or industrial lot, the comparable price should be on a square foot basis. For larger parcels of land, it should be on the basis of a price per acre.

Step 5. From the base value of the comparable, a price can be determined on the property being evaluated through interpolation. The subject property may not be as good as the highest priced comparable but is better than the poorest, so an evaluation is determined.

An example of the information required in Land Valuation through the use of comparables is as follows:

Sale #1— Location: Southeast corner of Indian Road and 19th Lane
Instrument: Warranty Deed Date: 7/16/77
Legal: The East 200 feet of Lot 48, Indian Tract
Size: 20,080 square feet
Zoning: C-2
Sales Price: $68,500
Unit Price: $3.41 per square foot
Remarks: Property has been improved since sales date.

Sale #2— Location: Northwest corner of 15th Ave. and Indian Road
Instrument: Warranty Deed Date: 5/25/77
Docket: 7852 Page: 612

Legal: Assessor's Parcel #125 - 37 -4
Size: 32,000 square feet
Zoning: C-0 (Commercial Office Building)
Sales Price: $130,000
Unit Price: $4.06 per square foot
Remarks: A new office building is to be constructed in the near future.

Sale #3— Location: Northwest corner of 19th Ave. and Highland
Instrument: Warranty Deed Date: 3/15/77
Docket: 5917 Page: 413
Legal: Assessor's Parcel #125 - 32 - 10
Size: 300′×150′ = 45,000 square feet
Zoning: R - 5
Sales Price: $96,000
Unit Price: $2.13 per square foot
Remarks: A new office building has been constructed on the site.

SUMMARY OF COMPARABLE SALES

Sale	Date	Sales Price	Size	Unit Price	Zoning
#1	7/16/77	$68,500	20,080 sq. ft	$3.41	C-2
#2	5/25/77	$130,000	32,000 sq. ft.	$4.06	C-0
#3	3/15/77	$96,000	45,000 sq. ft.	$2.13	R-5
	Subject Property		48,000 sq. ft.		C-2

ANALYSIS AND CONCLUSION OF LAND VALUE

The comparable land sales cited range from $2.13 to $4.06 per square foot. Sale #1 was located half a mile west of the subject site, was sold to a convenience market, and is considered a fair market value for its use. Sale #2 was located on the corner of a main arterial of the city, was considered superior, and would tend to set the extreme limit of value. Sale #3 was the lowest sale at $2.13 per square foot. However, this sale was zoned R-5 which is a lesser zoning than the subject property.

After adjustments for various factors, a value of $3.25 per square foot is indicated for the subject site or:

48,000 square feet @ $3.25 per square foot = $156,000

This same method of land valuation can be used in evaluating large parcels and farms.

Those steps necessary to evaluate land and farms are repeated below:

Step 1—Preparation of a Detailed Checklist
Step 2—Fact and Information Profile
Step 3—Selection of Comparable Values
Step 4—Sales Price of Comparable Values
Step 5—Interpolated Value of Subject Property

THE PROFESSIONAL APPRAISAL, THE SURE WAY TO DETERMINE VALUE

Sometimes another opinion on the value of a commercial or industrial property is wanted, and in some cases, required. One sophisticated investor may want an appraisal of the property to substantiate his own valuation. In another instance, a professional appriasal may be required by banks and other recognized lending institutions for mortgage purposes. Such formal appraisals are made by licensed appraisers and they clearly establish the value of a property.

There are several national appraisal organizations around the country. One such group, known as the American Institute of Real Estate Appraisers, advertise themselves as being the nation's oldest organization of professional real estate appraisers. Those qualified to appraise all types of real estate are designated as an MAI (Members Appraisal Institute). Others in the organization are designated as RM (Residential Members) and are qualified to appraise single-family residences. Many lending institutions, recognizing the qualifications of the members of this organization may require an MAI appraisal.

Another organization of appraisers is known as the Society of Real Estate Appraisers. They are an international association of professional real estate appraisers and evaluation analysts. There are three designations of members: Senior Real Estate Analysts, Senior Real Estate Appraisers, and Senior Residential Appraisers.

A third national organization is the American Society of Appraisers. They state that every member is qualified in his specialized field of appraising.

As you can see, it is not difficult to find a professional appraiser. There should be representatives of each organization in every major city in the country. While their methods in establishing the value of a property are similar to those shown in this chapter, the end result is a much more detailed explanation. The cost of such an appraisal will vary with the appraiser and the property being appraised. It is always wise to get an estimate of cost.

HOW AN ASTUTE INVESTOR PUT HIS KNOWLEDGE TO PROFITABLE USE: AN ACTUAL TRANSACTION

A number of years ago in Scottsdale a parcel of land was in a flood area known as the Indian Bend Wash. Since it was subject to periodic flooding, no one would buy the property. It was a long strip of land, extending a distance of one mile north to south, and its width varied from 800 to 1000 feet. It totaled approximately 120 acres. The western boundary was an existing street along the half-section line.

One astute investor had a plan and knew what to do with the property. His offer of $2,000 per acre was immediately accepted by a surprised and grateful owner who had visions of having to keep the land until the government finally decided to do something about Indian Bend Wash.

As soon as the escrow closed, the investor employed an engineer and a land planner, and discussed his development plan with them. The resulting master plan provided for 10 acres of townhouses along the northern arterial. The next 40 acres to the south was allocated for a 9-hole executive golf course, bordering along the street to the west, except for a 5 acre parcel jutting into the golf course which was to be zoned for apartments. Immediately south of the golf course, a new street was to be cut through about two-thirds of the way across the property and then extend south to the southern border of the property. Just south and west of the new street, 25 acres was shown as a park. East of the park and across the new street, 20 acres were to be for more townhouses. Extending south of the park and west of the new street, a strip of land several hundred feet wide was designated for the Indian Bend Wash after it flowed through the golf course and park. The remainder of the property on both sides of the Wash was designated for approximately 10 more acres of apartments, and about 20 acres on the southern arterial were marked as commercial.

After the master plan was completed, the investor applied for zoning changes as they appeared on the plan. Sometime later, the property was zoned as requested, and the investor donated the 25-acre park area to the city.

Soon after the zoning was granted, the golf-course land was leased based upon a $6,000 per acre valuation with a 10 percent yield. Following the completion of the golf course, the 10 acres zoned for townhouses along the northern arterial were sold at a price of $15,000 per gross acre. The city, in the meantime, began constructing a beautiful club house, small lake, tennis courts and softball diamonds in the new park. It was a wonderful addition to the city. At the same time, the new street was paved and two more sales made. The 5 acres jutting into the golf course were sold for apartments at $20,000 per acre, and the 10 acres opposite the park were sold for a townhouse development at $15,000 per acre. Later, as development moved to the southern portion of the property, the remaining apartment land was sold at $20,000 per acre and the commercial sales ranged from $1.00 per square foot up, depending on the location of the parcel.

Needless to say, the land that no one else wanted proved to be an excellent investment. It resulted in a profit in excess of one million dollars for an astute investor who was innovative in his ideas and had the knowledge and ability to accomplish what he set out to do.

KEY POINTS

1. Know how to obtain factual information on property
2. Learn to use public records
3. Study classification of commercial and industrial real estate
4. Use a property checklist
5. Use a Fact and Information Profile
6. Use Income Analysis and Evaluation
7. Use guidelines for determining values
8. Understand acceptable yields
9. Study capitalization
10. Evaluate land through the use of comparables
11. Understand the need for a professional appraisal

3

The Technique of Structured Financing to Increase Profits

Financing—the supplying of money—is the magic word in commercial and industrial investments. *The intelligent use of money, coupled with imaginative financing techniques, will produce far greater income and profits than would be possible if you stuck only to "normal" financing methods.* Smart, sophisticated investors know how to buy and how to get the maximum yield for their invested dollars.

One very knowledgeable investor, for example, used an innovative financing technique to purchase a large tract of acreage which he planned to develop. To reduce his initial outlay of cash and to lower his annual payments, including interest, to a minimum during the first years, he proposed the following method of payment to the seller: After a small down payment, the annual principal payments were to extend for ten years. The investor structured his purchase in such a manner that interest did not accrue until the end of the third year. Then, at that time, interest on the then unpaid principal balance would be paid at the same time and in addition to the regular principal payments.

This innovative financing technique resulted in a tremendous savings in interest because before interest commenced to accrue, the development was nearly completed and most of the land released. In this instance, the interest to be paid on the small remaining principal balance was just a fraction of what it would have been if "normal" financing procedures had been followed.

THE IMPORTANCE OF CREATIVE FINANCING

Many knowledgeable investors learned early in their investment careers that creative and innovative financing is an essential part of investing in commercial and industrial real estate. That such techniques would produce more income or a greater yield than "normal" methods of financing became known. Investment programs were enlarged to include many financing techniques in not only the purchase of land but also in methods of financing the purchase of an income property. To these investors, creative financing was important. It proved to be a method whereby the yield on invested dollars could be increased through the use and application of financing techniques designed to achieve that result. This chapter will illustrate a number of creative techniques and demonstrate how the desired result can be accomplished.

THE TECHNIQUE OF MAKING FINANCING WORK FOR YOU

The preceding chapters have explained that real estate investment in commercial and industrial property is divided into two major segments:

1. Income producing properties
2. Land and other commercial and industrial properties

The financing techniques used in the acquisition of income producing properties are entirely different from those used in acquiring land or any of the other types of commercial and industrial real estate. Therefore, being able to determine the best type of financing for both major types of property becomes most important. Whenever possible, an astute investor will structure the financing so that it will work for his benefit. With a little ingenuity this can be accomplished by creating as much leverage as possible through the use of maximum financing techniques. Usually there will be an existing mortgage on the property which can be assumed. Leverage can then be created by making as low a down payment as possible, assuming the existing first mortgage and giving a new second mortgage on the property for the remaining balance of the purchase price. The new second mortgage should be structured at an interest rate and with monthly or annual payments to give the desired yield on the investment. This type of buyer always has financing working for him. There are many other variations available to the astute and informed investor as will be brought out in subsequent sections of this chapter.

There are investors who like to buy land in certain ways to create maximum leverage. Whenever financing can be structured their way, they know that financing is working for them. To further explain some of their methods, some examples will be discussed as they relate to the sale of land:

> *Example No. 1.* There are investors who like to buy land with a low down payment—interest only for from three to five years and then principal and interest payments over the next ten years.
>
> *Example No. 2.* Another investor will want to buy land by prepaying interest as a down payment then regular terms on the balance.
>
> *Example No. 3.* Another method sometimes used in the purchase of land is paying interest only on a contract for a specified period of time before principal payments start.
>
> *Example No. 4.* Financing the purchase of land through the use of a series of options is a method used by the more astute investors of large parcels. This technique really makes financing work for the investor and will be more thoroughly explained in a subsequent section of this chapter.

TWENTY-FIVE WAYS TO FINANCE THE PURCHASE OR SALE OF A COMMERCIAL OR INDUSTRIAL PROPERTY

It is a well-known fact among investors in commercial and industrial real estate that the success or failure of an investment can depend upon the type of financing that was available and how it was structured into the transaction. Over the years, many different types of financing techniques have been developed and used. Each type was determined by the situation existing at the time of the investment. A number of the more useful financing methods are shown here along with a brief description of when to use them and what results they produce.

1. *A down payment with a new mortgage or Trust Deed on the balance.* This is usually the standard method of financing the purchase of a new structure, such as an apartment complex, an office building, warehouse, retail store, motels or similar structures. The builder will probably have made arrangements for a new permanent mortgage to be placed upon the completed structure. This method is also suitable for land purchases.

2. *A down payment with an Agreement for Sale on the balance.* Typical financing on an older structure that can be free and clear or with a small encumbrance that

can be paid off from the down payment funds. This can be applicable to smaller structures such as a small office building, older warehouse, small retail store, triplex or a fourplex. It may also be used in the purchase of land.

3. *A down payment with an assumption of the existing mortgage or Trust Deed.* This is the way most sellers like to sell—the old standby "cash to mortgage" method. This type of financing gets all the money for the seller at the close of escrow and can be used for apartments, office buildings, shopping centers, warehouses, motels and any other type of commercial or industrial property.

4. *A down payment with an assumption of an existing Agreement for Sale.* Another popular method with sellers—again it gets all their cash at the close of escrow. The difference between an Agreement for Sale and mortgage or Trust Deed is well known to all people who are familiar with real estate financing. The use of one or the other is usually determined by the seller as to which form of security he would rather have. This method is typical in land purchases or unimproved commercial and industrial lots.

5. *A down payment with an assumption of the existing encumbrance whether it be a mortgage, Trust Deed or an Agreement for Sale and a new second mortgage on the remaining balance due the seller.* This type of financing is used when the cash to mortgage method takes more cash than the investor wants to pay. This is another typical method of financing used primarily in the acquisition of apartments or other income producing properties.

6. *A down payment with an assumption of the existing encumbrance and an Agreement for Sale on the remaining balance due the seller.* The only difference in this method and that shown in 5 above is the use of an Agreement for Sale instead of a second mortgage. Again it is a preference on which form of security to use.

7. *A down payment with a wrap-around mortgage.* When the existing mortgage is small and at a low rate of interest, the seller sometimes wants the mortgage on the property to remain his obligation. In this instance, a wrap-around mortgage is the total of the existing first mortgage and the amount due the seller after the down payment. The interest due on this new mortgage can be more than that being paid on the first mortgage. A collection agency is usually used so that the total payment can be broken down with part going to the existing first mortgage and the balance to the seller. A buyer always wants to know that the first mortgage is being paid. This method is used in the purchase of older apartments, small office buildings or other smaller income producing properties.

8. *A down payment with a Trust Agreement on the balance due the seller.* This is the accepted and standard method of financing a sizeable purchase where the

property is to be developed requiring releases and other requirements of a subdivision trust. Usually a title company, as Trustee, administers the trust in accordance with its provisions. This method is used in the purchase of land to be developed wherein releases are required.

9. *A down payment with a Trust Agreement wherein the property is encumbered by an existing mortgage.* This method is somewhat similar to a wrap-around mortgage except much larger and more complicated but very workable. It is usable in land purchases and also in purchases of income producing properties, apartments, shopping centers, office buildings, warehouses, etc.

10. *Prepayment of interest as a down payment with balance payable in accordance with any one of the foregoing methods.* This is very usable in the purchase of land.

11. *A down payment with the principal balance payable in one of the above described methods with the exception that interest does not accrue and is not payable for a specified number of years.* This provides another method of buying land where leverage is created.

12. *Interest only for a number of years wtih principal and interest payments beginning at a specified time.* This method of financing can apply to any type of commercial or industrial property.

13. *A down payment with interest only paid for several years, then principal and interest payments can begin in the usual manner.* Another variation of land purchase financing, this is applicable when initial development costs are heavy.

14. *A down payment with the balance payable in any one of the previously described methods but with a rate of interest lower than the prevailing rate to compensate for a higher price.* This provides negotiating method of financing that can be used on any type of commercial or industrial property.

15. *A lease with an option to purchase.* This is a very popular method of financing especially when money is short. When the option is exercised, the plan of purchase can be any one of those covered in this chapter. It is applicable to the purchase of any type of commercial or industrial property.

16. *A lease with an option to purchase for cash.* This method is a very simple process—within the terms of the lease the property may be purchased for cash. It is also applicable to the purchase of all types of commercial and industrial property.

17. *An option to purchase for cash.* The terms of the option give the Grantee the right to buy the property for cash in accordance with the terms of the option. Buyers like any purchase plan that has to do with an option. It ties up the property

for relatively little money so that the purchase can be made at a more convenient time and may be used in purchasing any type of commercial or industrial property.

18. *An initial purchase and an option for the remainder of the property.* The terms of the initial purchase can follow any of the foregoing methods outlined. The terms of the option when exercised and purchased are usually on the same terms and conditions of the initial purchase. This is a popular method of purchasing land.

19. *An initial purchase with a series of options.* This method provides an excellent way to buy a large parcel of land. The method used by most investors is to make the initial purchase by making a down payment with terms on the balance secured by a Trust Agreement. Each option is exercised at a specific price and on specific dates with terms similar to those given in the initial purchase. Each option when exercised usually goes into another trust—again similar to the Trust Agreement entered into in the initial purchase. This is an excellent method of buying a large tract of land as it enables the buyer to schedule his development in a more orderly manner.

20. *Trade of property as a down payment with the balance payable by mortgage or Trust Deed.* This method of purchase is used when the person with the trade property wants to trade "up." It is also used when money is in short supply and is applicable to the purchase of land, apartments, office buildings, shopping centers, warehouses and, in general, any type of commercial or industrial property.

21. *Trade of property as a down payment with the balance payable by Agreement for Sale.* The only difference in this method and that shown above is the preference for an Agreement for Sale over a mortgage or Trust Deed.

22. *Trade of property as a down payment with the balance secured by a Trust Agreement.* This method is usually used when there is a sizeable parcel of land that is going to be developed requiring releases and other subdivision requirements.

23. *Trade of property as a portion of the down payment and the balance of the down payment paid in cash with the unpaid balance secured by a mortgage, Trust Deed, or a Trust Agreement.* This is a variation of the foregoing methods using a trade as the down payment.

24. *Sale and leaseback.* This is a method of financing that is not typical and is used when the owner of the property uses the facility in the operation of his business. At the time when his depreciation is running out, he usually considers selling the property, but since its location is good for his business, he desires to lease it back from its new owner. His selling price and the rent he is willing to pay

are relative, so any sales price consistent with the rent can be obtained. Typical sales would be owner-operated retail businesses, warehouses, distribution centers, small medical and dental offices.

25. *Lease land and buy improvements.* This provides a more sophisticated method of financing. Since land is not depreciable and rent is an expense, this method of purchasing allows the maximum tax shelter available. The purchase and its financing can be structured to provide for almost any type of tax shelter desired. It is very popular with some buyers and is applicable to income producing properties.

From the 25 methods discussed above showing various techniques used in purchasing commercial and industrial property, it becomes clear that different methods can be used to achieve desired results. Here's the story of an actual investment transaction which amplifies a principle of structured financing discussed in this chapter. . . .

How an investor used interest to "level" a price

A number of years ago, an investor was interested in buying an apartment complex. The owner was asking $260,000 which was more or less average for the apartments. After inspecting the property and analyzing its income and expense, the investor made an offer of $200,000 with a $50,000 down payment including $5,000 earnest money deposit. The balance was to be carried by the seller over a 20 year period and evidenced by an agreement for sale, payable monthly, and bearing interest at the rate of 6 percent per annum.

The owner was an elderly gentleman who had owned the apartments for many years and had finally decided to sell them. In reviewing the offer, he considered the price too low and the earnest money not enough. While he would not sign a counter-offer, he indicated to the real estate broker that he would accept $225,000 with the same $50,000 down, and the balance of $175,000 to be payable over 20 years at 6 percent interest. He also stated that the earnest money deposit should be increased to $25,000. The broker met later that evening with the investor and gave him a detailed report on the meeting with the seller. The investor had no objections to increasing the earnest money deposit to $25,000 even though it was considered quite large for the size of the transaction. On the change in price to $225,000, the investor said that he would buy at that price, but with a change in the rate of interest. The broker was instructed to prepare a second offer for $225,000 with $50,000 down, showing an earnest money deposit of $25,000 and the balance of $175,000 payable monthly over a 20 year period bearing interest at 4 percent per annum. When the broker attempted to return the original $200,000 offer to the investor, he was told to keep it and to let the seller take whichever offer he wanted.

The next day the new offer was presented to the seller. He was pleased that the price had been increased to $225,000 and also that the earnest money was a figure which he considered sufficient. While he objected somewhat to the lower rate of interest, the increased selling price was more than enough to offset his objections. The second offer was accepted; the escrow opened and later closed in accordance with the signed instructions.

In structuring the second offer, the investor was able to offset the increased price by a reduction in the rate of interest to be paid on the remaining balance. To further explain, the monthly amortized payment on $150,000 over 20 years at 6 percent interest was $1,074.70. The monthly payment on $175,000 over the same 20 years but at 4 percent was $1,060.50, a savings of nearly $15 per month. Actually, the second offer was less in actual dollars even though the selling price was $25,000 more—all of which amplifies a lesson in how to use interest to level a price.

MONEY, A NECESSARY COMMODITY, AND HOW TO FIND IT

Money is a necessary commodity in any real estate investment, especially in commercial and industrial property. It has to come from the buyer, from a lending institution in the form of a note and mortgage, trust deed or other device, or from the seller in some method of financing. Usually it comes from at least two of these sources. *Money is like anything else—when it is in short supply or when the demand is high its cost rises astronomically*—not only on the rate of interest but on the points that have to be paid plus whatever other fringe benefits the lender wants to demand. These costs can get so high that they affect the sale of everything.

The availability of mortgage money is a necessity for the development of commercial and industrial property under any economic conditions. No one wants to build anything out of his pocket. Borrowed money is the key to all development. Our whole system of business is built upon this fact.

Mortgage money can come from one of many sources—banks, savings and loan associations, insurance companies, pension funds, REIT's, trust funds, and numerous others. The supply and amount is determined by the conditions existing in the money market at the time of commitment.

It should always be a part of every investment program to keep in close contact with those in the money-lending business. This should be done not only to be knowledgeable about the current money situation, but also to know where to go when the need arises. Many large transactions are dependent upon the availability of development funds.

Therefore, this procedure is recommended:

1. Keep in close contact with those in the money-lending business.
2. Keep abreast of the current money market.
3. Understand the process of applying for and obtaining a new mortgage.
4. Know where to go when the need arises.

HOW TO BEAT THE HIGH COST OF MONEY, CREATING MORE PROFIT FOR YOU

With the purchase of land, many investors have been able to beat the high cost of money. Since it is very difficult to borrow money from regular lending institutions against unimproved land, all the necessary financing in the purchase of land must come from the seller. Consequently, no points have to be paid. In a large transaction this can represent a tidy sum. The seller, if he wants to sell, will carry the unpaid balance of the purchase in a note and mortgage, trust deed, agreement, or maybe a trust agreement. In most large transactions during the time when other interest rates have been extremely high, astute investors have been able to get the seller to carry his balance at an interest rate that varied from 7 to 8 percent and usually 7½ percent per annum. The difference in an interest rate of 7½ percent and 9½ percent on a large transaction can run into a lot of money. If the seller objects, he is told that he should be happy with his profit on the land and 7½ percent interest. However, sellers often object saying that if they can't borrow money from their banks at that rate why should they give it.

A smart investor will explain that the price per acre is no bargain and the interest factor is definitely a related cost. If the seller insists upon that high rate of interest, the investor may lower his offered price per acre to compensate for the increased interest costs. At the same time, the investor will point out the fact that the higher price per acre is more important to the seller because the profit from the sale would be subject to a capital gain tax, whereas interest is taxed as ordinary income. The investor then further explains that he prefers to buy the land at a lower price per acre and raise the interest rate because of his side of the ledger, interest is an expense and the cost of land must be capitalized. *In nearly all such cases, the rate of interest is not increased and the seller is very happy with his profit and the lower rate of interest.*

The practical application of some of the basic principles of financing can make financing work for the investor and at the same time beat the high cost of money—even in the purchase of an income property.

How to beat the high cost of money

Another example involved the purchase of a retail and service store building which was located on a major arterial street. The building was presented to an investor at its appraised value of $115,000. A savings and loan bank was contacted to determine the amount it would loan on the property and the terms and conditions. The investor was informed that the bank would loan 75 percent of its appraised value but wanted 3½ points to make the loan and 10¼ percent interest amortized over a 15 year period. This high cost of money was more than the investor wanted to pay so he presented an offer on the property based upon the unpaid balance being carried by the seller. His offer was for $100,000 with $10,000 down and the balance of $90,000 payable over fifteen years at 8½ percent. Because the owner was anxious to sell, he accepted the offer and the investor saved considerable money on points and accrued interest.

There was nothing fancy about this transaction. It just applied basic financing principles in a manner that produced results and at the same time beat the high cost of money.

AN INNOVATIVE APPROACH TO FINANCING AND TAXES

There are times when a new, innovative financing technique will increase not only the cash yield but will also change the tax liability for the advantage of the investor. This can be done by refinancing the investment either at the time of acquisition or at a later date. Such refinancing solves a lot of financial problems and changes a borderline investment to one which creates a more than acceptable yield.

When the encumbrances on a commerical or industrial property become so complicated and expensive, refinancing is necessary before the property can be considered a good investment. This has happened many times in the purchase of apartments. A typical example would be an apartment complex that had been sold several times. In each transaction the seller took a small down payment and carried the balance due him on a third, fourth or maybe even a fifth mortgage. When this happens, all of the income goes to pay off these short term mortgages. Finally, an investor comes along who likes the property and knows that its only salvation is through refinancing with a new first mortgage. He pays off all of the existing short-term debts plus the old first mortgage. Usually at this time, all of the second, third, fourth, and fifth mortgage holders are agreeable to a discount of their notes and mortgages for cash. *Thus a questionable purchase has turned into a good investment by the use of a refinancing technique to clean up a lot of cats and dogs.*

Shopping centers, office buildings, and other income producing properties can sometimes be made into better investments by refinancing. The name of the game in commercial and industrial real estate is to get the maximum use of dollars invested. If refinancing can accomplish this, then it should be done.

The situations applicable to apartments with their numerous mortgages are not usually the same as those with other income producing properties. As an example, the following actual transaction is described.

Using refinancing techniques for greater yields and more profit

A shopping center was offered to an investor at a price of $1,500,000. There were two existing mortgages on the center totaling $758,337, requiring a down payment of $741,663. The center's operating profit after deducting current operating expenses was $159,000. The debt service on the two mortgages was $108,355, leaving a cash spendable income of $50,645. This represented a cash yield to the investor of 6.8 percent. Since this yield was below that which was acceptable to the investor, he calculated a new yield based upon refinancing, changing a borderline investment to one showing an excellent return.

A new mortgage of $1,125,000 was obtained having an amortized debt service of $111,000. Deducting this debt service from the operating profit, a new cash spendable income of $48,000 was shown—a little less than the prior cash flow, but less cash was required from the investor. Instead of having to invest $741,663, he only had to come up with $375,000. This reduction in invested capital increased his cash yield to an excellent 12.8 percent, a substantial increase over the prior 6.8 percent. In addition, his tax picture changed considerably. Through refinancing, his book loss for the first year increased from a small $11,000 to a whopping $47,000. The additional tax shelter was an added bonus to this innovative financing technique.

This same situation will result with any income producing property whenever:

1. The existing mortgage is paid down to a point where the gain in equity is disproportionate to the cash spendable income.
2. There are several mortgages on the property, thereby causing the debt service to be disproportionately high.

3. The buyer wants to reduce his invested capital to increase his yield-cash on cash.
4. Older properties with a fixed amortized debt service and with increased operating expenses, have little or no provisions for escalation in the lease.

If you should encounter an investment where any of the foregoing situations exist, you will find that refinancing can be most helpful in improving the profit potential of the investment.

CREATIVE FINANCING—FINDING THE CONSTANT AND THE USE OF THE BALLOON PAYMENT

So far in this chapter you have been shown many ways to finance the purchase of a commercial or industrial real estate investment—from the normal, usual routine methods to the more innovative techniques necessary to accomplish a desired result. When the normal and routine methods do not work, it becomes necessary to be a little creative in your thinking and planning. Through the application of creative financing techniques, those profit opportunities which were recognized and evaluated as good can become excellent investments. The remaining sections of this chapter will show you a number of creative financing techniques which are designed to increase profits and yields.

Many knowledgeable investors will negotiate mortgage terms on the basis of a constant percentage factor. The constant factor can be described as being the percentage of the total loan payable each year to pay off the debt, including both principal and interest. To explain, a $150,000 loan amortized over a 20 year period at 8¾ percent interest is payable in monthly payments of $1,325.60 or an annual total of $15,907.20. By dividing the annual payment of $15,907.20 by the total loan of $150,000, the constant percentage factor is found to be 10.6 percent. Thus 10.6 percent of the loan is paid each year as principal and interest. By the same token, the same loan at the same rate of interest but for a term of 15 years has a constant of 12 percent, whereas the constant for 25 years is 9.87 percent.

To find the constant for any rate of interest for a specified number of years, the procedure is simple. A small book containing payment tables for monthly mortgage loans is available at any title company. Open the book to the required rate of interest and to the number of years of the loan and select the figure necessary to amortize $1,000. This time, using 9¼ percent for 20 years, you will find the monthly amount to be $9.16. Multiplying by 12, the annual amount is $109.92. By dividing $109.92 by the amount of the loan of $1,000, the constant is 10.99 percent.

Therefore, it is readily understandable that *the lower the constant, the less the monthly payments will be, resulting in a higher cash spendable income and cash yield.* A number of years ago an astute investor said that he didn't care what the rate of interest was as long as the constant was no more than 7½ percent.

One way to reduce the constant is through the use of the financing technique of the balloon payment. It is common practice for a lending institution to put a limit on the term of the loan. As an example, the term limit of the loan is 20 years and the amount is $500,000 at an interest rate of 9 percent. The monthly payments are $4,498.70 or $53,984 annually with a constant 10.8 percent. A smart investor would ask the lending institution to amortize the loan on a 25 year schedule with a 20 year balloon. His monthly payments would reduce to $4,196 or an annual amount of $50,352 and a constant of 10.08 percent. With the balloon payment, the lending institution is still being paid within the term limit specified, and the cash yield to the investor is increased $3,632.

HOW TO USE LONG-TERM INTERIM FINANCING TO INCREASE PROFITS

The normal procedure in financing a commercial or industrial development is to select and purchase the site, prepare plans and specifications, secure a lease or leases, obtain a mortgage commitment and make an interim loan for the money necessary to build the facility. Upon completion, the permanent mortgage is funded and recorded in accordance with the provisions of the commitment and the proceeds are used to pay off the interim loan.

To deviate from the normal procedure many builder/investors will make provisions for the interim loan to remain in effect for a longer period of time, beyond the completion of construction. This is usually done for several reasons, one of which is to pay interest only as is required on the interim loan for an extended period of time, thereby increasing the cash flow. Another procedure is to take a breathing spell during the opening stages of the project, possibly to secure more leases. If the interim construction loan is made entirely upon the provisions of the permanent mortgage commitment, then the interim loan can only be extended to the time limit imposed for recording of permanent mortgage. If, however, the interim loan is made upon the financial strength and capabilities of the builder/investor without the requirement of a permanent take-out commitment, then the interim loan can remain in effect as long as is provided in the loan provisions. This is usually done if the builder/investor wants to pay interest only for a considerable length of time or if he anticipates a reduction in interest rates which would be applicable to a permanent mortgage obtained sometime in the future.

An interesting use of interim financing

One such builder/investor used long-term interim financing in nearly every project he developed. His procedure was really quite simple. Since he had the financial strength and the reputation to perform, he was able to secure an interim loan large enough to build the entire project for a term of ten years. After completion, the operation of the project commenced as planned, interest was paid on the interim loan and at the end of each year, the cash spendable income was used to pay on the principal amount of the loan. Since the cash spendable income was completely tax-sheltered, this could be done because no income tax had to be paid. Over the years, the principal was reduced until it was time to place a permanent mortgage on the property, either because the term of the interim loan had expired or the time of good interest rates had been reached. As he had planned, *the reduction in the interim loan had been accomplished through the use of tax-sheltered dollars.* Many times this reduction amounted to as much as 33⅓ percent of the original loan.

ADVANCED FINANCING TECHNIQUES FOR LAND AND INCOME PROPERTY TO CREATE MORE PROFIT OPPORTUNITIES

In larger transactions, more sophisticated methods of financing can be used than those presented in this chapter. These more advanced techniques in financing usually separate the land from the improvements, making separate and distinct transactions on each.

A typical example is a large apartment complex which was presented to a group of doctors. This group of doctors invested in apartment projects and had their own special format of purchasing. Each apartment complex was purchased by a limited partnership made up of these investing doctors. They always liked new projects wherein they could qualify as a first user for the accelerated depreciation advantages. Also, if the permanent financing had not been finalized, they separated the land from the improvements, buying the land in one transaction and the improvements in another. One limited partnership was formed to purchase the land. It then leased the land to the group that would own the improvements, subordinating its interest in the land to a mortgage to be placed upon the improvements. The end result produced a very happy arrangement wherein all tax advantages were obtained along with maximum financing.

These more advanced techniques in financing are really not as complicated as they sound nor are they that advanced. By the time you break one of these large multiple transactions down to its various component parts, all you have is a number of transactions employing the sound financing techniques we have described in this chapter. *They may have become a little fancy, putting some variations to an old program, but the end results are the same.*

DEPENDABLE TECHNIQUES AND GUIDELINES ON HOW TO USE A SERIES OF OPTIONS FOR MAXIMUM PROFITS

Maximum profits can be realized in the development or resale of land if the purchase is financed by using the initial purchase and series of options method. By following this technique, a large parcel of land can be acquired *by making an initial purchase of a designated number of acres and then a series of options to purchase the remainder of the property at specified times on stipulated terms and conditions.* This procedure will enable the investor to make not only greater profits but also to provide more flexibility in development or resale.

This technique of purchase and financing is particularly attractive to sophisticated investors especially when the property is larger than would normally be purchased if the entire parcel was bought at one time. There are six distinct advantages, *each contributing to greater profits*, in purchasing land by this method.

1. *Smaller down payment.* Since the initial purchase is a small part of the entire parcel, the down payment can be proportionately smaller, making the initial outlay of cash much less—permitting a greater yield on cash invested.
2. *Smaller annual payments.* The annual payments on the initial purchase are also proportionately smaller. Any developer needs assistance in the beginning to conserve cash on land acquisition because the cash requirements for development purposes are quite large.
3. *Less interest to pay.* Interest under this method does not accrue on the options until an option is exercised resulting in a tremendous savings and far greater profits. If purchased as an entire parcel, interest would accrue on the large unpaid balance. In some of the large transactions, *the savings in interest over a ten year period is equal to approximately $1,000 per acre.*
4. *More orderly development.* By establishing options to conform to a predetermined plan of development or resale, the developer can eliminate the strain and worry of meeting large annual payments plus interest and concentrate on an orderly approach to his overall development.
5. *Maximum profits.* Over the term of the series of options, the optioned land will appreciate in value far above the purchase price established when the options were granted.

6. *No liability and less risk.* The investor is not obligated to exercise any of the options. If the development should bog down or turn sour, succeeding options can be passed and not exercised. However, if the entire parcel were purchased, the investor could be sued for specific performance in the event of default.

Even though this technique has been used successfully by informed investors, it is not always easy to accomplish. Not all owners will agree to sell their property under this method of purchase, but when it is properly explained, they will sometimes change their minds. The advantages are not all on the side of the investor. The following advantages can be explained to the seller:

1. *Continued use of the optioned property.* This is true in the sale of large farms that are ready for development. The options can be so structured to permit the farmer to continue farming the optioned property until the option is exercised.
2. *Foreclosure and repossession.* If an option is not "timely exercised," the land has never been conveyed, so the seller does not have to repossess.
3. *No taxable implications.* Again if an option is not exercised, there has been no sale and consequently, no profit or tax. A foreclosure and repossession can sometimes create a tax problem to the seller.
4. *Tax advantages.* Through the use of the sale by options, tax problems can be adjusted to meet any given situation.

In establishing a purchase utilizing this technique, these simple guidelines should be followed:

1. Plan the purchase
2. Designate the initial purchase
3. Establish option parcels
4. Structure contract of purchase to include series of options

More detailed instructions will be given in Chapter 7 on how to implement this plan of purchase with step-by-step procedures to follow.

KEY POINTS

1. Use creative financing—deviating from the "normal"
2. Understand how to make financing work for you through innovative techniques
3. Know the 25 ways to finance a real estate purchase
4. Understand that money is a necessary commodity

5. Learn to beat the high cost of money
6. Use the refinancing technique to increase profit and yield
7. Know how to find the constant
8. Learn the advantages of the balloon payment
9. Understand that long-term interim can increase profits
10. Discover the use of options for maximum profits

4

How to Make Big Profits from a Small Investment—Individually or as a Group

There are many people who would like to invest in real estate but do not because they feel either that they don't have enough money or lack the knowledge and confidence to enter a program of commercial and industrial real estate investing. However, there are many profit opportunities available today that can be purchased under terms and conditions structured to fit any purse or situation. All an investor must know is how to do it with a minimum of cash and risk. The suggestions, guidelines and procedures outlined and explained in this chapter should be most helpful in making that first commercial and industrial real estate investment.

The belief that it takes a substantial amount of money to invest in commercial and industrial property is not necessarily true. Naturally, the more expensive properties require more cash, but smaller, less expensive properties can be purchased with much less.

Each investment must be analyzed and evaluated not only from the standpoint of its value and yield potential but also in terms of whether or not it can be purchased with a minimum of cash and risk. This procedure will bring out innovative financing techniques, interest saving features, cost-cutting operation procedures and maintenance standards. In the end, you may find that an investment group should be formed to make the purchase.

HOW SMALL PARCELS CAN LEAD TO BIG PROFITS

One investor liked to purchase smaller parcels in the city which had been by-passed by development. Some consisted of several acres while others were smaller pieces with frontage on a good street. All were already zoned for either multiple, commercial or industrial. He liked this type of investment because the down payments were never too much and development or resale of those parcels was sure to happen sooner or later. One such purchase is worthy of description.

This particular parcel was not large, consisting of five 50 foot lots on a main arterial going back in depth 150 feet to an alley. The parcel was zoned R-5, permitting either apartments or an office building. Being an interior piece and not having a street corner at either end, it was not too expensive for its location and zoning. The investor's offer of $37,500, calculated at $1.00 per square foot was accepted by the owner. The 15 percent down payment and 10 year term with only 6 percent interest made the purchase all the more appealing.

After two years but before the third annual payment, the parcel was sold to a developer for an office building. By that time, developers had begun to move back into the inner-city, picking up desirable parcels which had been passed over earlier. The sales price was $150,000, computed at $4.00 per square foot, and the terms were cash upon the close of escrow since the buyer's request for subordination was refused. His profit of $108,319 for such a small investment in just over two years was excellent. His total cash outlay was only $16,080, including the down payment of $5,500, two annual payments of $3,200 each, $3,418 in interest and $763 in closing costs.

HOW ONE INVESTOR USED HIS RENT PAYMENTS TO PURCHASE AN OFFICE BUILDING

Another astute investor began his commercial and industrial investments by purchasing the office building in which his insurance business was located. The building contained 4,200 square feet of rentable area of which he was occupying 1,800 square feet with the remaining 2,400 square feet leased to other businesses. The building was priced at $120,000 with an approximate $100,000 current mortgage balance at 8½ percent interest, amortized at $11,595 annually. The income of the building including the rent was $27,300, and the expenses including real estate taxes and insurance was $13,000, leaving a cash spendable income of $2,705. On a cash to mortgage basis the yield would have been 13½ percent. The investor agreed to pay $10,000 less credit for $7,000 in security lease deposits, $3,000 of which was his own and $4,000 of the other tenants at the close of escrow, assume the existing mortgage in the amount of $100,000 and pay the remaining $10,000 in five equal annual payments of $2,000 each plus interest at the rate of 7½ percent per annum.

In calculating the return of his investment, he did not consider yield but determined that his rent was reduced from $6.50 per square foot to a little over $5.00, plus the gain in equity through amortization and the additional savings in his income taxes through ownership of the building. All this was accomplished with a $3,000 down payment.

The largest tree started as a small seed, and it is not uncommon for big investments in commercial and industrial real estate to begin on a small scale. *Whether the investment is big or little, the principles of investing are the same—only the amounts differ.*

Many investors prefer small investments. They like to diversify and not have all of their eggs in one basket. *The secret of converting a small investment into a large profit is to plan small but think big.* This was obviously the case with the investor who converted a small option into a tremendous $5,000,000 profit as told in Chapter 1.

THE ESSENTIALS OF A PROFITABLE SMALL INVESTMENT

The eight key principles of successful investments were outlined and explained in Chapter 1. These same key principles are applicable in making small investments with the added consideration of size and amount.

The limiting factor in most instances is money. Either the investor is in short supply, or he wants to use it in small amounts creating leverage for maximum profits. As a result the investor should only consider those investments which he can afford or those investments where the desired leverage can be used. The many profit opportunities are also present in small investments and, proportionately, the profits are as large if not larger than those where a lot of dollars are necessary. As was pointed out in the foregoing section, many investors prefer a number of small investments instead of a large one. Their risks are less and their yields are higher.

In structuring your small investment, consideration must be given to *the purpose of your investment,* whether the investment is for income or resale. Also, such consideration must include methods of determining *the type of property most suitable* for your purpose, keeping in mind your financial limitations. In addition, *procedures of selection* by a proper analysis of suitable properties must be followed as described in Chapter 2. Once the property has been selected, you must provide for *methods and strategies of acquisition* to use in purchasing the selected investment. The many techniques of financing must be studied and mastered.

It is in the acquisition phase of small investments that special consideration must be given. Innovative financing techniques must be used to create maximum yields and the required leverage. Such techniques will be more specifically described in subsequent sections of this chapter, outlining procedures and guidelines to follow.

THE INVESTMENT GROUP—A SYNDICATE APPROACH TO INVESTING FOR PROFIT

In an active real estate market everyone at one time or other has the desire to own a piece of real estate. Those with that desire but insufficient capital usually join others in pooling their resources to buy a selected commercial or industrial property, opening the door to the many profit opportunities available. This practice began in our area about 1958.

At first several friends would join together in buying something they all wanted in commercial or industrial real estate. Each would contribute a portion of the required funds necessary to purchase the property and would own an undivided interest in the property in a percentage amount equivalent to the value of their contribution. The amounts did not necessarily have to be equal and in many instances were in differing percentages. In fairness to those who contributed the most, it was generally agreed by the members of the group that the *majority in interest* could decide questions relating to the operation or disposition of the property. In other words, those participants who had contributed more than 50 percent could make the required decisions.

Later small investment groups were formed by friends contributing a stipulated amount each week or month to be used at some point to invest in commercial or industrial real estate. In this instance, since each member had contributed an equal amount, decisions were made by a majority vote. Such small investment groups were not necessarily limited to men but many were formed by housewives, secretaries and other women participants. They, too, were interested in investing in commercial and industrial properties.

HOW ONE GROUP OF INVESTORS POOLED THEIR MONEY FOR A SMALL INVESTMENT

A group of ten investors that I knew contributed $10 a week into their investment plan. At the end of their first year, they had $5,200 to invest. Selecting a commercial lot on a highly traveled street, they purchased the property for

$25,000, paying $5,000 down with the balance payable $4,000 annually plus 7 percent interest for the next five years. In the event the property didn't sell for a few years, they were prepared to continue their weekly contributions to make the annual principal and interest payments.

Shortly after making the first annual principal and interest payment, the property was sold for $55,000, netting an excellent profit for their investment club. After paying accrued interest and closing costs, they received a check from the title company in the amount of $38,335.50. After reimbursing the investment club with the $9,000 paid into the property, they realized a nice big profit of $29,335.50. They voted to distribute the proceeds in equal amounts of $2,933.55 to the ten members, leaving the $9,000 in the investment club for a future investment.

Syndication soon became more complex and sophisticated. Large investment groups were formed by realty organizations made up of investors who were not friends, relatives or neighbors. The purpose of these larger groups was to buy bigger, better and more expensive commercial and industrial real estate. The groups were not necessarily controlled by the realty organization which had formed it, but were guided by that organization in its decision-making process.

As the technique grew in size and scope, the Securities and Exchange Commission stepped in with their ruling. They decided that syndication shares were securities and that salesmen who sold such shares must be licensed securities salesmen and that such investment groups would be governed by the rules and regulations of that governmental body. All of this dictated that those real estate salesmen active in that market should obtain a Securities License also. This edict was the forerunner to the use of Limited Partnerships where large groups joined together in acquiring real estate. It did not, however, preclude small groups joining together as individuals in buying property, a practice which is still prevalent today.

TESTED TECHNIQUES TO USE IN BUYING COMMERCIAL AND INDUSTRIAL PROPERTY AS A GROUP

Usually a small investment group or syndicate is formed for the purpose of acquiring a specific commercial or industrial property. There are dependable and necessary procedures to follow in this type of real estate investing. The seven steps necessary in the successful operation of an investment group are as follows:

1. Purpose of the investment
2. Formation of the group
3. Analysis and evaluation of properties under consideration

4. Selection of the property
5. Calculation of financial requirements
6. Partnership agreement
7 Making the purchase

STEP 1. Purpose of the investment

Most groups usually begin with one or two investors who conceive the idea of investing in one of the many profit opportunities available in commercial and industrial real estate. It is decided generally at that time whether the investment will be for income or for resale at a profit or if it will be land or income property.

STEP 2. Formation of the group

After the purpose of the investment has been determined by the founding member or members, additional members are enlisted. Each agrees at the time to the purpose of the investment. Based upon the size of the proposed investment, the number of participants is determined and agreed upon by those initial members. Their decision is usually based upon the amount of money each will have to contribute. By the same reasoning, the more participants sharing in the profits will reduce the amount to be distributed to each member.

STEP 3. Analysis and evaluation of properties under consideration

Following the procedures outlined in Chapter 2, a Fact and Information Profile should be prepared on each property under consideration. From the information contained in the profile, an analysis and evaluation must be made and each value determined in accordance with the guidelines shown in Chapter 2.

STEP 4. Selection of the property for investment

As a group, it is then decided which property best suits the purpose of the investment and provides the profit opportunity desired by the investment group. This selection process is determined by majority vote, either in interest or by number, whichever is applicable.

STEP 5. Calculation of financial requirements

In determining the amount of money to be contributed by each participant, consideration must be given not only to the funds necessary to close the escrow including the down payment, prorations and other related closing costs, but also to future contributions to make the deferred payments and accrued interest plus maintenance and other operating costs and expenses if required. Every participant should be obligated and prepared to pay his proportionate share during each and every year until the property has either been paid for or sold.

STEP 6. Partnership agreement

It is necessary and essential that an agreement between the members of the investment group be signed and the terms and conditions agreed to by all members. The agreement should include, but not necessarily be limited to, the legal description of the property being purchased, the terms and conditions of the purchase, and the amount of contribution each member will be required to make not only for the initial purchase funds but also to define and identify the amount of contribution to be required of each member for each year during the entire term of his ownership. In addition, the document should state the percentage of *undivided interest* each member will own. Provisions should also be stipulated as to what happens when one of the members is unable to continue his contributions or just decides to pull out of the group. Also, the procedures to follow in making decisions relating to the operation or disposition of the property should be detailed and explained. Just remember that the palest ink is better than the most retentive mind. Even with close friends, relatives or neighbors, the terms of the agreement should be reduced to writing and executed by all parties.

STEP 7. Making the purchase

Following the procedures outlined in the partnership agreement, the property has been selected, analyzed, evaluated and an offer made for its purchase.

HOW TO PREPARE AN OFFER

In preparing the offer, great care and consideration should be given to every avenue that will *increase profits, reduce interest costs, increase yield, lower operational and maintenance costs, and minimize risks of ownership*. This can be done by following the step-by-step procedure outlined below:

1. *Purchase price*. After the property has been analyzed and evaluated, the purchase price should be an amount which will create the desired yield on an all cash basis or be a price that will produce the greatest profit when resold. In most cases this can be a price that is considerably less than what the seller is asking. By

the process of offers and counter-offers, the best price can be obtained. It is readily understandable that the lower the purchase price the higher the yield or profit when resold.

2. *Terms of purchase*. First, of course, is the amount of the *down payment*. The seller will have an amount he considers necessary while the investment group may have another amount in mind, taking into consideration their cash position. Usually the amount of the down payment can be agreed upon if both parties are interested in making the transaction. The amount of the *earnest money deposit* that is to be given with the offer should be consistent with the purchase price and the down payment. The terms of purchase must now be determined if the purchase is not for cash. These terms can be simple or complicated depending upon the type of purchase. In Chapter 3, *The Technique of Structured Financing to Increase Profits*, various methods of financing a real estate purchase are outlined. One of these methods is usually acceptable to both the investment group and the seller. Based upon the requirements of the seller and the needs of the investment group, a financing plan for the purchase can be determined.

3. *Conditions of Purchase*. In the purchase of commercial and industrial property, there are usually special conditions related to the close of escrow. These special conditions are identified as contingencies and become a requirement of the purchase. Such contingencies can include but not be limited to the following:

1. Approval of the Preliminary Title Report
2. Rezoning if required
3. Boundary surveys
4. New mortgage financing
5. Subordination if required
6. Engineering and feasibility studies
7. Soil tests
8. Approval of existing mortgage
9. Obtaining leases
10. Annexation
11. Leaseback if required
12. Options if requested
13. Assignment of leases
14. Verification
15. Plus other items which may be necessary and required.

A more detailed explanation of *Making the Purchase* will be given in subsequent chapters describing specific purchases of different types of commercial and industrial real estate.

HOW TO SAVE ON INTEREST IN PURCHASING COMMERCIAL AND INDUSTRIAL PROPERTY

Profits can become larger, yields increase and savings made by an astute and knowledgeable consideration of the rate of interest which will be included in any financing necessary in the purchase of commercial and industrial property and also the method and time of payment.

The normal and customary method in financing a real estate purchase requires that interest either be included in the amortized payments or be paid at the same time and in addition to the regular principal payments. Mortgage companies and other lending institutions charge rates of interest consistent with the current economic situation. It can sometimes be difficult to negotiate a better rate with them. Sellers, on the other hand, can be more flexible and liberal in the rates of interest they will require in the payment of an unpaid contractual balance due them. Being able to obtain a rate of interest from the seller which is considerably less than the currently established rates is one way to save on interest charges.

Interest prepaid or deferred is not interest saved. However, interest forgiven for a period of time is money saved. A contract which stipulates that interest will accrue on the unpaid principal balance beginning with a date one, two, three or more years from the close of escrow and then paid at the same time and in addition to the regular principal payments results in a large savings in interest.

The use of options is yet another way to achieve big savings in interest. It was explained in Chapter 3 how maximum profits can be realized if the purchase is financed using an initial purchase and a series of options. Since interest does not accrue on property under option until the option is exercised, the savings in interest can be sizeable whether there is a single option or a series of options.

HOW ONE INVESTOR SAVED A "BUNDLE" ON INTEREST

There is still another way to save on interest and that is to have a long escrow which provides for payment in cash at the close. This method was used by an investor who saved nearly $90,000 on interest!

This investor wanted to purchase a commercial property that was very important to the overall development plan he had under consideration. The purchase price of the property was to be $900,000, and he wanted to structure a purchase plan that could save him money on the high rate of interest being charged at that time. He knew that he would be able to pay cash in a year but wanted to buy now.

He devised a plan wherein he would not have to pay any interest at all and not be obvious about it. The plan was to enter into an escrow with a sizeable earnest money deposit and close the escrow one year later. He realized that the seller would probably want the earnest money released to him at some point in time.

The investor, in structuring his offer of purchase, included an earnest money deposit of $100,000 with the remaining $800,000 to be paid upon the close of escrow one year later, subject only to his approval of the Preliminary Title Report. The offer was accepted by the seller with the stipulation that the $100,000 earnest money deposit be released to the seller upon the approval of the Preliminary Title Report by the buyer.

Later the earnest money was released, and one year from the opening of the escrow it closed according to the terms of the Escrow Instructions. This maneuver saved the investor one year's interest on $800,000 which at that time was at a very high rate.

THE IMPORTANCE OF HOW TO TAKE TITLE

How title should be held as an individual or as a member of an investment group is most important to every investor in real estate. It can have a far-reaching effect not only on the quiet enjoyment of ownership but also on income taxes and other related problems of ownership.

Laws of each state govern the types and rights of ownership. Before taking title in any real estate transaction, an attorney should be consulted to explain the various types available and recommend the type best suited for the situation at hand, the interest of such ownership being the governing factor.

As an individual, there are a number of ways that title can be held:

1. A single man
2. A single woman
3. A divorced man
4. A divorced woman
5. A married man, as his sole and separate property
6. A married woman, as her sole and separate property
   (In the two separate property types above, a disclaimer deed must be signed by the spouse.)

As an entity, a corporation can hold title also.

Where two or more individuals join together in the ownership of real estate, the following estates can be created:

1. Husband and wife, as community property
2. Tenants in the entirety

3. Tenants in common
4. Joint tenants with right of survivorship

PROVEN PROCEDURES TO USE IN SELLING COMMERCIAL AND INDUSTRIAL PROPERTY TO CREATE MAXIMUM PROFITS

When a commercial or industrial real estate investment has been purchased to create a maximum yield or big profit potential, every known money-saving method is utilized. Escrow procedures, financing with interest saving techniques, and convenient and extended terms with required special conditions are structured into the agreement. After acquisition, cost-cutting operational and maintenance procedures are followed, all of which tends to make the property more desirable, saleable and valuable.

Once your buyer cap has been replaced by a seller's cap, the techniques and procedures of selling take over. While your technique in purchasing was to buy for less and less, the technique in selling is to make more and more profit.

With an income producing commercial or industrial property, this can be done by following the step-by-step procedure outlined below:

1. Establish a larger selling price consistent with a lower yield. (If the purchase is based upon a 13 percent yield, establish a price with a 10 percent yield to the new buyer.)
2. Through better management techniques, reduce maintenance and operating costs. Also determine if rents can be increased.
3. Structure the sale with a down payment sufficient to recapture your invested capital plus your profit.
4. Permit the buyer to assume the existing debt.
5. If unable to sell on a cash to existing debt basis, structure the sale with a financing technique which will pay your profit as quickly as possible.

If your sale of commercial and industrial property is something other than income producing, such as land, the following procedure can be followed to create those maximum profits.

1. Establish a larger selling price consistent with the higher comparables in the area.
2. Anticipate an up-grade in zoning and price the property accordingly.
3. Keep aware of changes in value through appreciation.
4. Sell subject to rezoning if necessary.

5. Sell with a down payment sufficient to recapture your invested capital plus your profit.

6. Permit the buyer to assume the existing debt.

7. If unable to sell on a cash to existing debt basis, structure the sale with a financing technique to pay your profit as quickly as possible.

HOW ONE GROUP OF INVESTORS CREATED A LARGE PROFIT IN THE SALE OF A SMALL OFFICE BUILDING

This investment group purchased a 6,060 square foot neighborhood office building for $160,000. It was an older building but was well-located with an excellent rental record. The terms of the purchase included a down payment of $10,000, assuming the existing $120,000 mortgage payable $15,907 annually at 8¾ percent interest, and giving a second mortgage on the property in the amount of $30,000. This was to be paid monthly in the amount of $251 at 8 percent interest with a balloon payment at the end of the sixth year. The building produced an income of $31,087. After amortization of the 1st and 2nd mortgages and operating expenses, the cash flow was $2,288.

At the beginning of their second year of ownership, they decided to sell the property. During that year they were able to reduce the operating and maintenance expenses by $1,780, thus increasing the cash flow to $4,068. Through amortization their equity had also increased another $6,180.

After evaluating the property based upon a 10 percent yield to a new buyer, they arrived at a price of $217,500. A short time later, they received an offer of $205,000 from a buyer who wanted to make at least 12 percent on his investment. His offer was not acceptable but they signed a counter-offer at $207,500 which the buyer accepted. In calculating the amount of profit made in that one year, they deducted the existing debt of $143,820, leaving a balance of $63,680. From that figure, they further deducted the total amount of their invested capital, including down payment and the amortized payments on the two mortgages, leaving a profit of $34,760. The 120 percent profit could be considered excellent especially since they also earned an additional $4,000 cash flow in that one year of operation.

TECHNIQUES OF FINANCING TO INCREASE PROFIT YIELDS

The best way to increase profit yields is through the application of innovative financing techniques. In Chapter 2, 25 different ways to finance the purchase of a commercial or industrial property were shown. It goes without saying that the method which produces the greatest yield should be the one to use.

Any method which will reduce the amount of the regular monthly payments on the debt will directly increase the yield or cash flow. This can be done by utilizing one of the following financing techniques:

1. Interest only for a few years before amortized payments begin
2. Long-term interim financing
3. Reduction in the rate of interest
4. Extend term of mortgage payment to maximum limits
5. Use of low constant
6. Use of balloon payment

THE STRATEGY OF REZONING FOR ADDITIONAL PROFITS

It has been said that most of the great wealth in this country came through the sale or exchange of real estate. When a person realizes the amount of money that can be made in real estate, he can believe that statement. The impact of zoning in increasing the value of property is sometimes unbelievable.

A five acre parcel located within the city that is zoned for single family residences *can be increased in value four or five times when its zoning is changed to multiple*—maybe more depending upon the density obtained. *A change to commercial or industrial zoning can result in an even greater increase in value.* An astute investor who owns a property that is ready for such commercial or multiple development will establish a price on his property as if the new zoning were already on the property. *Under these conditions it is not difficult for the investor to sell his property subject to the new zoning being obtained.* In addition, he can provide in the sales' escrow that *the buyer secure the change in zoning at his own expense, thereby eliminating the cost of rezoning to the seller.*

To beat this game an investor has to move farther out from the main core of the city and acquire a larger parcel of property, land-plan the property to include a variety of zonings, develop as much as he wants, and sell the balance in accordance with the type of existing zoning. If the parcel is large enough, it can include acreage for single-family residences, apartments, townhouses, commercial and other types of development that may be needed or required. *It is not inconceivable for a small amount of commercially zoned portions of the property to be valued at an amount equivalent to what the entire parcel cost when it was acquired.*

There will be more on the necessity of zoning and the impact of zoning on values and sales along with proven methods and procedures to use in rezoning a property in Chapter 7, ***How to Make Big Profits in Commercial and Industrial Land.***

HOW TO CREATE MAXIMUM LEVERAGE WITH A SMALL INVESTMENT

Leverage can be expressed as gaining the advantage in the purchase of a commercial or industrial property through the use of a variety of innovative financing techniques, utilizing money from other sources with a minimum of your own capital.

Leverage can be created particularly in a small investment by any one or all of the following financing techniques:

1. Little or no down payment
2. Financing the proportionately large unpaid balance on long and extreme terms and conditions
3. Keeping the interest at a level well below existing percentage rates
4. Prepaying one year's interest as a down payment
5. Paying interest only on the first years of the contract before principal payments begin
6. Paying principal only during first years of contract with interest commencing to accrue at a later date

Generally, small investments which are purchased with the thought in mind of reselling at a profit are sold within one and not more than two years. Therefore, the profit realized from the resale should be measured from the standpoint of capital invested. True, profit is determined by the amount of the sale, less expenses, over the base cost of the property; however, the amount of profit in proportion to the amount of cash invested is the important factor to consider.

If commercial or industrial property requires a cash investment of $50,000 to make a profit of $20,000 in a little over one year, it would be considered a good investment, making a 40 percent profit on cash invested. If, however, through leverage and astute financing techniques that same $20,000 can be made with a cash investment of only $16,000, then a good investment has turned into a great investment, with its 125 percent yield on cash.

This can be done and has been done by knowledgeable investors who followed the above guidelines, investing as little cash as possible and reselling the property as quickly as possible. It's a good way to make a fast buck.

KEY POINTS

1. Understand how to convert small parcels to big profits
2. Know how to use rents to purchase an office building

3. Learn the necessary essentials for a small investment
4. Form the investment group
5. Know the techniques of buying as a group
6. Understand interest-saving procedures
7. Learn how to take title
8. Use procedures of selling for maximum profits
9. Know the techniques of financing to increase profit yields
10. Learn to rezone for more profit
11. Understand how to create maximum leverage

5

Investing or Speculating: How to Analyze Risk, Timing, Location and Salability

There is sometimes only a fine line which separates investing from speculating. It can be said that the elements of risk, timing, location and salability of the property are the determining factors which indicate the difference.

In this chapter, the difference between the two approaches to investing in commercial and industrial real estate will be illustrated. With the element of risk ever present, techniques to use to minimize those risks through intelligent buying will be explained. The security of an assured income and the tax advantages in an income producing property will be described along with the beauty of a large Capital-Gain profit. In addition, you will be shown whether to hold for appreciation or operate for depreciation. Investor speculating and the risks of speculating for profit are explained in detail. Also proven guidelines on carefree, risk free investments are given followed by profit opportunities for the informed, knowledgeable investor who speculates on certain types of commercial and industrial property. Scattered throughout the chapters are interesting and informative stories of actual transactions as they apply to investing or speculating.

THE ELEMENT OF RISK IS EVER PRESENT

There is an element of risk in almost every commercial and industrial real estate investment. While some may be small and insignificant, others can be large and problematic. Each must be recognized for what it is and given much thought and consideration.

In determining the risk element in any real estate investment, every investor should know what to look for and where to look. The fact and information profile, income analysis and evaluation forms will provide much needed information. The following lists for both income producing properties and land show those areas where risk problems can exist.

Key risk factors in income producing properties

1. Existing mortgages, trust deed or trust agreements
2. Continuation of income
3. Excessive operating expenses
4. Insurance coverage
5. Real property taxes
6. New financing
7. Construction
8. Equipment

Key risk factors in land and other properties

1. Financing
2. Zoning
3. Topography
4. Drainage
5. Timing
6. Resale
7. Location
8. Development

There will be those risks which are *recognized for what they are*. There will also be those *risks that should be anticipated and resolved*. In addition, there is the *unknown risk that is neither recognized nor anticipated because the investor did not make a thorough analysis and evaluation of the property.*

For those investors who rely on luck and intuition rather than an intelligent study of the facts, each purchase can be more or less speculative. Other investors who structure their purchase after a proper and detailed analysis to minimize whatever risks are present, can make a wise, intelligent and very profitable investment.

HOW TO MINIMIZE THOSE RISKS THROUGH INTELLIGENT BUYING

Once a risk or problem has been recognized for what it is or has been anticipated, consideration should be given to how to minimize those risks. A brief description of each problem is outlined below along with what can be done to minimize the effect of each through intelligent buying procedures.

Minimizing risks in income properties

1. *Existing mortgage, trust deed or trust agreement.* Any existing indebtedness should be understood by reading the documents covering and securing such debts. Special attention should be given to the term of the loan, rate of interest, amortization, acceleration or balloon payment, and other related items. Objectionable portions of the documents should be noted and taken into consideration. It is difficult and most times impossible to obtain permission to change any of the provisions of an existing document. Refinancing under more favorable conditions, however, can be considered.

2. *Continuation of income.* A reduction in income is always a possibility. It is, therefore, essential to read and approve each lease with tenants before assignment and close of escrow. Special consideration should be given to the term of each lease, space occupied, rent, services provided, cancellation rights of the tenant, if any, options to renew and at what rent plus all other items related to income and occupancy. Those items that are objectionable should also be noted and taken into consideration.

3. *Excessive operating expenses.* An operating statement of the property for the prior three to five years should be obtained from the seller. All operating expenses should be studied and analyzed. If the expenses are considered to be excessive, they should be reviewed. If such expenses can be reduced, it will mean additional profits. If they cannot, then the property should be evaluated as it exists and proper consideration given to the high expenses.

4. *Insurance coverage.* All existing insurance policies should be reviewed. If coverage is sufficient, the policies can be retained and assumed or cancelled. If

coverage is inadequate or should be changed, it can be cancelled and new policies issued from the insurance agent of the investor's own choosing.

5. *Real property taxes.* Property taxes should be compared with existing comparable structures as to rate and taxable amount. If found to be excessive, an appeal should be made to the Board of Adjustments for a reduction in rate and valuation. Any lowering of taxes will directly increase profit and cash flow.

6. *New financing.* If new financing is required, there is always a risk in obtaining a satisfactory mortgage loan at a rate of interest and on terms and conditions that will be acceptable. It is, therefore, always wise to make the purchase subject to the obtaining of a satisfactory and acceptable mortgage commitment.

7. *Construction.* A personal inspection of the property should be made to determine not only the quality of the construction but also to determine if extensive repairs are required. If such repairs are needed or if the property needs to be cleaned up and painted, the seller should be required to make such repairs or painting. Your purchase can be made subject to such repairs being made before the close of escrow as a contingency in the purchase agreement.

8. *Equipment.* All equipment, including refrigeration and heating, should be inspected by a qualified person who will determine the condition and serviceability of each item. There is always a risk in existing operating equipment and those items in need of repair or replacement should be noted for appropriate action.

Minimizing risk in land and other properties

1. *Financing.* If the property is purchased with an existing debt, the security documents, whether a mortgage, trust deed or trust agreement, should be studied and understood, giving special attention to those areas that indicate a risk or a problem. If financing is necessary, there is again the risk of obtaining a satisfactory loan. Any purchase, therefore, should be made subject to securing an acceptable loan. In purchasing land, however, the seller will in many instances own the property free and clear of debt and will be willing to take a mortgage on the unpaid balance. Under these conditions, it is possible to structure the financing along terms and conditions acceptable to the investor thereby eliminating the many risks of financing.

2. *Zoning.* The property will either be zoned for the purpose intended or the property will have to be rezoned to permit the planned use. If rezoning is necessary and required, every purchase should be made subject to obtaining the required zoning. This procedure will eliminate the risk of owning a piece of property that can't be used for the desired purpose.

3. *Topography.* If the property is a parcel of land, a topographic survey should be studied and the land inspected to determine if the parcel is completely usable or how much will be lost in development due to the conformation of the land. A good land planner can eliminate all risks that might be present in the usability of the land. Knowing how much of the parcel is usable is very important to every investor or developer and should be taken into consideration in structuring the purchase.

4. *Drainage.* This item is one of the most important physical features to check. It can be a controlling factor in zoning, financing, building permits and development in general. An on-site inspection of the property is mandatory to determine whether the property is subject to flooding. This inspection should be made in addition to a topographic study. In addition, soil tests and percolation tests should be made. The risks of buying a parcel of land that is subject to flooding is too great to take without a proper and adequate inspection.

5. *Timing.* Being at the right place at the right time is not an act of luck but is the result of careful study and a thorough analysis of the facts. The risk of poor timing can lead to an unsuccessful investment while good timing can assure success.

6. *Resale.* Suitability, feasibility and salability are three very important factors to consider in the resale of an investment property. If an investment is made in a parcel of land that is suitable for development by its location, physical characteristics and zoning and if such development is feasible as to need and timing, then the property is salable. The purchase of a property that does not fit this criteria is a risk too great to take and would be considered speculative.

7. *Location.* This is another very important factor that should be analyzed and checked thoroughly. The story at the beginning of this chapter amplifies the importance of location and the risks of a poor selection. An astute investor will always select a location for his investment that is either ready for development or is at least in the path of future growth.

8. *Development.* An investment in commercial or industrial property is usually made for development or for resale to a developer. It is essential that your purchase be structured to permit an orderly and profitable development, not only by a financial technique which will permit and facilitate such development but also by a careful study of the suitability and feasibility of the project.

If every item on the foregoing lists is investigated and checked, keeping in mind those areas where the element of risk can occur, your investment will be made on sound business procedures and will become a very profitable venture. Relying on luck, intuition, price and terms without regard for all of the other important items can result in a very speculative investment with little chance of profit or success.

HOW TO ACHIEVE THE SECURITY OF AN ASSURED INCOME

Making an investment in commercial and industrial property with the security of an assured income and eliminating the risk element, are the aims and desires of all sophisticated investors.

Whether the investment is an apartment complex, a shopping center or an office building, the rental history of the facility should be investigated thoroughly. Those buildings with a high vacancy factor can be speculative investments with no assurance of continued or sufficient income. An astute and knowledgeable investor will want to know and will determine whether his income is secured by advantageous and binding leases, providing for tax, insurance and maintenance increases and will include percentage and escalation factors which will increase the income through greater sales volume and/or a rise in the rate of inflation.

How one investor achieved security

The quality of the tenants should also be investigated as to their financial and performance capabilities. One friend of mine who invested in shopping centers insisted that the tenant ratio in any center under consideration be 75 percent nationals and 25 percent local tenants. By having that ratio, his income was assured for at least a sufficient amount to pay operating costs and to service the debt by the performance and financial stability of the nationally-rated tenants. He was willing to let his profit and cash flow be produced by the selected local tenants. His yield could have been higher with a smaller percentage of nationals but he slept better at nights knowing the security of those national tenants.

THE TAX ADVANTAGES OF INCOME PROPERTY

Tax shelters in income producing commercial and industrial properties were explained in Chapter 1. The tax advantages available to a sophisticated investor can change what would normally be considered a speculation into a sound investment. Some investors with large ordinary incomes will make investments in income properties which show little or no cash flow but produce a large operating loss. To them, this type of investment is considered sound and prudent since the loss can be used to offset other income while increasing their equity position in the investment through amortization.

The same investment to another investor who needs the cash flow as income would be considered speculating since the income produced might not be sufficient to service debt in addition to the operating expenses. A large loss to him is not as important as cash flow. He can, however, through the same tax advantages offset a positive cash flow with the book loss produced by the investment.

THE BEAUTY OF THE CAPITAL GAIN PROFIT

Profits made from the sales of a capital asset are subject to an income tax; however, the profits may be considered a Capital Gain if certain requirements are met.

The Internal Revenue Service has ruled that a capital asset must have been acquired and held for investment for a required length of time to qualify for the preferred Capital Gain's Tax. A number of years ago, this time factor was only six months; however, during the succeeding years it has been extended several times. It is therefore essential and advisable to check with your accountant to determine the prevailing time factor at the time of sale. The amount of Capital Gain's Tax can be calculated two ways.

The first way permits you to add one-half of the profit to your other income and then calculate your tax as ordinary income. The IRS also permits an alternate method whereby the Capital Gain's Tax from the sale is limited to a maximum percentage of the profit. A number of years ago this maximum percentage was 25 percent; however, this limitation has been increased several times. Therefore, it is again necessary to consult with your accountant to determine the best method to use at the time of sale.

Whether you are speculating for a high profit or making a routine sale of an income producing property, the same guidelines are applicable. Many knowledgeable investors in commercial and industrial property always try to qualify the profits made from the sale of an investment for a Capital Gain's Tax. *It is still the best way to retain a higher profit after taxes.*

HOLDING FOR APPRECIATION OR OPERATING FOR DEPRECIATION

In Chapter 1, the significance of appreciation in property and the recovery of capital investment through depreciation were discussed. In Chapter 2, it was pointed out that an investment in commercial and industrial property is usually made for income or resale for profit. Astute investors do one or the other, but seldom both.

Land, whether it is a large parcel, small acreage or lots will appreciate more in percentage of value than an income producing property. Speculative land will increase in value more than any other type of land but the risks are greater. Many investors, however, who specialize in such land are willing to take the risk for a chance at those huge profits. Other more astute investors prefer to eliminate the element of risk and purchase only those parcels of land that are either ready for development or are in the path of future development. Even though the cost per acre is higher and the anticipated percentage of profit is lower, the security of the investment is greater.

An investment for appreciation

One knowledgeable investor explained his choice of land to hold for appreciation this way: A 320 acre parcel of land was under consideration as an investment. The property was located in an undeveloped area about thirty miles from the city. It was essentially speculative land since it was not near or in the anticipated path of development. The price was $300 per acre and the terms of purchase were simple and easy. Its chances of being sold quickly for a nice profit, however, were slim. If the property were held for five years or more, the value might double or even triple. However, it was determined that selling at that time and at that price would be governed by a number of factors over which the investor would have no control. At the same time another property was considered for investment. This parcel totaled 20 acres and was situated on a section line corner near the outskirts of the city and was in the path of development. Its price was $5,000 per acre.

The investor chose the smaller, more expensive parcel because its chances of appreciation far exceeded the more speculative property and in a much shorter time. He realized that through rezoning the commercial value of the property would increase to $40,000 per acre.

Income producing commercial and industrial properties, on the other hand, are usually purchased for income and not for resale by investors who have determined that the security of income is more important than the profits gained by the resale of the property. The many tax advantages available through the application of depreciation is the predominant factor which governs their decision. *It is not uncommon for such depreciation to result in a completely tax-sheltered cash flow.*

WHEN IS AN INVESTOR SPECULATING

Some investors continue to speculate in cheap desert or mountainous land knowing the risks involved. They are willing to take the chance for the high profits that might be made. They give little thought or consideration to the lack of water or other utilities, thinking only of the price and extremely favorable terms available in buying such speculative land.

In 1958, many investors speculated in cheap desert land in an area known as Harquahala Valley. Actually, there was nothing in the area except rocks, sand, a few hills and several roads leading to the numerous mines in the valley. For some reason, speculators started buying land in this huge area. In the beginning, land sold for $6 per acre in large parcels of 160 acres to a section of 640 acres. As the sales boom continued, the price of land jumped about $10 per acre with each sale and at the time of the following story the price was $85 per acre.

One day a man and his wife went into a real estate office and inquired about land in Harquahala Valley. They were from Detroit, Michigan and some friends had told them all about the money that could be made in Harquahala Valley land. The realty company had a number of good listings in the area and these were shown to the man and his wife. Plotting each location on a large map of the area, they selected a half section of 320 acres which was listed at $85 per acre.

They asked if the salesman would drive them out to the area so that they could see the land. This was a normal request except that Harquahala Valley was not a normal area. There were very few roads in this desert. The salesman was quite frank and said that if they went out there, he would not know whether he was within a mile or two of the property they wanted to see. He explained that there were very few roads or landmarks and said, "Frankly, if you go out there and look at that stuff, you won't buy it." They asked if it was really that bad and the salesman had to admit that it was. He did say, however, that people were making money on the land just selling it to the next man that came along. Also, he felt that sales activity in the area would continue to drive the price higher and higher. Since they were determined to buy some Harquahala land, they purchased the 320 acres that they had selected. When the escrow closed, they re-listed the property with the realty company at $125 per acre and another salesman in the office sold it a short time later.

The investor from Detroit made money on his speculative investment because he was lucky in getting in and out at the right time. Not so fortunate, however, were those investors who bought land in the same area at its peak price of $300 per acre. The land boom ended at that price level and those with land are still trying to find a buyer.

Other investors, either through a lack of knowledge or by not investigating the investment thoroughly, purchase a property that they are unable to re-sell at a profit. In their anxiety and desire to make an investment in real estate, they failed to determine the salability of the property and as a result made a speculative purchase without realizing it at the time.

THE RISKS OF SPECULATING FOR PROFIT

During the 1960's, many thousands of acres of cheap, barren, desert land were purchased by land speculators whose only aim was to subdivide the land into smaller parcels and sell them to an unwary and unsuspecting investing public. Their brochures were beautiful and inviting but were only pictures. Their sales techniques were hard, cold and efficient, promising huge profits to be made for those who purchased parcels of land in a proposed community that was never developed.

The many thousands of small investors all over the country who invested in those speculative parcels of land never bothered to check into the risks involved in purchasing such land. They seemed satisfied with the representations made in the beautiful brochures or by the glib and convincing salesman. Their only questions were: how much was the property, what was the down payment and how many years did they have to pay out the contract. They never checked into the background or performance of the developer or the actual location of the property. They never checked when the proposed improvements on the property would be made and whether there was water or other utilities on the property. Very few bothered to look at what they were buying. Needless to say, their speculative purchases never produced the profits they so eagerly anticipated.

Those investors who speculate in land for profit should at least be cognizant of the following risks which will determine the degree of speculation:

1. *Being in the path of possible or continued development.* Select property that has a chance at some sort of development in the foreseeable future.
2. *Have a desirable location.* The property should be located in an area where someone else might want to live, vacation, develop or play.
3. *Timing.* Proper timing can lessen the degree of speculation.
4. *Money Market.* Terms of purchase will be better and prospects of sales improved during a favorable money market.
5. *Economy.* The pulse of the nation's economy should be determined—a rising economy makes resales easier while a falling economy will have an adverse effect.
6. *Water and utilities.* The availability of all utilities to the property greatly enhances the suitability, feasibility and salability of the property. Land without water and power is very, very speculative.
7. *Roads and accessibility.* Land-locked property should be avoided. Every property under consideration should be on an identifiable road with reasonable access to the public.

8. *A planned use.* Property purchased without reason is pure speculation. Even a speculative investor should have some preconceived use for the property.
9. *Rezoning.* If rezoning is necessary, make certain that such zoning is practical and possible. In every instance, such rezoning should be a condition of purchase.
10. *Finding a buyer when ready to sell.* The greatest risk in purchasing speculative land is in finding a buyer when the property is to be resold. If the risks can be minimized and the property made presentable, the chances of a sale increase. At the very least buy something that someone else might want to purchase.

DETAILED GUIDELINES ON CAREFREE, RISK FREE INVESTMENTS

Every investor in commercial and industrial real estate is always looking for a carefree, risk free investment—one that requires very little, if any, maintenance or supervision, yet yields an acceptable return on the invested capital. Such profit opportunities may be found in the following types of commercial and industrial property:

1. Industrial warehouses
2. Commercial buildings
3. Single tenant office buildings
4. Ground leases
5. Service stations
6. Government buildings

To determine the quality of each investment, the following items should be thoroughly checked using the guidelines shown below:

1. *Location.* While the tenant has already approved the location for his use as evidenced by the terms of the lease, it is always important to look at the location as to its future importance beyond the term of the existing lease.
2. *Tenant.* The quality of the tenant must be known and approved. While the lease may stipulate certain terms and conditions, the document is only as strong as the strength of the tenant signing the lease. All investors want to lease to a national tenant with an AAA rating but many have to settle for less. Therefore, it is mandatory to determine the financial strength of each tenant and his performance ability.

3. *Construction*. Even though the lease states that the lessee will maintain the property, it is wise to personally inspect the building and equipment to determine if such maintenance is being performed adequately and properly.
4. *Financing*. Existing financing should be checked and analyzed in detail. The note and mortgage or other security document should be read and understood, making certain that there will be no surprises before the maturity of the note.
5. *Leases*. The income of a property is determined by the terms and conditions of the lease. The security of that income is determined by the performance and quality of the lessee. All details of the lease should be checked and evaluated. Such items as term of the lease, rent to be paid, percentage factors as additional rent, real property taxes, insurance, occupancy, options to renew, cancellation, partial destruction, maintenance of building and equipment are all important. The most desirable lease is one that is described as triple net. It specifies that the lessee will pay real property taxes, insurance and maintain the property.

By following the foregoing guidelines, every investor will know just how secure the income from his investment will be.

HOW TO GAMBLE ON BIG PROFITS

Many times an astute investor will purchase a commercial or industrial property which borders on speculation. As discussed in the beginning of this chapter, there is often only a very fine line which separates investing from speculation.

Gambling on timing

Some investors will gamble on timing. They realize that good buys in commercial and industrial property can be made during periods of tight money or a downturn in the economy. They also know that they may have to hold the property for a longer period of time but are willing to speculate on being able to sell the property at a much higher price when the timing is better or the economy begins to rise.

One such investor purchased 320 acres of land in an area northwest of the city. He knew that in time the area would explode with development everywhere, but at the time of his purchase, land was just not being sold. The housing market was at its lowest level and commercial development was extremely slow. Having the knowledge and foresight with the necessary financial strength, he purchased the property at an excellent price and on extreme terms including an initial purchase and a series of options. In a few years the housing market began to improve and builders were again looking for good land. Along with other increased housing came the demand for more commercial development, and this investor was ready. Having already zoned the property for development into single-family residences, apartments, townhouses and a large shopping center, the investor began to reap the rewards of having made a good investment. His profit was tremendous since he only paid $3,500 per acre for the entire parcel. His sales of the 40 acre commercial corner, 60 acres of apartment and townhouse land plus over 200 acres of residential housing totaled over $4,500,000.

Gambling on occupancy

Other investors will gamble on occupancy. Not long ago Phoenix was overbuilt with office buildings as were many other cities around the country. More square footage of office space was available than could be absorbed through normal demand and expansion.

A number of years ago, a large national development corporation acquired 10 acres of land fronting on Central Avenue with plans to develop the property into a beautiful commercial complex encompassing office buildings, a bank, hotel and large parking garage. The first project was a high-rise office building followed closely by the bank building. The next building was to have been an uptown hotel; however, the insurance company providing the funds had some thoughts about the success of such a hotel at that location. As a result, they approved the construction of a high-rise combination of hotel and office building with the lower floors for the hotel and the upper floors for offices. It was later proven that the developer was right and the insurance company wrong. The hotel was an immediate success while the office portion of the building had vacancies due to a progressive over-building of office space in Phoenix. To satisfy the demand for more hotel rooms, a hotel annex was built along with a large parking garage.

According to their master plan, the last project was to be another high-rise office building. Even though the vacancy factor in office space continued to rise, the developing corporation commenced construction on their last 23-story office building. By the time construction was completed, the vacancy factor was at its highest level. Because it was a part of a beautiful complex, the first three floors were rented to various local companies on short-term leases, and it began to look as if the developer might be in real trouble.

For quite some time the upper 20 floors of this beautiful building remained empty. Then, one day, much to the relief of everyone, an announcement appeared in the local paper stating that the building had been leased in its entirety to one of the largest corporations in the country and that the huge corporation would move its national headquarters to Phoenix. Needless to say, such a transition provided a tremendous boost in the real estate market in Phoenix with several hundred executives and their families moving en masse to the city. This certainly took the developer off the hook with his 23-story building that was practically empty.

KEY POINTS

1. Understand the elements of risk involved in income producing and other types of commerical and industrial property
2. Minimize risks through intelligent buying
3. Evaluate the security of an assured income
4. Learn the tax advantages of income property
5. Study the importance of a Capital Gain Profit
6. Know whether to buy for appreciation or operate for depreciation
7. Realize when an investor is speculating
8. Be familiar with the risks of speculating for profit
9. Be ready to take risks and speculate in certain types of commercial and industrial property

6

Making the Most of Profit Opportunities in Apartment Investments

As a real estate investment, apartments offer more profit opportunities than any other type of commercial or industrial property. From the large 200-unit complex down to the smaller apartments, there is an opportunity to fit any size investment. The following case examples show the profits that can be made in any type of apartment investment.

One investor purchased an older 36-unit apartment building. After remodeling and increasing the rental income, he was able to sell the apartments at an excellent profit of $210,000.

Another investor who purchased a $950,000 apartment complex with a relatively small down payment and innovative secondary financing, was able to make a cash flow of nearly $25,000 which represented a yield of almost 20 percent on his cash invested. In addition, he was able to enjoy the tax shelter provided by the investment.

The young investor who purchased a four-plex was extremely happy when, at the end of the year, he discovered that he had been living for free in one unit while the rent from the other three units paid the mortgage, insurance, taxes and incidental expenses and at the same time showed a cash flow of a little over $150 a month.

In this chapter, techniques, procedures and guidelines for evaluating the many profit opportunities available in apartment investments will be discussed. In addition, actual transactions will illustrate details of numerous apartment purchases and sales.

THE IMPORTANCE OF APARTMENT LOCATION

A good location is one of the most important factors to consider in evaluating an apartment investment. It is a proven fact that a nice apartment complex in a poor location has less chance of being a good investment than one not so nice but situated in an area offering the required conveniences.

In analyzing the location as to its desirability, the following checklist can be most helpful:

1. *Accessibility*. The apartment complex should be located in an area that is on or near major arterial streets which provide easy access to all points of the city.
2. *Schools*. It is essential that the apartment facility be located within walking or busing distance to both elementary and high schools. Parochial and private schools are not as important.
3. *Churches*. The apartment complex should be in the vicinity of churches of the various denominations.
4. *Shopping*. Being near a neighborhood shopping center which can provide tenants with the everyday necessities is very important. The location should also be within an easy driving distance to a regional shopping center where the larger department stores are located. Neighborhood shopping centers are usually scattered throughout a city while the larger regional centers are situated in the midst of a heavily populated area.
5. *Employment Centers*. While it is not necessary for the location to be close to an employment center, it should be on a street with easy access to freeways for movement to all points in the city.
6. *Transportation*. Having public transportation available is not mandatory but it will ease the transportation problem for many.
7. *Recreation*. Certain recreation facilities will probably be included within the apartment complex. It is also advisable for the location to be near or within a reasonable distance to other public recreational facilities.

All information concerning location of the apartment complex should be shown in the Fact and Information Profile on each apartment investment under consideration. A sample profile is shown in Chapter 2, providing a ready reference to every question regarding location.

SELECTING THE PROPER INVESTMENT FOR YOUR PROGRAM WITH GUIDELINES AND CHECKLISTS

A knowledgeable investor who is considering making an investment in an apartment complex will follow an established procedure in selecting the proper apartment. Those apartments under consideration are investigated and checked thoroughly using the Property Check List as shown in Chapter 2.

Step 1. The first step in the selection process will be the preparation of a Fact and Information Profile as described in Chapter 2. The following information is most important and should be included in the Profile:

1. Price
2. Description of property
3. Location of property
4. Type of construction
5. Land area
6. Present zoning
7. Size of buildings—Rentable area
8. Number of Units—Types
9. Parking facilities
10. Services provided
11. Furnishings
12. Income and expenses
13. Taxes and Insurance
14. Encumbrance
15. Amortization
16. Tenants—leases—rates
17. Quality of area
18. Distances to: City business area
Employment center
Airport—bus—rail
19. Public transportation
20. Nearest shopping center

21. Schools
22. Churches

Step 2. An analysis of the income and expense should be made not only for the current year but also for the past several years of operation. The following section describes in detail the procedure to follow in verifying and analyzing the operating statement.

Step 3. A personal inspection of the property should be made, checking the construction, maintenance, equipment, and general condition of the buildings. What to look for and where to find it is shown in a subsequent section of this chapter.

Step 4. A detailed and comprehensive evaluation of the property should be made using the Income Analysis and Evaluation form as shown in Chapter 2. Other dependable techniques to use in evaluating an apartment investment are described in a subsequent section.

Step 5. This is the moment of decision. As a result of the foregoing steps, a selection can be made as to which investment is most suitable and satisfies the requirements of the investor. How to make that decision is explained and described in subsequent sections of this chapter.

VERIFYING AND ANALYZING THE INCOME AND EXPENSE

As shown in Step 2, the income and expense should be verified and analyzed. To do this, the investor must be given an operating statement showing the actual total income and expense of the project. In addition to the current year, similar statements should be obtained for the past three to five years. By having the figures on several years operation, the true income and expense of the property can be determined.

If the seller wants to provide a pro-forma operating statement, showing an income when fully rented less a 5 percent vacancy factor and estimated expenses, *insist upon actual income and expense figures.* Vacancy factors can be misleading and very inaccurate while estimated expenses can be understated. After an acceptable operating statement has been provided, both income and expense totals should be verified as being correct.

Verification of rental income can be made by an inspection of bank deposits and leases with tenants. Other income from laundry facilities and coin-operated vending machines can be verified by a statement from the concessionaire or again by bank deposits.

Verification of all operating expenses should be made by a detailed inspection of the charges for services which would include the following:

1. Utilities
2. Janitor
3. Equipment repairs and maintenance
4. Landscaping and lawn service
5. Pool
6. Painting and decorating
7. General repair and maintenance
8. Management and housekeeping

In addition, real property taxes and insurance should be checked and verified as to amount and coverage. After all income and expenses have been verified, both should be analyzed and placed in the proper perspective.

In analyzing the income, every investor should be interested in the relation between actual income and the total potential income. In other words, he should want to know how much vacancy actually existed during the current year of operation. Also his analysis should include thoughts and plans to increase income to 100 percent occupancy.

Each item of expense should be analyzed as to whether it is low, normal or excessive. Much thought and consideration should be given to those items that can be reduced since a reduction in expenses will increase profits. In our area, operating expenses total between 30 to 36 percent of gross income, depending upon location and type of operation.

THE STRATEGY OF THE PERSONAL TOUR

A personal tour of the apartment complex is a definite part of the selection process, detailed in Step 3. An investor should always see the property under consideration. The checklist for a personal tour should include the following items for verification:

1. Location
2. Size of Property
3. Zoning
4. Size of Buildings—Number of Units
5. Parking—Number of Spaces
6. Physical Condition

7. Good features
8. Bad Points
9. Quality of Area
10. Accessibility

During the tour, the investor should be shown the property to his satisfaction. Every item in the above checklist should be checked and verified, as he makes note of good and bad points. The inspection tour should last as long as the investor has items and areas to check. Often a personal tour can be conducted with a ''get it over with'' attitude. Since the purchase of a sizeable apartment complex can be a million dollar or more investment, the astute and knowledgeable investor will take time and thoroughly check each item on his list.

CHECKING THE CONSTRUCTION AND MAINTENANCE—WHAT TO LOOK FOR AND WHERE TO FIND IT

Of all the items on the checklist for the personal inspection tour, the most important is the physical condition of the property. Not every investor is qualified to properly inspect and determine the structural quality and physical condition of the apartment complex. Many times it is necessary to use the services of a plumber, electrician, heating and refrigeration engineer or some other specialist to inspect these structural parts of the buildings. As a guide for future use, the following checklist shows those items that should be thoroughly and expertly inspected.

1. General building structures
2. Roof
3. Plumbing
4. Electric facilities
5. Elevators, if any
6. Refrigeration equipment
7. Heating equipment
8. Painting—both exterior and interior
9. Pool
10. Pool equipment
11. Recreational equipment
12. Landscaping
13. Gas and electric meters
14. Laundry, washers and dryers, if included
15. Carports
16. Driveways and paving

It is important to know, *before the purchase,* the condition of the following critical items:

1. If the plumbing is faulty
2. Whether the electrical system is overloaded and if circuit breakers are used
3. If the heating and refrigeration systems are adequate and in good working condition
4. Whether the exteriors of the buildings need repainting
5. Or, if the apartment units need redecorating
6. Whether the landscaping is being properly maintained and growing
7. If the roof leaks or needs repairing
8. If the buildings are structurally sound
9. Whether the pool equipment is in need of repair
10. Plus numerous other items so important to the operation and enjoyment of the apartment complex

In addition, all warranties and guarantees covering equipment should be noted. It is important to know those items still under warranty or guarantee. Those items in need of repair or replacement should be noted and become a condition of purchase, requiring the seller to repair or replace those items.

A good approach to inspections

One investor was very particular about the condition and maintenance of the heating and refrigeration equipment. As a result, he would always inspect the equipment room first. Often he would not purchase an apartment complex because the heating and refrigeration room was dirty and the equipment showed signs of not being properly maintained. He felt that if the owner was that sloppy in maintaining this important and expensive equipment, he would be equally as careless in maintaining everything else.

Not long ago, he was shown an apartment complex which he had under consideration as an investment. Following his usual procedure, he asked to see the refrigeration equipment room first. When he stepped into the room, he was pleasantly surprised to see an immaculate and spotless equipment room. Tools and supplies were hanging or neatly stacked. The motors and compressors were running quietly and efficiently. He listened attentively and respectfully as the owner explained and described each piece of equipment.

After leaving that room, he inspected other items on his checklist and found the same neat, clean and well-maintained condition throughout the complex. Returning to his office, he prepared an offer to purchase the property after a comprehensive evaluation. However, being an astute and prudent investor, he made his offer contingent upon a more detailed and thorough inspection of the property by his team of specialists and his approval of their report.

WHAT TO DO ABOUT POOR CONSTRUCTION AND BAD MANAGEMENT

After a complete and thorough inspection of the apartment complex, it can be determined if the structure is well-built or poorly constructed. If there is evidence of poor construction, the property should normally not be considered as a good investment. If, however, the property can be improved with new construction techniques and can be purchased well below its market value, a second evaluation should be made. This time the cost of improvements should be added to the purchase price to determine its true value. At that time a decision can be made as to whether the investment is worth the trouble and work. With so many good profit opportunities available in apartments, it is seldom worthwhile to try to make a silk purse out of a sow's ear.

It is not uncommon for a well-located apartment complex to show a high vacancy factor and to have a rapid turnover in tenants. Generally, this problem is the result of bad management. There are some management firms and apartment managers who feel their only responsibility is to collect the rents. They lack the initiative or interest to maintain a clean, orderly and well-run apartment operation—by listening not only to the complaints of tenants but also having the ability and foresight to satisfy those complaints.

An old boss once said to me many years ago, "You can stipulate in a contract what a contractor must do but you cannot, thereby, endow him with capabilities he does not possess." There are many good, reputable and efficient apartment management firms that can provide excellent management. It is advisable, however, to investigate each company as to their performance capabilities before entering into a management contract.

DEPENDABLE TECHNIQUES IN ANALYZING AND EVALUATING AN APARTMENT INVESTMENT

In Chapter 2 we discussed how to analyze and evaluate any type of income producing commercial and industrial property. Now it is necessary to follow those same steps and procedures to properly analyze and evaluate an apartment investment.

Step 1. Using the Property Check List, all known facts and information relative to the property should be itemized.

Step 2. From the information gathered in the Property Check List, a Fact and Information Profile should be prepared. A sample profile is shown in Chapter 2.

Step 3. An Income Analysis and Evaluation Form should now be completed. Applicable information from the Fact and Information Profile can be used to complete the form through Cash Spendable Income. The last four entries on the form can then be calculated as shown in Chapter 2.

Step 4. The three steps shown above assist in analyzing and evaluating an apartment investment based upon the asking price of the seller. This fourth step is a procedure whereby the investment is evaluated as to its value to the investor. By consulting the table in Chapter 2 on acceptable yields for apartments, the investor determines the yield he expects on his cash investment. If he decides that 13 percent is an acceptable yield to him, he divides the Cash Spendable Income by that desired yield. The resulting amount is then added to the current mortgage balance for a value of the property. In the event the current mortgage balance is unusually small and a distorted value results, the investor should follow the procedure of capitalizing the operating profit before debt service as shown in that Section of Chapter 2, *A Simple Method in How To Capitalize an Income Investment.* By using this technique, an investor can accurately evaluate an apartment investment and determine what his offer should be.

HOW ONE REAL ESTATE INVESTMENT CORPORATION ANALYZED AND EVALUATED A LARGE APARTMENT COMPLEX

Following their established procedure, a Fact and Information Profile was prepared by one successful investment corporation, using information from the Property Check List. Their profile contained items shown below:

FACT AND INFORMATION PROFILE
LINCOLN VILLA—DATED 11/1/77 OWNER—LINCOLN VILLA, INC.

1. Price—$4,726,000
2. Description of Property—Lots 4, 5, 6 and 7, Block 1, Lincoln Heights
3. Location of Property—23rd Avenue and Indian Road—Phoenix

4. Type of Construction—Block
5. Land Area—10.1 acres
6. Present Zoning—R-4
7. Size of Buildings—14 Apartment—1 other
8. Number of Units—128 Studios
   144-1 Bdrm.-1 Ba.
   4-2 Bdrm.-1 Ba.
   4-2 Bdrm.-2 Ba.
9. Parking Facilities—1:1 Ratio
10. Service Provided—All utilities paid by Lessor
11. Furnishings—All units furnished
12. Income and Expenses—Total Income $693,490
    Total Expenses $258,724
    (See attached Operating Statement for breakdown)
13. Taxes and Insurance—Taxes - $67,310
    Insurance - 4,896
14. Encumbrance—$3,089,645—National Bank
15. Amortization—$298,672.00—8⅝%—25 years
16. Tenants Leases—Rates—See attached rental schedule
17. Quality of Area—Medium Income
18. Distances to: City business area - 6 miles
    Employment centers - 3 miles - 5 miles
    Airport - bus - rail - 6 miles - 9 miles
19. Public Transportation—Indian Road
20. Nearest Shopping Center—1 mile
21. Schools—2 mile College—1 mile Elementary and High School
22. Church—1 mile

From the information contained in the above profile, an Income Analysis and Evaluation form was completed on the apartments as shown below:

INCOME ANALYSIS AND EVALUATION
LINCOLN VILLA DATED 11/1/77 OWNER: LINCOLN VILLA, INC.

Total Listed Price - $4,726,000
Current Mortgage Balance - $3,089,645
8⅝% - $24,889.33 Mo. P+I
Cash Required - $1,636,355
Total Effective Rental Income:

Gross Rent	$697,236.00
Other Income	32,760.00
Sub-Total	729,966.00

Vacancy (5%)	36,500.00		
Effective Income			$693,496.00
Operating Expenses:			
Salaries	$45,000		
Advertising	9,800		
Maintenance	40,000		
Management	33,119	(5%)	
Utilities	63,099	(actual)	
Real Estate Taxes	67,310.00	(actual)	
Insurance	4,896.00		
Total Expenses			$258,724.00
Operating Profit			$434,772.00
Less Debt Service			298,672.00
Cash Spendable Income			$136,100.00
Gain in Equity			32,500.00
Total Gain			$168,600.00
Yield—Cash on Cash			8.3%
Total Yield			10.3%

By consulting the tables on acceptable yields on apartments as shown in Chapter 2, the corporation quickly determined that the yield as shown in the above Analysis and Evaluation was too low to be acceptable.

To evaluate the property using more acceptable yields, cash on cash, the corporation determined the following high, medium and low values of the apartments:

13%	$4,136,568.00
14%	4,061,787.00
15%	3,996,978.00

To explain, the above valuations result from dividing the Cash Spendable Income by the desired yield and then adding the current mortgage balance.

TESTED GUIDELINES ON HOW TO BUY—WITH CHECKLISTS ON PRICE, TERMS AND CONDITIONS

After the decision has been made to purchase a specific apartment complex following the analysis and evaluation of the property, consideration must be given to the preparation of an offer to purchase.

The three main parts of the offer should be:

1. Price
2. Terms
3. Special conditions

Price. The purchase price should be the result of a careful analysis and evaluation of the property. In determining that price, the technique of capitalizing income to an acceptable yield is the procedure to use, as shown in Chapter 2 and again in the foregoing sections of this chapter.

Terms. The terms of the purchase should include the following items:

1. *Down payment, including earnest money deposit.* This amount represents the cash invested and should be given careful consideration. The amount should be that which will produce the desired yield.
2. *Existing encumbrance.* Before assuming the encumbrance, the security documents should be carefully studied and understood, making certain that all conditions are as represented.
3. *New financing.* If secondary financing is to be considered in addition to the assumption of an existing indebtedness, one of the financing methods shown in Chapter 3 should be used, making certain that such secondary financing accomplishes the leverage desired. In most cases, the seller will provide this type of financing, taking a second mortgage on the property. In the event refinancing is required, the new financing should be structured to include the needs of the investor as to term, rate of interest and at an acceptable constant which will create the desired yield.
4. *Prorations.* The following items should be prorated as of the close of escrow or a specific date:
   a. Real property taxes
   b. Insurance
   c. Assessments
   d. Interest
   e. Rents
   f. Other applicable items

Special Conditions. Any of the following items could become a condition of the purchase:

1. *Approval of the Preliminary Title Report.* The purchase should be contingent upon the investor's written approval of the Preliminary Title Report. This report indicates the condition of title, making reference to easements, mortgages, restrictions, leases and other matters important to the ownership of the property.

2. *Verification of income and expense.* If the investor is not satisfied as to the accuracy and reliability of the information provided prior to the offer, such verification should become a condition of the purchase.
3. *Inspection and approval of all existing leases.* Leases with all tenants should be read, understood and accepted in writing.
4. *Assignment of Leases.* All leases should be assigned to the investor at the close of escrow.
5. *Rent Statement.* The seller should be required to furnish a rent statement showing the status of rents paid or to be paid by each tenant as of the close of escrow. Prepaid rent or rent deposits are to be credited to the investor at the close of escrow.
6. *Warranties and Guarantees.* Any repairs that should be the responsibility of the seller should be itemized, described and become a condition of the purchase.

THE TECHNIQUE OF FINANCING TO INCREASE LEVERAGE

A knowledgeable investor can structure the financing to minimize his invested cash and at the same time increase not only his leverage but also his yield.

To explain this procedure, the purchase of the large 280-unit apartment complex by the real estate investment corporation will be continued. The corporation decided to purchase the property at a price that would yield 13 percent. In accordance with their evaluation, the offered price was to be $4,136,568. After deducting the existing mortgage of $3,089,645, the cash required would have been $1,046,923.

To conserve cash, the corporation decided to pay $500,000 down and have the seller carry the balance on a five year, interest-only note and mortgage, with the entire principal balance due at maturity but with the right to prepay portions of the principal amount at any time. The rate of interest was to be the same as on the existing first mortgage—8⅝ percent. Since the cash spendable income of $136,100 was tax free, it was further decided to apply that amount to the principal and interest due on the secondary note, thereby paying off that note within five years. In this manner, half of the down payment was paid from operations and with tax-free money. In addition, the reduced down payment and leverage financing increased the yield to 18 percent. At the end of the initial five years, the yield further increased to 25 percent—cash on cash.

Since all of the cash spendable income was being used to pay off the note, the lack of a cash yield on the $500,000 invested was not disturbing to the corporation. The book loss of more than $100,000 for the first year of operation was equivalent to a 20 percent yield when it was calculated into their overall extensive apartment investments.

HOW TO CALCULATE YIELD TO PURCHASE PRICE

How the corporation determined a purchase price for the large apartment complex by capitalizing the cash spendable income for a specific yield has been briefly explained. To further illustrate the technique, the following step-by-step procedure is outlined:

Step 1. The Cash Spendable Income must be determined. This is done by preparing the Income Analysis and Evaluation form as explained in Chapter 2. In the foregoing transaction that amount was $136,100.
Step 2. The Cash Spendable Income is then divided by the desired yield. Again, using the foregoing transaction, the desired yield of 13 percent was divided into $136,100, resulting in an amount of $1,046,923.
Step 3. Add the above resulting amount to the current mortgage balance.

Shown below is the result of the corporation's calculations.

Capitalized Cash Spendable Income	$1,046,923.00
Current Mortgage Balance	3,089,645.00
Offer Price at 13% yield	$4,136,568.00

DETERMINING WHETHER TO OPERATE FOR TAX-SHELTERED INCOME OR SELL FOR CAPITAL GAIN PROFIT

In the beginning, investors generally consider an investment in an apartment complex for its tax-sheltered income. The purchase is structured to provide the maximum yield with the minimum of risks. As long as the income is sufficient and the tax advantages remain in effect, the investor usually continues to own and operate the apartments for the tax-sheltered income. However, many things can happen to change an investor's mind during the initial months of operation.

After the property has been held the required length of time to qualify for Capital Gain, a decision can be made at that time—whether to continue ownership or sell. The following section will describe a technique which will be helpful in making that decision.

THE TECHNIQUE OF INCREASING YIELD FOR MORE PROFIT IN SELLING

It should be readily understood that any change in the income, expenses and amortization will directly affect the yield. Therefore, the technique is to increase the income while decreasing the expenses and, if possible, lower the monthly payments on the mortgage.

Income can be increased by renting the vacant apartments and by periodic rental increases of all apartments. Operating expenses can be decreased by a careful and thorough study of those expenses. It is prudent and wise to make certain that the real property taxes are no more than they should be. Insurance premiums should be checked every year also.

As a general rule, it is very difficult to reduce the monthly payments on the existing mortgage; however, there are times when a difficult mortgage may be renegotiated to the advantage of the investor. If this fails, refinancing is sometimes the answer.

One apartment investor makes a specialty of upgrading the income of his apartments. In so doing, he makes a nice profit each time he sells one of his apartment complexes. One apartment complex that he purchased had an annual income of $102,784 with a 7 percent vacancy existing at the time. The operating expenses were a little high at $39,058. The existing $340,000 mortgage was payable at $3,020 a month, prinicpal and interest. The resultant Cash Spendable Income was $27,486. His offer of $550,000, which was calculated to produce a 13 percent yield, was accepted.

As a result of a good advertising campaign, he was able to not only rent the vacant apartments but also to increase the overall rent by 7 percent. At the same time, he reduced his operating expenses. After operating the apartments for one year, he prepared the new Income Analysis and Evaluation form on the property as shown below:

Total Income	$118,256.00	
Operating Expenses	37,858.00	
Operating Profit		$80,398.00
Less Debt Service		36,240.00
Cash Spendable Income		44,158.00
Gain in Equity		6,500.00
Total Gain		$50,658.00
Yield—Cash on Cash ($210,000.00)		21%
Total Yield		24.1%

Since he had purchased the property a year before based upon a 13 percent yield, he was pleased to see that his cash on cash yield had increased to 21 percent on his original investment of $210,000.

He then capitalized the increased yield into new valuations and possible selling prices as shown below:

12% yield - $700,000.00
13% yield - $675,000.00

Needless to say, it was a difficult decision to make—whether to continue operating the apartments at the new increased income or to sell for a fast Capital Gain Profit.

HOW TO SELL FOR MAXIMUM PROFIT

After the income of the apartment complex has been increased and the operating expenses decreased, the Cash Spendable Income will automatically increase. As a result, the yield will also increase proportionately. At that time the investor usually gives consideration to selling the investment. Once he decides to sell, his thinking centers on a plan to make the maximum profit possible. The increase in yield will assure a nice profit and structured financing will further increase that profit to the maximum.

In the foregoing example, the investor had increased the cash yield to 21 percent on his invested capital. When he considered selling, he capitalized the yield at 12 percent and discovered that the apartment complex was worth $700,000 for another investor who would pay cash to mortgage. Since a purchase under this type of financing would require $366,500 as a down payment, the number of investors capable and willing to make such a cash investment were very limited.

By structuring additional financing on a portion of the down payment through the use of a second mortgage, he found that the selling price could be increased and still yield 12 percent to a new buyer. With this financing technique, the new evaluated selling price was $750,000. At this price, he decided to sell because the profit would be $200,000.

His sales plan at $750,000 required the buyer to assume the existing mortgage of $333,500, leaving a balance due the investor of $416,500. The down payment would be $216,500 and the remaining $200,000 would be financed on a second mortgage, payable interest only at 9 percent with the entire balance due at the end of five years. His calculations under this sales plan are shown below:

Total Income	$118,256.00	
Operating Expenses	37,858.00	
Operating Profit		$80,398.00
Less Debt Service:		
1st Mortgage	36,240.00	
2nd Mortgage	18,000.00	
Total Debt Service		54,240.00
Cash Spendable Income		$26,158.00
Gain in Equity		7,500.00
Total Gain		$33,658.00
Yield—Cash on Cash ($200,000.00)		12%
Total Yield		15.5%

It can be seen by an analysis of the above evaluation form that the investor, through an innovative financing technique, was able to increase the selling price an additional $50,000 and at the same time produce an identical 12 percent yield to the new buyer. Also the down payment recaptured his original invested capital of $210,000.

Another financing technique to increase yield for more profit in selling is refinancing. Many times this technique is particularly applicable to apartments. When, through a number of sales, the apartment complex is encumbered with not only a first mortgage but also a second, third and maybe even a fourth mortgage, refinancing is the only solution to a profitable investment. Since the additional mortgages are generally short-term, the cash flow diminishes considerably with the accelerated debt service. By consolidating all of the mortgages into one new long-term first mortgage, the cash spendable income will immediately increase. Also, as an extra profit technique, those second, third and fourth mortgages can usually be discounted for cash.

Needless to say, an astute and wise investor will utilize the most productive financing techniques to realize the maximum profits when selling his apartment investment.

KEY POINTS

1. Understand the importance of location
2. Use guidelines and checklists in selecting the proper investment
3. Know ways to verify and analyze the income and expense
4. Learn which strategies to use in the personal inspection tour of the property
5. Understand the importance of checking the construction and maintenance

6. Use guidelines for coping with poor construction and bad management
7. Use dependable techniques in analyzing and evaluating an apartment investment
8. Know the procedures used by a real estate investment corporation in analyzing and evaluating a large apartment complex
9. Learn positive guidelines for buying apartments
10. Study the techniques of financing to increase leverage
11. Learn how to calculate yield to purchase price
12. Understand the considerations concerning whether to operate for tax-sheltered income or to sell for a Capital Gain profit
13. Study the techniques of increasing yield for more profit in selling
14. Use guidelines for selling for a maximum profit through the use of innovative financing techniques

7

How to Make Big Profits in Commercial and Industrial Land

Big profits have been made and can still be made by the smart, innovative investor in the sale, development and exchange of land. Those huge profits are sometimes unbelievable but the opportunities are available as will be pointed out and explained in detail.

Beginning with the many uses in land development, we will discuss the importance of location for immediate use or future appreciation. The ten steps to follow in finding a commercial or industrial lot for a specific purpose are most informative. Equally important is the list of items to thoroughly check before a purchase is made. The necessity of zoning and its impact on values and sales is descriptively explained. In addition, the ten important steps to follow in rezoning land will be detailed. Structured financing techniques to use in purchasing and selling land are described along with proven and tested examples, followed by a story of how one investor made an additional profit through the use of structured financing. Also, illustrations will be given on how profits can be increased through the use of options along with techniques and methods to use in planning a Multiple Sale Project with its three-phase program. Throughout the chapter actual transactions are described, amplifying these salient points. To whet your appetite, the following examples are given as the transactions actually occurred.

One investor and businessman always bought more land than was needed for his particular purpose. He realized that his development would enhance the value of the adjacent land. Rather than make that additional profit for someone else, he would purchase acreage or frontage on both sides of where he intended to build.

In one location he needed 100 feet of frontage for his new building. Selecting a parcel with 300 feet of frontage on the main arterial, he paid $300,000 for the property. When he commenced building, he sold the remaining 200 feet as a location for a large bank. This maneuver resulted in receiving free land for his building or a parcel worth in excess of $150,000 after both his building and the new bank were constructed.

In another city he needed about 2½ acres for another building. Again, he purchased more than was required for his development. This time he selected two adjacent 5 acre parcels on a main thoroughfare and paid $360,000 for the 10 acres. When he had completed construction of his new theatre and had opened for business, he sold the remaining frontage on one 5 acre parcel and sold the other 5 acre parcel in its entirety for an amount well in excess of $1,000,000.

These are only two representative examples of how this investor made tremendous profits in land. He recognized the potential of location, rezoning and land development in increasing the value of his adjacent property. Other land investors have been equally as successful by following the procedures, techniques and principles as outlined in this chapter.

THE FLEXIBILITY OF MULTIPLE USES IN LAND DEVELOPMENT

Under everything is the land. As the foundation for all real estate development, its uses are many and varied. Astute and knowledgeable investors know this and shape their investment programs accordingly.

The list below outlines a few specific uses and real estate developments that are most prevalent today.

1. Single-family residences
2. Townhouses
3. Apartments
4. Condominiums
5. Office buildings
6. Shopping centers
7. Stores, shops and service buildings
8. Medical buildings

9. Industrial warehouses
10. Distribution centers
11. Manufacturing facilities
12. Recreational facilities
13. Mobile home parks
14. Garage and service stations
15. Automobile dealers
16. Theatres

Some investors may specialize in purchasing and operating any one of the foregoing commercial or industrial properties. Others may develop and sell specific projects while a few will package large parcels of land for sale and development by still other investors and developers. It is a continuing process that grows with the economy of the country and the need for such facilities. This flexibility in multiple uses in land development is what makes investing in commercial and industrial real estate both challenging and very rewarding.

THE IMPORTANCE OF LOCATION FOR IMMEDIATE USE OR TO HOLD FOR APPRECIATION

In an investment in land, one of the most important factors to consider is location. Whether the land is being purchased for immediate development or whether it is to be held for appreciation or later development, a complete and thorough analysis of the location should be made.

In the foregoing section a number of the most prevalent types of development, both residential and commercial/industrial were given. Location is most important to all of them; however, the requirements of some may differ from others.

Land for development into residential uses, whether single-family, apartments, townhouses or condominiums must be situated in an area with easy access to schools, churches, employment centers, and shopping and recreational facilities. While commercial developments should be on land in a densely populated area, the size and type of facility will determine the population required as well as its drawing radius. A regional shopping center requires much more population than a neighborhood center but has a much wider drawing area. Industrial development should be near or have easy access to highways, freeways, truck routes, rail and all other transportation facilities.

An investor who is considering a land purchase to hold for appreciation in value must by all means study future growth projections of the city, making certain that the location is in the path of future or proposed development. One astute investor once told me that the three most important factors to consider when buying land are: 1. Location, 2. Location, and 3. Location.

THE TECHNIQUE OF FINDING A COMMERCIAL OR INDUSTRIAL LOT FOR A SPECIFIC PURPOSE

Finding a location for a specific development is a technique which utilizes proven procedures followed by the most informed and knowledgeable investor/developers. As a general rule, the commercial or industrial lot is required for the development of a facility for use by one or more tenants. The need could be for apartments, stores, shops, service buildings, an industrial warehouse, medical building, automobile dealer or an office building.

With the exception of an apartment development, the following step-by-step procedure can be used to find an acceptable site for the commercial or industrial facility:

STEP ONE. *Requirements of tenant or tenants.* It is important for the investor/developer to know the requirements of the tenant or tenants as to size of lot, building area, rentable space, floor plan and parking requirements. He can determine these requirements by having the tenant or other prime tenants list their needs with a rough sketch of a floor plan.

STEP TWO. *Location of general area defined.* The location of the development will be described as being within a given area. In Phoenix, a prime tenant will indicate that he is interested in locating in an area bounded by Central Avenue on the west, 24th Street on the east, Thomas Road on the south and Camelback Road on the north. This description covers an area of six square miles.

STEP THREE. *Tour of the designated area.* The investor/developer should now tour the area looking for suitable lots or parcels for the intended development. Knowing the size required, all suitable parcels should be noted as to size, address and general description.

STEP FOUR. *Secure plat maps of all lots.* Plats of each parcel can be secured from a title company using the services of their title plant. By a study of the plats of each lot or parcel, it can be determined which parcels are suitable as to size, shape and location.

STEP FIVE. *Check zoning and availability of utilities.* By checking with the Planning Department of the City, the existing zoning of each lot or parcel can be determined. The location and availability of utilities can be established by a call to each municipal department of the city. These should be noted on each plat.

STEP SIX. *Contact owners.* The owner of each parcel should be contacted to determine not only the availability of the property but also the price and terms under which the owner is willing to sell. At that time, it would also be wise to verify the zoning and any other facts pertaining to the property such as easements, dedications, and other restrictions.

STEP SEVEN. *Prepare a Fact and Information Profile.* From the information obtained in the previous steps, a Fact and Information Profile should be prepared on each lot or parcel under consideration.

STEP EIGHT. *Analyze and evaluate each parcel.* Each parcel should be analyzed as to its availability, suitability and feasibility for the intended development using the procedures outlined in Chapter 2. In addition each should be evaluated through the use of comparables as described also in Chapter 2.

STEP NINE. *Availability of mortgage money.* It is necessary to know whether mortgage money is available, and at what cost, for the intended development at the locations under consideration. This can be determined by talking to mortgage companies, outlining the proposed development.

STEP TEN. *Selection of specific lot or parcel.* Through a careful analysis and evaluation of all of the information obtained on each lot in this step-by-step procedure, a selection can be made as to which lot or parcel should be purchased for the intended development.

STRUCTURING THE PURCHASE TO PERMIT DEVELOPMENT AND ITS ULTIMATE USE

It is sometimes too late, after the purchase has been made and the escrow closed, to discover that the planned development cannot be built because of a poorly structured purchase agreement. There are many factors to consider before construction can commence and the facility can be used for the purpose intended.

The following items should be checked thoroughly before the purchase is made and/or the escrow closed:

1. Easements
2. Dedications
3. Deed restrictions
4. Existing mortgage

5. Leases
6. Financing
7. Zoning
8. Utilities
9. Soil
10. Percolation
11. Drainage
12. Feasibility of project
13. Land releases
14. Building permit

Easements, dedications, deed restrictions, existing mortgage and leases will be shown in the Preliminary Title Report furnished by the title company after the escrow has been opened. It is always wise and prudent to make the purchase subject to the approval of the Preliminary Title Report, in the event that something appears that would preclude the development of the property.

Financing can be a matter of necessity or choice. If construction funds are required to build the facility, the purchase should be subject to the obtaining of a satisfactory mortgage for construction purposes.

Zoning is most important. If the property is not zoned to permit the intended development, then rezoning must be considered to obtain the required zoning. Again, the purchase should be subject to the property being rezoned.

Utilities are sometimes taken for granted; however, the availability of water, power, gas and sewer to the property should be checked.

Soil, percolation and drainage can be determined by engineering studies of the property. All three items are most important to construction on the site. Therefore, the purchase should be subject to and contingent upon an engineering study of the building site for soil tests, percolation and drainage.

Feasibility of the project is a seldom used contingency but can be important if the investor/developer wants to continue his studies during the escrow period to determine if the intended project is feasible.

Land releases can be most important if the property being purchased is larger than the initial phase of development. Unless releases are provided in the purchase documents, the seller can demand that the entire purchase price be paid before any construction can commence. It is sometimes an overlooked item but it can be a problem if the investor/developer is unable to pay all cash for the property.

Building permits are usually obtained without any real problems if the planned construction conforms to the building and zoning requirements of the city. There are times, however, when height limits, parking requirements and land coverage are subject to dispute and review. Such matters can cause expensive delays and should be reviewed and reconciled with the municipal departments involved prior to close of escrow if possible.

After every item related to the development of the property has been considered and its status determined, the purchase agreement can be structured to meet the requirements of building the project. Those items that are to be resolved during the escrow period should become a contingency to the closing of the escrow. Leave nothing to chance or interpretation. Remember, a poorly constructed purchase agreement can lead to costly problems.

How poor planning can be costly

Several investors that I know of have learned their lesson the hard way. One investor failed to check the Preliminary Title Report closely and discovered too late that a deed restriction was recorded on the property which precluded the development he intended.

Another investor assumed that mortgage funds for development of his project would be available. After the escrow closed and plans were nearly completed, he was told by the mortgage company that his location was not acceptable.

Still another investor learned the hard way that rezoning is not automatic. When the City Council denied his request for a change in zoning, he had to dispose of the property he had purchased—a costly oversight.

Not thoroughly checking the availability of all utilities to the property caused some anxious moments and additional cost to another investor. He assumed that the sewer line had been completed to the property line only to find out later that the anticipated completion date would not be for another year.

The most common mistake of many investors is not providing for releases of portions of the property so that the initial phase of development can commence. Those that were unable to amend the purchase agreement to provide for such releases had to pay off the entire unpaid balance due on the property before construction could begin.

THE NECESSITY OF PROPER ZONING AND THE IMPACT OF ZONING ON VALUES AND SALES

A commercial or industrial property that is being considered for development is either zoned for the intended purpose or its zoning has to be changed to permit such development. Therein lies a real problem. This can apply to apartments, shopping centers, office buildings, industrial warehouses, distribution centers, stores, shops, and service buildings to name a few. Investors and developers are continually striving to rezone a property to permit its development into a project that seems to be both worthwhile, and an asset to the community. The city or county does not always agree.

Investors have learned through experience that a particular property is very seldom zoned for its ultimate, best use. This can apply to the whole spectrum of commercial and industrial developments. In the beginning, location and accessibility are more important than a specific zoning. If the property selected is not zoned properly, then rezoning has to be considered and planned accordingly. Finding a suitable commercial or industrial property that is zoned properly is the exception rather than the rule.

The value of a property is based entirely upon what can be done with it. The controlling factor that governs the use of a property is the type of zoning that has been placed upon it. If the existing zoning is not suitable for the intended use, the zoning must be changed before development can proceed. An investor wants to purchase a property for a specific use which in most cases requires a change in zoning. If he cannot get the property rezoned, he does not want to buy it. The purchase then becomes contingent upon the property being rezoned.

It has been said that most of the great wealth in this country came through the sale or exchange of real estate. When one realizes the amount of money that can be made in commercial and industrial property, that statement is not hard to believe. The impact of zoning in increasing the value of property is sometimes unbelievable.

A five-acre parcel located within the city that is zoned for single-family residences *can be increased in value four or five times when its zoning is changed to multiple*—maybe more depending on the density obtained. *A change to commercial or industrial zoning can result in an even greater increase in value.* This is true if the owner of the property is changing the zoning. His base or cost is usually in accordance with the existing zoning. An astute seller who owns a property that is ready for such multiple or commercial development will establish a price on his property as if the new zoning were already on the property. *Under these conditions it is not difficult to sell a property subject to the new zoning being obtained.*

To beat this game an investor has to move farther out from the main core of the city and acquire a larger parcel of land, plan the property to include a variety of zonings, develop as much as he wants and sell the balance to developers in accordance with the type of existing zoning. If the parcel is large enough, it can include acreage for single-family residences, apartments, townhouses, commercial and such other types of developments that may be needed or required. *It is not inconceivable for the small amount of commercially zoned portions of the property to be valued at an amount equivalent to what the entire parcel cost when it was acquired.*

Packaging property for huge profits

Not all investors who buy land want to actually build and develop the property themselves. One investor friend of mine likes to buy a large parcel on the outskirts of the city that is in the path of development, plan the property for a neighborhood development having a combination of houses, apartments, maybe some townhouses and a shopping center plus other individual commercial developments. He then sells the entire parcel after the zoning has been obtained or sells specific zoned parcels to specific builders who want to develop that particular parcel. In other words, he prepares a package all tied up with a pretty ribbon for the developers. He has the financial capabilities to purchase a sizeable piece of property, pay for the expense of land planning, secure the necessary zoning, and carry the property in his inventory until it has been sold.

His profit in each such investment is considerable. *In a well-located area where the development of the property is immediate, he usually doubles and sometimes triples his cost.*

PROVEN METHODS AND PROCEDURES TO USE IN REZONING A PROPERTY

There are attorneys who specialize in zoning actions. However, an investor may want to secure the required zoning change himself. In this event, the following procedures and guidelines can be most helpful.

In most areas property is usually zoned in the following *general* classifications:

1. Residential
2. Commercial
3. Industrial
4. Rural
5. Planned Area Development

Through zoning ordinances adopted by a city or county, these general classifications are further identified for specific uses and at densities regulated by such ordinances. Copies of all published zoning ordinances can be obtained at the Planning and Zoning Department of each city or county administrative office.

There are certain established procedures that are required to successfully change the zoning of a property. The following step-by-step technique is recommended.

Step 1. Determination of required zoning

By referring to the zoning ordinances applicable to the intended use of the property, the proper required zoning can be determined. To explain, the property is presently zoned for apartments and the intended use is for a neighborhood shopping center. It is found that a shopping center is a permitted use in a commercial zoning district. Therefore, the zoning of the property has to be changed from multiple residential to commercial.

Step 2. Preliminary meeting with planning director

Every city or county administration has a Planning Director and a Planning Staff which is responsible for the orderly development of that city or county. It is considered wise to have a preliminary meeting wtih the planning director prior to the preparation of a detailed plan for the proposed development or before submitting an application for rezoning.

The purpose of this preliminary meeting is to outline, in general, the proposed development. You should be prepared to present all facts relating to the property and its location. Also, it will be helpful to present your initial plot plan along with any letters of intent from potential tenants. With this information, the planning director can determine if such a planned development at your location is in keeping with the master plan of the city or county. His concern is not one of economics but of traffic flow, impact on the neighborhood, population movement, transportation, providing services for the planned development and future planning.

The approval of the planning director is not automatic. He may not agree with your thinking, so it is necessary to counter his objections with plausible reasons for granting the zoning change. If he still does not agree, do not give up—continue with your plans for rezoning. Many zonings are changed over the objections of the planning director.

Step 3. Meeting with planning staff

At the suggestion of the planning director, you will meet with the planning staff. You will again present the facts relating to the site for the proposed development along with the preliminary plot plan. The staff will review your plan and will make suggestions as to parking, set-backs, landscaping, traffic flow, entrances, exits, and exterior lighting—all to conform to the requirements of the city ordinances. This review by the planning staff will follow their established procedure regardless of the merits of the case or the thinking of the planning director.

Step 4. Prepare new development plan

Following the recommendations of the planning staff, a new development plan should be prepared by your architect. He will be familiar with the requirements of the city and will prepare a plot plan suitable for zoning purposes.

Step 5. Obtain zoning application

At the time of obtaining an application for the zoning change, the new development plan should be presented to the planning staff to make certain that the plan has been prepared in accordance with their recommendations. Along with the application to change the zoning, you will be given a petition to be signed by adjacent property owners within 300 feet of the property, indicating their approval of such change in zoning.

Step 6. Secure approval of adjacent property owners

This next step is most important. You now must obtain the approval of the adjacent property owners to the change in zoning. You do not need all of those within 300 feet of the planned project—only 51 percent in both area and number.

Those who approve will sign the petition, but those who are against the change in zoning will not sign and will probably appear at the Planning and Zoning Commission hearing in opposition to your project. Therefore, it is essential to get as many owners as possible to approve your proposed development. To combat the opposition that may appear at the Planning and Zoning Commission hearing, try to get as many people to appear who are for the change in zoning. Many times a planning commission can be influenced by a show of numbers—either for or against the zoning change.

Step 7. Submit completed zoning application

The request for the change in zoning should now be completed, signed by the applicant and accompanied by the petition of the adjacent property owners. After paying the required fee, the application is processed by the Planning Department and assigned a date upon which the application will be submitted to the Planning and Zoning Commission. During the interim period, the planning staff will review the proposed development and make written recommendations to the Planning and Zoning Commission.

Step 8. Secure copy of staff recommendation

It is most essential that you obtain a copy of the staff recommendation on your proposed development prior to the date of the Planning and Zoning hearing. This report will give not only their recommendation to the Commission but also will itemize by stipulations everything that must be done to the property before the zoning can become effective. Since it is the usual practice of the Planning and Zoning Commission to follow the recommendations of their planning staff, it is well to know in advance just what those recommendations are going to be.

If the planning staff recommends approval of the change in zoning, the stipulations imposed by the staff should be studied carefully to determine if they are acceptable. If the planning staff recommends denial of the change in zoning, meetings can be held with the staff prior to the Planning Commission hearing to resolve the problems. Sometimes their objections can be overcome prior to the commission meeting.

Step 9. Planning and zoning commission hearing

The Planning and Zoning Commission is not empowered to grant a change in zoning but can only recommend approval or denial of such change. Nevertheless, you should prepare a detailed and effective presentation to be given at the Commission hearing. A technique to remember in any presentation: *Words cannot adequately describe your development—you need drawings, plot plans, pictures, renderings—anything that the members of the Commission can see.*

Each zoning case has been assigned a number. When your application is presented to the Commission, the chairman will ask if the applicant is present. From this point on, the application can move in several directions. If the planning staff has recommended approval, the chairman will ask if there is any opposition to the change in zoning. If no one present opposes, the chairman can then ask for a motion in accordance with the recommendation of the planning staff. When this happens, it will not be necessary for you to make a presentation. On the other hand, if there is opposition, those opposing will be given an opportunity to state their reasons. Following the opponents, you will then be given an opportunity to make a presentation for the change in zoning. When both sides have presented their cases and have been questioned by the members of the Commission, the chairman will ask for a motion on the case. As a general rule, if the planning staff has recommended approval, the Commission will act accordingly and recommend approval regardless of the opposition.

On the other hand, if the planning staff has recommended denial, the Commission can go either way. With little or no opposition, with adjacent property owners appearing on behalf of the zoning change and with a good presentation of your application, the Commission can recommend approval without the concurrence of the planning staff.

Step 10. City council meeting

The City Council will now hear your zoning case. The moment of truth has arrived. The Council can either grant your change in zoning or deny your request. The hearing can be short and sweet or it can be long and drawn out. As with the Planning and Zoning Commission, the mayor, as the chairman of the council, will ask for those opposing to present their opposition. If there are no opponents and the Planning and Zoning Commission has recommended approval, the Council action is usually automatic in granting the change in zoning. On the other hand, if there is opposition, both sides will be heard before the Council makes its decision. It is the exception rather than the rule for the City Council to override a recommendation of the Planning and Zoning Commission. It can happen, however; so always be prepared to make a thorough and plausible presentation.

This did happen to one investor in a very important zoning case. The planning director and his staff recommended denial of the change to the Planning and Zoning Commission. They in turn recommended denial to the City Council. During the interim period before the Council meeting, the investor worked harder than ever preparing a more detailed and comprehensive presentation for the Council hearing. The hard work paid off. The City Council voted to grant the zoning—overriding the recommendation of their entire Planning Department.

The foregoing 10 steps, if followed as outlined, should result in obtaining the required zoning, thereby enabling you to conclude your purchase and commence construction on your planned projects which you have worked so hard to develop.

STRUCTURED FINANCING—A SPECIALIZED TECHNIQUE IN PURCHASING AND SELLING LAND

The financing techniques used in the sale and purchase of land are entirely different from the techniques used in the sale and purchase of income producing properties. Therefore, being able to determine the best type of financing is most important in concluding the purchase or sale.

Whenever possible, the financing should be structured so that it can be an aid to the purchase rather than a hinderance. *Tough terms make land hard to buy.* An astute investor will begin his financing technique when he first talks to the owner about buying the property. At that time, the usual information is obtained—size, price, terms, existing encumbrances if any, and other necessary information. The investor usually has some preconceived ideas about what he wants to do with the property and how he would like to buy. The owner also has his ideas about how he wants to sell and the terms he is willing to give. In determining how flexible the owner will be in finalizing a sale, the investor will ask various questions regarding the terms. Those questions will center around several of the 25 different ways to finance this real estate transaction. If there is a particular type of financing the investor would like in buying the property, he will dwell on that method more than others, just to plant a seed and to get the owner thinking.

There are certain investors who like to buy land in specific ways to create maximum leverage. Whenever they can structure the financing their way, they feel that financing has become a most useful tool. To better explain some of their methods in making financing an aid to the purchase, let me describe some examples as they relate to the purchase of land.

Example No. 1. Some investors like to buy land with a low down payment—interest only for from three to five years and then principal and interest payments over the next ten years. Whenever they can get these terms, they will most generally purchase the land.

Example No. 2. Another investor will want to buy land by prepaying interest as a down payment and then regular terms on the balance.

Example No. 3. There are times when the investor can get the owner to permit him to place a mortgage on the property to make the down payment and then take a trust agreement to secure the balance of the trust agreement. One time this was the beginning of a series of resales that resulted in tremendous profit to the investor. I must say, though, that it is not often that the owner of a property will let a buyer use his property to enable him to buy it.

The "series of options" technique

Another method of structured financing in a land purchase is with a series of options. Financing becomes a technique when the land can be acquired, using this method. In setting up this type of purchase, the property is divided into several parcels depending upon the number of options desired. One parcel is designated as the initial purchase and the remaining parcels become a series of options. The terms of purchase of the initial parcel can be in the usual and customary manner, making a down payment and the balance payable over a number of years. Options are granted for the remaining parcels, each to be exercised at specific times, at a specific price, and usually on terms consistent with the terms granted in the initial purchase. This type of structured financing is particularly attractive to an investor, and more so when the property is quite large—larger than he would normally buy if he had to purchase the entire parcel at one time. Since the inital purchase is a small part of the entire parcel, the down payment is proportionately smaller, making his outlay of cash much less. It is in the interest, however, where the real savings occur. The investor does not have to carry that large unpaid balance upon which interest accrues everyday. In some larger transactions, the savings in interest over a ten year period is equal to approximately $1,000 per acre. When this can be accomplished, financing has played an important part in the purchase. Also, this technique enables the investor to carry a larger inventory in land for future development without the interest and principal payments breaking his back.

Not all owners will entertain the sale of their property under this format, but when it is properly explained they will sometimes change their minds. This has been true in the purchase of some large farms that were ready for development. The options are so structured that the farmer can continue farming the optioned property until the option is exercised.

HOW ONE INVESTOR MADE AN ADDITIONAL PROFIT THROUGH THE USE OF STRUCTURED FINANCING

One investor structured his financing of land purchases in a way that not only conserved cash but also saved considerable money. Much has been said about prepaying interest as a down payment and paying interest only for a few years, but neither of those financing plans saves any money. Interest deferred to be paid later or paid in advance does not save money, but interest forgiven does and lots of it!

In one very profitable transaction, he purchased a 160 acre parcel at $5,500 per acre totalling $880,000. He agreed to pay $180,000 down for which he would be permitted to release 20 acres. The $700,000 was to be paid in ten annual installments of $70,000 or more on or before each principal payment date. Interest at the rate of 8 percent per annum was not to accrue until three years following the close of escrow and at that time would be paid at the same time and in addition to the regular principal payments. This unpaid balance was secured by a trust agreement which provided for the release of land upon payment of an amount equivalent to $6,000 per gross acre but only in parcels of no less than 10 acres. Since the purchase was subject to the property being rezoned, the escrow closed after the new zoning was obtained.

During the first three years of the development through release payments, the trust agreement had been paid down to a balance of $220,000. This period of time before interest commenced to accrue saved the investor over $110,000 in interest payments that normally would have been paid.

This investor recognized that interest is a directly-related cost and any savings that can be made is the same as additional profit.

PROFITS CAN BE INCREASED THROUGH THE USE OF OPTIONS

It was explained in a foregoing section of this chapter how a series of options is a structured financing technique which can lead to increased profits in the purchase of land and its ultimate resale.

This can be done because of the following reasons:

1. *Smaller down payment.* Since the initial purchase is a small part of the entire parcel, the down payment can be proportionately smaller, making the initial outlay of cash much less resulting in a profit but for much less cash invested.
2. *Smaller annual payments.* The annual payments on the initial purchase are also proportionately smaller. Any developer needs to conserve cash on land acquisition so that more money can be put into the development which ultimately leads to more profit.
3. *Less interest to pay.* Interest under this technique does not accrue on the options until an option is exercised, resulting in a tremendous savings and more profit. If purchased as an entire parcel, interest accrues on the large unpaid balance. *In some of the larger transactions, the savings in interest over a ten year period is equal to approximately $1,000 per acre.*
4. *More orderly development.* By establishing options to conform to a predetermined plan of development, the investor can eliminate the strain and worry of meeting large annual payments plus interest and concentrate on an orderly approach to his overall development—all of which is conducive to more profits.
5. *Increased profits through appreciation.* During the option period and other development, the optioned property will increase in value without the usual cost of carrying the property in the normal manner, resulting in still more additional profits.

Not all owners will agree to sell their property under this type of purchase, but when it is properly explained, they will sometimes change their minds. The advantages are not all on the side of the buyer. The following advantages can be explained to the seller:

1. *Continued use of optioned property.* This is true in the sale of large farms that are ready for development. The options can be so structured

to permit the farmer to continue farming the optioned property until the option is exercised.

2. *Foreclosure and repossession.* If an option is not timely exercised, the land has never been conveyed, so the seller does not have to repossess.
3. *No taxable implications.* Again if an option is not exercised, there has been no sale and consequently, no profit or tax. A foreclosure and repossession can sometimes create a tax problem to the seller.
4. *Tax advantages.* Through the use of the sale by options, tax problems can be adjusted to meet any given situation.

HOW ANOTHER INVESTOR USED THE TECHNIQUE OF A SERIES OF OPTIONS, RESULTING IN BIG PROFITS

Another very knowledgeable investor purchased 345 acres of land which was in the path of development. The owners were asking $3,500 per acre, totaling $1,207,500. Since the cost of carrying such a large purchase would be quite heavy until the property was actually ready for development, the investor structured a plan of purchase wherein a small portion of the property was purchased initially with a series of options on the remainder of the property. In this manner, he would be able to conserve cash while waiting for its ultimate resale for development.

The basis of his offer was to be an initial purchase of 60 acres and then a series of five options exercisable one each year. Each option was to be for a specific parcel varying from 40 to 60 acres each. The down payment of the initial purchase would be $32,000 and the down payment due on the exercise of each option would be 15 percent of the total purchase price. The balance due on the initial purchase and on each option when exercised would be payable in five equal annual payments bearing interest at the rate of 7½ percent per annum. The balance due was to be evidenced by a Trust Agreement providing for all of the necessary items to permit development of the property. The offered price was $3,000 per acre on the initial purchase and also $3,000 per acre on each option.

When he presented his offer to the owners and their attorney, the option plan of purchase did not cause nearly as much conversation as he thought it would nor did the 18 months zoning contingency period. The only changes made to the contract were in the prices of the optioned property. The initial purchase remained at $3,000 per acre and so did the first option. The remaining options were graduated in price from $3,200 per acre to $3,800 per acre. The average price per acre was approximately $3,360, which was close to the asking price of $3,500. With these changes, the contract was accepted by the sellers and later approved by the investor.

During the escrow period, the property was rezoned into a neighborhood development plan including a 40 acre commercial corner. After exercising the first option, the investor sold the package to a developer. After cutting out the 40 acre commercial corner, there were 305 acres to sell. The final agreed sale price per acre was $4,750, making a total sale price of $1,448,750. There were left a total of 223½ acres under options at prices varying from $3,200 to $3,800 per acre—totaling $777,300 in options yet to be exercised. The value of the options was deducted from the total selling price, to arrive at an amount representing the value of the 81½ acres being actually purchased in the transaction—that amount being $671,450. The options were assigned to the buyer with the provision that each option must be exercised upon a date thirty days prior to the exercise date shown in each option. This thirty days would enable the seller to exercise any option by the automatic re-assignment provision in the event the developer should fail to exercise such option.

In this transaction, my investor friend made nearly $425,000 cash and retained ownership of the 40 acre commercial corner on an initial investment of $32,000. While this return on his cash invested was fantastic, the value of that 40 acre commercial corner exceeded the total amount paid for the entire 345 acres in the beginning.

TECHNIQUES AND METHODS TO USE IN PLANNING A MULTIPLE SALE PROJECT

There are some investors who utilize a special technique for a large parcel of land by dividing it into a number of separately zoned smaller parcels and selling each one to different developers according to a master plan of development. This is not something that can be done week in and week out. Certain conditions have to exist or be made to happen to make a Multiple Sale Project possible.

The following three phases are necessary in preparing and implementing a Multiple Sale program:

Phase 1. The initial purchase

This initial purchase is the most important and usually the hardest. The investor must have the financial capability to purchase the land, pay for the expense of land planning, secure the necessary zoning and carry the property until the program has been successfully completed.

In Phase 1 it is necessary to set the stage for everything that follows. By analyzing the property, a complete plan is determined and includes the development phase. The most important part of Phase 1 is structuring the purchase to facilitate all phases of the development. There is usually a down payment which may or may not release land, depending upon the terms of the sale; however, acreage should be released with such payment because it can become important in later phases. The remaining balance of the purchase price is secured by a Trust Agreement wherein the Title Company acts as trustee and administers the trust in accordance with its provisions. The Trust Agreement should provide that the Second Beneficiary, who is the buyer, may plot and subdivide the property, rezone if required, dedicate streets, be granted subordination for offsite and onsite improvements, release property in accordance with the release schedule as shown, sell all or part of the trust property, be granted time sales privileges, and be payable in minimum annual payments over a long enough period of time to permit the entire project to be concluded. The rate of interest should be at a negotiated percentage and the entire unpaid balance may be paid at any time without penalty. The reason to have everything but the ''kitchen sink'' in that Trust Agreement is because it is almost impossible to renegotiate terms after the property has been sold.

Phase 2. Planning the development and zoning

During the escrow period, the property is planned for development and rezoned. This procedure is outlined below in a step-by-step description:

Step 1. Land Planning. The more astute investor employs the services of a professional land planner, who will probably plan the development to include a shopping center, apartments, possibly an office building, medical and dental clinics, single-family residences along with the usual amenities required for such a development. He will show how to plan the property in a manner that will be acceptable and approved by the planning and zoning staff.

Step 2. Zoning. In a project of this size, most investors will use an attorney who specializes in zoning matters to secure the zoning changes required for the complete development of the property. During the zoning period, the attorney is usually assisted by the land planner and the investor who form a team that is most generally very successful.

Step 3. Preparation for Sale to a Developer. The property has now been zoned for a shopping center, apartments, an office building, medical and dental clinics plus acreage for single-family residences. At this point, the property is analyzed, evaluated and prepared for sale to a developer or developers. The sale price of the property is now determined by the new existing zoning that has been obtained and not by the base cost of the land. The package is now ready for multiple sales.

Phase 3. Sale to developers

To achieve the maximum profit from this program, the investor will sell each zoned segment of the property to different types of developers—shopping centers, apartments, office and medical buildings and single-family residences. The amount of profit that can be made in this Multiple Sale program is sometimes unbelievable.

KEY POINTS

1. Understand the flexibility of multiple uses in the development of land
2. Know the importance of location for immediate use or for appreciation
3. Learn the technique of finding a commercial or industrial lot for a specific purpose
4. Structure the purchase to permit development and ultimate use
5. Realize the necessity of zoning and its impact on values and sales
6. Use proven methods and procedures in rezoning a property
7. Utilize structured financing—a most important technique in purchasing and selling land
8. Read how one investor made an additional profit through the use of structured financing
9. Understand how profits can be increased with the use of options
10. Learn how another investor made it big by using the technique of a series of options
11. Know techniques and methods to use in planning a Multiple Sale Project

8

Shopping Centers: A Flexible, High Profit Investment

If you can find a successful shopping center for sale, grab it. That advice appeared in one of the leading business publications recently and the subsequent sections of this chapter will tell you *why* and *how* A few brief examples of how other investors found shopping centers to be a very flexible, high profit investment are shown in the following paragraphs.

One investor, after analyzing and evaluating a shopping center, determined that through the technique of refinancing he would be able to double the cash yield while reducing his down payment in half. The result was an excellent shopping center investment.

Another investor needed tax shelters more than additional income. The flexibility of financing and the high yield of the shopping center enabled him to structure his purchase to gain the much needed tax shelters while gaining equity in his investment.

Still another investor recognized the potential of excess rentals to increase the income of the shopping center. After the income had reached a peak, he capitalized the increased Cash Spendable Income to establish a value of the center. The resultant sale produced a fantastic profit of nearly $400,000.

In addition, this chapter illustrates a simple procedure to follow in analyzing and evaluating a shopping center along with major points and terms to look for in leases. How to verify and analyze income and expense followed by checklists to use in your personal inspection of the property should be informative and useful. Also, the technique of buying a shopping center with procedures and proven practices to use will be explained in detail. How income and profits can be increased and operating costs reduced through escalation clauses in the leases are shown. Other case examples are also given to further explain the main thrust of the chapter.

ANALYZING THE NEED FOR SHOPPING CENTERS

As cities grew beyond the limits of their urban centers with their downtown business sections, the need for small neighborhood shopping centers became increasingly evident. The buying public quickly recognized the ease of shopping for their everyday needs with the trouble-free parking and accessibility of these neighborhood shopping centers. As a result, the continued urban sprawl demanded more and more shopping centers to satisfy the needs of the growing cities.

Regional shopping centers began to be built when the large department stores which had traditionally been located in the downtown section began to move into the suburban areas. The choice was really simple—either move into one of the new and fashionable regional centers located in heavily populated suburban areas, or die downtown.

Using the city of Phoenix as an example, neighborhood shopping centers began to be built all over the city, but generally at the intersection of two heavily traveled, arterial streets. As the city continued to grow, these small centers were built on nearly every section line corner where the people lived. Those in the real estate business began to wonder just how many shopping centers could be built and operated profitably.

This question came up one day during lunch with two friends of mine. One of the men was a radio executive who later became mayor of the city and after that became governor of the state. The other was his campaign manager during both elections. At one point, the subject of shopping centers came up and they both felt that there just couldn't be anymore built—that the saturation point had been reached. I disagreed and explained why.

It was my belief that as the city grew and prospered, there would be many more shopping centers constructed. My reasoning was that as long as Safeway, Walgreen, Skaggs, Thrifty, Lucky, Penney, Sears, Kresge and numerous other strong national tenants would sign leases for space in new shopping centers and the leading lending institutions would continue to loan money for their construction, shopping centers would be built. Now, nearly 15 years later that statement is still correct.

TYPES OF SHOPPING CENTERS: KEY POINTS TO CONSIDER

As a general rule shopping centers are classified into three types:

Regional shopping centers are built on the concept of bringing downtown to the people. The primary tenants are several large department stores and usually require a land area of 80 to 160 acres with 800,000 to over one million square feet of buildings. It is recommended that this type of shopping center have a market area of approximately 500,000 people and have an 8 to 15 mile radius without major competition. Within the center can be every conceivable retail or service type of business. Since the large department stores are required to create the attraction and foot-traffic necessary to a successful center, their low percentage rent can sometimes reduce the overall return to the developer. This is sometimes solved by either selling or leasing that portion of the shopping center land to the department store. In this manner, the remainder of the center produces an excellent yield and still has the advantage of having the drawing power of the department store. Therefore, each regional center must be analyzed to determine the status of the department stores.

Community shopping centers are somewhat smaller than regional centers and are usually anchored to a supermarket, junior department store, drug store and a variety store. The land area required is 15 to 20 acres with approximately 150,000 to 200,000 square feet of building. Its market area should number about 60,000 residents and should have no sizeable competition within three to five miles.

Neighborhood shopping centers are built around a supermarket with a drug and variety store along with other service-type tenants. Customarily, neighborhood centers are constructed on 8 to 10 acres of land averaging 80,000 square feet of buildings. The population requirement is much less, being from 10,000 to 20,000 people and can be built within a mile of another such center. In fact one supermarket chain is willing to be within one mile of competition and within two miles of one of their own stores.

THE IMPORTANCE OF LOCATION: A REQUIREMENT OF EVERY SUCCESSFUL CENTER

Even though the shopping center is open and operating with acceptable tenants, the importance of its location is ever present. Many of the older shopping centers were built at the intersection of two good streets without regard for future growth or future business patterns.

In growing cities today, location is concerned with directional business growth and activity. The complex patterns of population movement, new growth areas, the constant shifting of traffic flow, the decline of certain neighborhoods and the renewal of others, changes in the function of such major factors as downtown, expansion and implementation of numerous governmental controls, environmental requirements and new city planning techniques, all contribute to obsolescence and change. Such characteristics are becoming increasingly critical for existing shopping center locations and for the analysis of the future volume of business that can mean continued success or failure to retail business.

As with apartments, a good location is an important factor to consider in evaluating a shopping center investment. In analyzing the location as to its desirability, the following checklist can be very useful:

1. *Population.* The number of people living within a radius of one mile from the neighborhood shopping center should be determined. This area will cover approximately four square miles and as a good location for this type of shopping center should include from 10,000 to 20,000 people. If the population is not given in demographic information, an aerial photo of the four square miles will show the number of houses and apartment buildings. By multiplying the number of houses and apartment units times the average family size, the estimated population can be determined. Naturally, the more people living within the prescribed area makes the location more desirable.
2. *Accessibility.* The shopping center should be located in an area that is on major arterial streets which provide easy access from all points of the city.
3. *Competition.* The location of each competitive shopping center within three miles of the center under consideration should be identified and shown on a map of the general area. In addition, the size of the center should be noted along with the principal tenants and the square footage each occupies.
4. *Future growth patterns.* It is wise to study the future growth plans of the city to determine if such plans will enhance or be a detriment to the operation of the shopping center. The path of freeways are known well in advance of construction, so a visit to the proper municipal department will determine whether a freeway is planned through the area under consideration.
5. *Quality of the area.* The quality of the neighborhood should be checked for not only the number of dwellings but also the average price of homes, rent paid, the number of people in each household, the

average family income, number of children in school, and the family shopping habits. All of this type of information can be obtained from the local Chamber of Commerce from demographic studies made of the area.

All information relative to location of the shopping center should be shown in the Fact and Information Profile on each shopping center investment under consideration. A sample profile is shown in Chapter 2. Such information will provide a ready reference to every question regarding location.

A SIMPLE PROCEDURE TO FOLLOW IN ANALYZING AND EVALUATING A SHOPPING CENTER

Investors who are knowlegeable about shopping centers follow a definite procedure in their analysis and evaluation of a center which they have under consideration as an investment. This simple procedure is outlined in the following step-by-step guide:

Step 1. All pertinent information is obtained using the property checklist and methods described in Chapter 2. From this information a Fact and Information Profile is prepared using the technique shown in Chapter 2. The following information is necessary as is shown in the profile of a neighborhood shopping center:

East Plaza Shopping Center — Date: 7/15/77
Owner: East Plaza, Inc.

1. Price: $2,100,000.00
2. Description of property: Neighborhood Shopping Center
3. Location of property: 3120 E. Dunlap Road
4. Type of Construction: Masonry
5. Land area: 7.3 acres
6. Present zoning: Planned Shopping Center
7. Size of buildings—rentable area: 64,170 square feet
8. Number of units-tenants: 13
9. Parking spaces: 400
10. Services provided: See leases
12. Income and operating expenses: Income - $239,300.00
    Expenses - $ 55,822.00
    (For breakdown see attached operating statement)
13. Taxes and Insurance: Taxes - $35,460.00
    Insurance - $ 2,750.00

14. Encumbrance: $1,350,000.00 - 9% - 25 years
15. Amortization: $11,340.00 P+I
16. Tenants—leases—rates: See leases
18. Quality of area: Medium income
19. Distances to: City business area - 8 miles
    Employment center - 3 miles
    Airport - bus - rail - 10 miles
20. Public transportation: Yes
21. Nearest shopping center: Neighborhood - 1 mile
25. Population within: 1 mile - 30,000
    2 miles - 90,000
    3 miles - 150,000

Step 2. Study and analyze existing leases of all tenants with special emphasis on those leases with the key national tenants. Major points and terms to look for in all leases are shown in the following section.

Step 3. An analysis of the income and expense should be made for not only the current year but also for the past several years of operation. A subsequent section of this chapter will describe in detail methods to follow in verifying and analyzing the operating statements.

Step 4. A personal inspection of the shopping center should be made—checking the construction of the buildings, paved parking area and lighting, equipment, maintenance of the structures, roofs, and general condition of the property. How to conduct your tour of inspection is outlined and described in a following section.

Step 5. A detailed and comprehensive evaluation of the shopping center should be made using the Income Analysis and Evaluation form as described in Chapter 2. Other dependable techniques to use in evaluating a shopping center are shown and explained in a subsequent section of this chapter.

Step 6. The time of decision. As a result of the five preceding steps, a decision can be made as to whether the shopping center is suitable and satisfies the requirements of the investor. How to make that decision is fully explained and described in a following section of this chapter.

TWENTY MAJOR POINTS AND TERMS TO LOOK FOR IN LEASES

Each lease will legally describe the location of the shopping center and the portion of the center under lease. Following that general description, a number of the major and most important points along with other items of the lease are outlined below:

1. *Term of lease.* In this paragraph the date of the commencement of the lease and the expiration date will be shown.

2. *Rent.* The total rent to be paid during the term of the lease will be shown along with the amount to be paid each month. In addition to the rent, this paragraph will show that applicable city, county and state sales taxes will be paid each month.

3. *Additional rent.* The lease will state that additional rent will be due from sales in excess of a stated amount. The percentage factor is usually determined by the type of business and the gross volume of sales expected from such a business. For some businesses, it might be 1½ percent others might be 2 percent while some may be as high as 6 percent. It is through excess rentals that the income of a long-term lease can increase. Major stores in shopping centers with percentage leases should be expected to reach excess rental after a few years.

4. *Real property taxes.* With property taxes increasing every year, it is absolutely necessary that the lease provide for tax escalation. Any increase in property taxes above the base year of the lease should be paid proportionately by every tenant.

5. *Insurance.* Each lease should provide for the tenant carrying the proper and sufficient amount of personal liability insurance to protect the landlord along with the necessary plate glass insurance covering its premises and such other insurance considered necessary to the type of business conducted.

6. *Common area maintenance.* The common area is all of that part of the shopping center used by all of the tenants and their customers—parking, unloading docks, malls, driveways, signs, walks and such other areas of common usage. The cost of maintaining these areas is charged proportionately to all tenants including insurance and utilities. The cost to each tenant can be an amount per square foot of leased space or can be an agreed upon fee with selected larger tenants. In any event the total cost should be paid by the tenant and collected as additional rent.

7. *Utilities.* Lessee shall be required to pay for all water, gas, heat, electricity and other utilities furnished to or used in or about the premises by the lessee during the term of the lease.

8. *Taxes.* Lessee should pay all taxes levied upon fixtures, furnishings, equipment and other personal property belonging to the lessee contained on the premises.

9. *Use of leased premises.* This paragraph usually states that the lessee may occupy and use the leased premises for the type of business specified for the sale of items customarily sold in similar types of businesses in the area.

10. *Nuisance, dangerous trade, compliance with law.* The lessee is prohibited from any nuisance or dangerous trade practices and shall comply with all laws, regulations and ordinances of public authorities.

11. *Maintenance of premises.* Any damage to the interior of the premises shall be repaired by the lessee and at his sole cost and expense. This paragraph usually stipulates that the lessor will keep the roof and outside walls in repair, except that lessee shall replace any glass or doors therein broken during the terms of the lease.

12. *Surrender of premises.* The lease should provide that the lessee shall, upon expiration of the term hereby created, or upon early termination hereof for any reason, quit and surrender said premises in good order, condition and repair, reasonable wear and tear excepted.

13. *Fixtures.* Lessee should provide, install and maintain, at his own expense, fixtures of a special nature that may be required by the lessee's business. All trade and other fixtures, equipment and furniture placed on the premises by the lessee shall remain the property of the lessee; however, such items may not be removed prior to the expiration of the term of the lease and at that time the leased premises shall be restored thereafter. All such fixtures, equipment and furniture not so removed shall become the lessor's property.

14. *Subletting.* Lessee is usually permitted to assign or sublet the premises; however, lessee shall agree to obtain an experienced and responsible person who is experienced in the operation of the type of business and such person be bound by and accept the obligations of the lease. Neither the assignment or subletting of the premises shall relieve the lessee of the obligations or responsibilities of the lease.

15. *Default, Re-entry remedies.* This paragraph should fully describe what happens in the event of default in the payment of rent.

16. *Insolvency of lessee.* This paragraph explains what happens when a petition in bankruptcy is filed and not dismissed or lessee makes an assignment for the benefit of creditors, or a Receiver is appointed to take charge and conduct the affairs of the lessee.

17. *Option to renew.* The terms and conditions of any option to renew the lease should be spelled-out in this paragraph.

18. *Condemnation Clause.* A lengthy, wordy paragraph regarding the taking or damage of all or any part of the leased premises or any interest therein by reason of any exercise of the power of eminent domain, whether by condemnation proceedings or otherwise is a part of all leases.

19. *Merchant's Association.* The tenant shall agree to become a member of a Merchant's Association which will consist of the landlord and all of the tenants of the shopping center according to the terms and conditions outlined in the paragraph.

20. *Security deposits.* The amount and conditions under which the security deposit is made are fully described in this paragraph.

The investor should study and analyze each lease as it affects the income, expense and operation of the shopping center as explained in Step 2 in his analysis and evaluation of the investment.

VERIFICATION AND ANALYSIS OF INCOME AND EXPENSE ALONG WITH PROPERTY TAXES, INSURANCE AND MAINTENANCE COSTS

As recommended in Step 3, the income and expense figures should be verified and analyzed. In an early meeting with the owner, the investor should have been given an operating statement showing the total income and expense of the shopping center for the current year. In addition, he should have asked for and received operating statements for prior years to determine when and if excess rentals have been reached by those tenants having percentage escalation clauses in their lease.

Verification of the income can be made by checking the leases of tenants as to what the rent paid by each should be. Accounting records and bank deposits of the owner can substantiate the amounts. Special note should be made of additional income such as percentage excess rentals, common area maintenance fees, and the tax escalation of the lease.

Verification of all operating expenses paid by the owner should be made by a detailed inspection of the charges for services which would include the following:

1. Utilities for the common areas such as parking lots, unloading areas, walks, malls and other areas of common use
2. Janitor and cleanup service for the common areas
3. Repair and maintenance of the common areas
4. Equipment repairs and maintenance
5. Landscaping
6. Painting and decorating
7. General repair and maintenance including roof and exterior walls
8. Management
9. Accounting
10. Legal

In addition real property taxes and insurance should be checked and verified as to amount and coverage.

Following the verification of all income and expense, the investor should analyze both and place them in their proper perspective. In analyzing the income, every investor should be interested in not only the guaranteed minimum income but also in the amount of excess rental paid through the percentage factor in the lease. As sales increase by those tenants, the excess rental will increase proportionately.

Every item of expense should be further checked and analyzed as to whether it is low, normal or high. Since a reduction in expenses will increase profits, much thought should be given to reducing those items that are considered to be excessive. It will probably be in the common area maintenance where savings can be made.

THE IMPORTANCE OF THE PERSONAL INSPECTION WITH CHECKLISTS TO USE

Unlike the inspection of an apartment complex where it is sometimes difficult to inspect each apartment because of tenant occupancy, the inspection of a shopping center can be more detailed and orderly. The spaces occupied by each tenant can be thoroughly inspected including equipment rooms and storage facilities.

A checklist to use for a personal inspection tour of the shopping center should include the following items for verification and condition:

1. Location
2. Size of land area
3. Zoning
4. Type of construction
5. Size of buildings
6. Tenants and space occupied
7. Parking—number of spaces
8. Condition of parking lot and other common areas
9. General condition of building—structural
10. Painting and decorating
11. Landscaping and lighting
12. Good features
13. Bad points
14. Quality of area
15. Accessibility

During the tour, the investor should inspect the property to his complete satisfaction. Every item on the above checklist should be checked and veritifed no matter how long it takes. An astute and knowledgeable investor will not rush through his inspection but will satisfy himself as to the physical condition of the property.

As with the inspection of an apartment complex, the most important items on the above checklist are those relating to the physical condition of the property. A knowledgeable investor will know that he is not qualified to properly inspect and determine the structural quality and physical condition of the shopping center. Often he will use the services of a plumber, heating and refrigeration engineer, electrician and other specialists to inspect the structural parts of the building and other improvements. The following checklist can be used as a guide, showing those items that should be inspected by qualified personnel:

1. General building structures
2. Roof
3. Plate glass
4. Electrical facilities
5. Plumbing
6. Refrigeration equipment
7. Heating equipment
8. Painting and decorating
9. Landscaping
10. Paving

Those items in need of repair or replacement should be noted and become a condition of the purchase, requiring the seller to repair or replace those certain items.

HOW TO MAKE A DETAILED AND COMPREHENSIVE EVALUATION OF A SHOPPING CENTER

The technique of evaluating any type of income producing commercial and industrial property was shown and described in Chapter 2. Using those same steps and procedures, a shopping center investment can be evaluated as shown below:

Step 1. Using the Property Check List as a guide, all known facts and information about the shopping center should be itemized.

Step 2. From the information in the Property Check List, a Fact and Information Profile should be prepared. A profile of the East Plaza Shopping Center was shown in a preceding section of the chapter and for the purposes of evaluation the information contained in that profile shall be used.

Step 3. An Income Analysis and Evaluation Form should now be completed. Applicable information from the preceding Fact and Information Profile will now be used to complete the form as shown below:

INCOME ANALYSIS AND EVALUATION

EAST PLAZA SHOPPING CENTER DATED: 7/15/77
OWNER: EAST PLAZA, INC.

Total Price		$2,100,000.00	
Current Mortgage Balance		1,350,000.00	
9%–$11,340.00 Mo. P+I			
Cash Required		750,000.00	
Total Guaranteed Income		$ 239,300.00	
Operating Expenses			
Property taxes	$35,460.00		
Insurance	2,750.00		
Management	5,000.00		
Maintenance + Repair	$ 7,200.00		
Common Area Maintenance	5,412.00		
Total Expenses		$ 55,822.00	
Operating Profit		$ 183,478.00	
Less Debt Service		136,080.00	
Cash Spendable Income			$46,398.00
Gain in Equity			15,080.00
Total Gain			61,478.00
Yield—Cash on Cash			6.2%
Total Yield			8.2%

Step 4. By following the foregoing three steps, the shopping center has been evaluated based upon the asking price of the owner. This fourth step is a procedure whereby the shopping center is evaluated as to its value to the investor. By consulting the table in Chapter 2 on Acceptable Yields for shopping centers, the investor decides the yield he wants on his cash invested. If 10 percent is the yield he wants to receive, he will divide the Cash Spendable Income by that yield. The resulting amount is then added to the current mortgage balance for his value of the property. As with other types of income producing commercial and industrial property, if the current mortgage balance is unusually small, the operating profit before debt service should be capitalized as described in Chapter 2.

By following the procedure outlined above, the shopping center based upon a 10 percent cash on cash yield would be valued at $1,813,980. This value is determined in the following manner:

Cash Spendable Income of $46,398.00 ÷ 10% =	$ 463,980.00
Current Mortgage Balance	1,350,000.00
Value based upon 10% yield	$1,813,980.00

If an 8 percent or 9 percent yield on cash invested is desired, the same procedure will evaluate the shopping center accordingly.

THE TECHNIQUE OF BUYING A SHOPPING CENTER

The investor, after finding a shopping center that is available, follows the procedures outlined in the preceding sections of this chapter in checking the location, reading and understanding the leases with tenants, analyzing and verifying the income and expense, making his personal tour of inspection along with certain specialists, evaluating the shopping center from the owner's asking price and finally making his own evaluation.

After all of these steps have been taken, the investor gives thought and consideration to making an offer on the shopping center. His technique of buying such an investment follows an established and proven procedure as outlined below:

1. Determine the purchase price
2. Decide upon a plan of purchase
3. Specify the most advantageous terms and conditions
4. Prepare the offer
5. Present the offer for acceptance by the seller
6. Open and close the escrow

The following remarks on each of the foregoing items can be most helpful:

Determine the purchase price. As was shown in Step 4 of the preceding section, the investor calculates his purchase price by capitalizing his cash on cash yield.

Decide upon a plan of purchase. In addition to the purchase price, the plan of purchase will include the amount of the down payment and earnest money deposit, terms of the purchase, special conditions and the opening and closing dates of the escrow.

Specify the most advantageous terms and conditions. The terms of the purchase should be structured to achieve the yield required on the cash invested including the amount of the down payment, assumption of existing mortgage, secondary financing and other items affecting the cash yield of the shopping center. Those special conditions under which the shopping center is purchased should be itemized as contingencies and become a part of the purchase agreement.

Prepare the offer. Many investors use Escrow Instructions as their purchase agreement since it is simple and easy to prepare. The following procedure and guidelines can be most helpful.

The front side of the escrow instructions are prepared in the normal and customary manner, identifying both the seller and the buyer and showing the close of escrow date. The legal description is then shown in the proper space.

The price and terms are shown in the spaces provided down to the unpaid balance, if any. The total amount of the unpaid balance is shown and also the form of security to be used, whether an agreement for sale, note and mortgage, a trust deed or maybe a trust agreement. In the space provided for the payment schedule, a method of paying the encumbrance is described. A typical example of how the payment schedule can be shown is as follows:

> "$27,500.00 or more on or before each principal payment date with the first principal payment beginning one (1) year from the close of escrow and the same amount on the same date each year thereafter until paid in full. Interest shall accrue on the unpaid principal balance at the rate of 8 percent per annum and shall be paid at the same time and in addition to the regular principal payments."

This paragraph can be modified to show any payment schedule required. If interest is to be included in the payment and not in addition thereto, it should be so stated. All of the proper boxes are then checked showing how the various fees and charges are to be paid and those items that are to be prorated are shown as to who gets charged for what.

On the back side of all escrow instructions is a page full of fine print which states everything legal and otherwise about the instructions. Usually, there is a blank space for other information and instructions. In this space, other items and conditions of the sale and purchase are shown.

Since the sale of a shopping center is more complex than a simple house sale, it is necessary to attach supplemental sheets describing in detail those additional terms and conditions. This attachment can be identified as a rider, supplemental instructions or an addendum. Reference is made on the escrow instructions to see the attached for such additional terms and conditions and, by reference, becomes a part of the agreement.

The first paragraph of this attached rider is a standard paragraph wherein the escrow instructions are made a binding agreement between the parties. This paragraph is numbered consecutively from the last number on the reverse side of the escrow instructions and reads as follows:

> "These Escrow Instructions, in addition to being instructions to the Escrow Agent, shall when executed constitute a binding agreement between the parties relating to the sale and purchase of the within described real property subject, however to the conditions herein provided."

Now the escrow instructions have become a binding agreement between the parties. Immediately following this "Binding Agreement" paragraph, succeeding paragraphs, numbered consecutively, are written to show all of the additional terms and conditions of the purchase—the "nitty-gritty" of the agreement.

These are all of the items that must be resolved or accomplished as imposed by the investor as his condition of purchase plus other statements of fact relative to the sale and purchase. The first of these succeeding paragraphs shows the contingencies. Typically this paragraph will begin: "*This purchase shall be subject to and contingent upon the following.*" All of the items upon which the agreement is subject to and must be resolved or satisfied are shown. A concluding subparagraph should state that in the event any or all of the foregoing contingencies are not satisfied or waived by the buyer, these instructions shall be cancelled and the earnest money deposited by the buyer shall be returned. Succeeding paragraphs usually cover other items of fact and responsibility that are required and necessary to the consummation of the transaction.

The concluding paragraph states that the escrow will be opened upon the execution of the agreement by the parties and shall close a certain number of days thereafter.

Presentation and acceptance by the seller. The offer of purchase is then presented to the seller for his acceptance.

Open and close the escrow. In accordance with the provisions of the escrow instructions, the escrow is opened at the agreed upon title company. During the escrow period those special conditions of the escrow are satisfied or waived.

HOW ONE KNOWLEDGEABLE INVESTOR PURCHASED A SHOPPING CENTER ON EXCELLENT TERMS AND CONDITIONS

One investor was interested in purchasing the neighborhood shopping center described in the preceding sections of this chapter. In accordance with his proven procedures, he followed each step through the evaluation of the shopping center. In his evaluation, he determined the value of the shopping center based upon a 10 percent cash on cash yield to be $1,813,980 as was shown in a previous section. In addition, he calculated the value using other acceptable yields as shown below:

8%	$ 1,929,975.00
9%	1,872,000.00

After these calculations, the investor determined that he would be willing to pay from $1,800,000 to $1,900,000 for the shopping center.

He then prepared his offer to purchase, using Escrow Instructions as the agreement between the parties as was shown in the preceding section. The purchase price was $1,800,000 with a $50,000 earnest money deposit, assuming the existing mortgage in the amount of $1,350,000 and the balance of $400,000 to be paid at the close of escrow. In an attached rider to the escrow instructions he listed the special conditions of purchase—none of which would prove to be a problem for either himself or the seller.

When he presented the offer to the seller, it was rejected, but the seller countered at $1,900,000 with $550,000 down. All other terms and conditions remained the same.

Knowing that the counter-offer from the seller would produce a yield of 9 percent on cash, he still wanted to make 10 percent. Recalculating the transaction, he decided to pay $1,900,000 for the center if the down payment could be reduced to $350,000 with a 6 percent interest only note on the remaining balance of $200,000 to be paid in full at the end of ten years. His further calculations are shown below:

Cash Flow	$46,398.00
6% Interest on Note	12,000.00
Net Cash Flow	$34,398.00
Yield—Cash on Cash	9.8%

Since the recalculated yield was so close to 10 percent, he did not change the figures. His new offer was prepared showing the above changes and was accepted by the seller.

THE DIFFERENT TYPES AND CLASSIFICATION OF TENANTS ALONG WITH AN ACCEPTABLE TENANT RATIO

There are many types of businesses that are suitable for shopping centers. Most generally are retail sales oriented or of a service type business. Occasionally offices, theatres and recreational facilities are acceptable tenants.

National tenants are those large corporations who operate retail businesses on a national scale, locating in selected shopping centers all over the country. Their leases are much sought after and are necessary in securing attractive mortgage financing.

Regional tenants are those large, well-financed businesses who operate on a regional rather than a national scale. Sometimes for mortgage purposes their leases are as acceptable as a national lease.

Local tenants are those small businesses both retail and service type that become a part of every shopping center. Without them no center would be really successful. It is their leases that raise the income level of a shopping center to the point where it is a profitable enterprise. If the current rate for a national grocery chain is $3.00 per square foot, the rate to the local tenant would probably be $5.00 per square foot or maybe more.

The income from the national and regional tenants is usually required to pay the insurance, taxes and service the debt. Many times the income from the local tenants, less applicable operating expenses, is profit.

Purchasing a center with the proper mix of national and good local tenants is most important. Since the national tenants usually occupy the larger spaces, they will comprise the bulk of the square footage available in the shopping center; however, the rent per square foot is always much less than that paid by local tenants.

A good ratio of tenants will range from 75 percent national and 25 percent local down to 60 percent national and 40 percent local. Mortgage lenders like those centers that are on the heavy side with the national tenants because of the security of their income. Investors like fewer nationals and more locals because it raises the level of income of the shopping center. Somewhere in between is usually the most acceptable ratio.

HOW INCOME AND PROFITS CAN BE INCREASED AND OPERATING COSTS REDUCED THROUGH ESCALATION CLAUSES IN THE LEASE

In a previous section of this chapter, major points and terms to look for in leases were outlined with pertinent comments. The paragraph describing additional rent is one of the most important parts of any lease for space in a shopping center.

Not all tenants operate businesses where percentage leases are applicable. Those leases with percentage factors, however, can produce additional rent in proportion to their total sales and can become an important part of the income produced by the shopping center.

An astute investor in evaluating a shopping center under consideration as an investment always investigates the status of the excess rentals—whether the larger stores have reached the percentage factor of the lease and how much in additional rent was paid for the preceding year and what is anticipated during the current year.

Let's assume that the percentage leases in the neighborhood shopping center shown in a foregoing section increased the gross income from $239,300 to $249,300, an increase of less than 5 percent. Since this type of rental increase does not incur a proportionate increase in operating expenses, the Cash Spendable Income is also increased from $34,398 to $44,398. Such an addition to income from excess rentals increased the cash on cash yield from 9.8 percent to 12.7 percent, an increase of nearly three percentage points. Likewise, a reduction in the cost of operating expenses will produce the same results in the cash flow and yield.

Therefore, it is readily understandable why astute and knowledgeable investors always investigate thoroughly the status of excess rentals and the cost of operating the shopping center.

THE FLEXIBILITY OF YOUR INVESTMENT, HOW LONG TO OPERATE AND WHEN TO SELL

The profit opportunities in a shopping center make it a very safe, secure, and profitable investment with the flexibility of long-range ownership or planned sale at an appropriate time.

With the security of income through long-term leases further enhanced by increased rental income through percentage leases, plus operating costs of the base year protected through the escalation features of each lease, shopping center investments are very desirable to many investors in commercial real estate.

Those investors usually retain ownership for many years, enjoying the assured income and tax advantages available in shopping centers.

Other investors own and operate their shopping center investment until such a time as the tax advantage diminishes to the point where they consider it advantageous to sell. At that time they either sell or trade the center, re-investing their cash in other, and more often, larger shopping centers.

How long to operate and when to sell are two questions that can only be answered by the economic conditions and the investor's own tax situation at the time of sale. Everyone likes to make a big, fat, profit. When a shopping center has been owned a number of years, purchased on a 12 percent to 15 percent cash yield, as was expected during that period of time, big profits can be made if rentals have increased through excess rentals and the center can be sold at an 8 percent yield. The result sometimes presents a profit that is hard not to accept.

KEY POINTS

1. Understand the need for shopping centers
2. Know the difference between a regional, community and neighborhood shopping center

3. Realize the importance of location and know the requirements for a successful center
4. Know the simple procedure to follow in analyzing and evaluating a shopping center
5. Recognize the major points and terms of a shopping center lease
6. Study how to verify and analyze the income and expense in the operation of a shopping center
7. Understand the importance of the personal tour of inspection
8. Know how to make a detailed evaluation of a shopping center
9. Master the technique of buying a shopping center using the procedures and practices shown
10. Learn how one astute investor purchased his shopping center and the special technique used
11. Understand the need for an acceptable tenant ratio along with the different types of tenants
12. Study how income and profits can be increased
13. Recognize the flexibility of the investment in shopping centers
14. Decide how long to operate and when to sell—two important questions that someday may need to be answered

9

Profitable Investments in Neighborhood Office Buildings

Many times the real estate entrepreneur who visualizes his dream of developing or owning a magnificent, high-rise office building in the center of his dynamic city lets his ambition and desire far exceed his capabilities and the basic need for more office space.

Not long ago a beautiful 22-story office building in the center of a downtown city was under construction. Even though over a third of the building had been leased to one of the leading banks in the state, the building was in trouble from the beginning. With two other larger office buildings (which had only been completed a year or so before) having vacancy problems, this new building was unable to attract enough new tenants in the required time to fulfill the lease requirements in the mortgage commitment.

Needless to say, in time, the large insurance company which had given the mortgage commitment and had provided the initial interim funds for construction, foreclosed and repossessed the unfinished building. As a result, the investors in the project lost all of the money they had invested. The building has since been completed by the lending institution but with many vacancies. The insurance company is now looking for a buyer.

It is always a gamble and the element of risk is ever present in the building of large, high-rise office buildings unless the developer has sufficient capital to weather the initial vacancy problems or has the building at least 75 percent leased before construction commences. Even then, consideration should be given to current vacancies in comparable office buildings. In cities where tenants are moving out of the inner-city and not moving in, this condition is more pronounced.

Some astute investors say that large office buildings constructed without proper and adequate feasibility studies need to be ''wrung out'' a couple of times before they become a good investment. Therefore, two important factors govern the profit opportunities available in today's market—vacancy and overbuilding.

In this chapter a new concept in neighborhood office buildings will be discussed along with how to analyze the risks and investment potential of such an investment. In addition you will be given guidelines and checklists to follow in studying and analyzing current leases. Proven techniques to use in evaluating an office building are provided with guidelines and checklists for purchasing a building with maximum yield on invested cash. The concluding section on recognized tax advantages of ownership with sheltered income should be most interesting.

THE CONCEPT OF OFFICE BUILDINGS IN NEIGHBORHOODS

Following the same reasoning behind the movement of large department stores from downtown into regional shopping centers, tenants are moving from large, city office buildings into the neighborhoods. Convenience for their customers and clients is the predominant factor which has led to the exodus from downtown. Accessibility and the ease of parking in these new neighborhood buildings has eliminated the congested traffic, parking costs and elevators confronting their customers and clients.

As new office buildings were constructed in the outlying areas and filled with tenants, many profit opportunities in this type of investment become available. With the lower cost of land and smaller buildings, the cost of such projects came within the financial capability of more investors.

A typical example of this movement was shown by a group of attorney friends of mine who occupied two floors of one of the high-rise office buildings downtown. Prior to the expiration of their lease, they contacted an investor/developer about constructing a new neighborhood office building in a location of their selection. They would initially lease 15,000 square feet with a projected need in the future for an additional 10,000 square feet.

After inspecting and analyzing their site selection, the developer agreed to construct a 25,000 square foot office building on the site, providing the terms and conditions of his lease to them were acceptable. The attorneys agreed, since finding an office building in the area they wanted with that much vacant floor space and a floor plan suitable for their needs would be impossible.

In this day of specialization, neighborhood office buildings have been constructed for related businesses, such as lawyers, accountants, real estate, title insurance companies, mortgage companies, advertising and insurance companies. By leasing space in a building to similar businesses, the buildings can become known as the Law Building or the Financial Center or the Insurance Building.

Investors soon realized the investment opportunities in these specialized office buildings. The locations were usually excellent—the income high and stable and vacancies were more or less non-existent.

MINIMIZING THE 10 BIGGEST RISKS IN OFFICE INVESTMENTS

Since there is an element of risk in all real estate investments, the secret of success in commercial and industrial properties is to recognize those risks for what they are and to minimize their effect on your investment.

Listed below are the risks which may be present in any office building investment, along with pertinent remarks regarding the effect of each and what should be done to minimize their effect on your operation:

1. *Suitable location.* Every knowledgeable investor should know that a suitable location is one of the most important factors to determine when a neighborhood office building is being considered as an investment. It should be located on a highly traveled and well known arterial street, providing access from all points of the city. In addition, other neighborhood conveniences should be nearby, such as shopping centers, branch banks, service centers and other consumer-oriented businesses.

2. *Costly financing.* The existing financing on the office building should be thoroughly investigated. If its high cost is a controlling factor in whether the investment produces an acceptable yield, other financing techniques should be considered. One would be to modify the existing finance, but this is sometimes impossible. Another would be to offset this high cost by offering only what your evaluation indicates regardless of the owner's asking price. Still another would be refinancing.

3. *Low rental rates.* A thorough investigation of the rental rates charged by other comparable office buildings will indicate the prevailing rental in the area.

Some developers will enter into short-term leases of one year or less in order to achieve a higher occupancy level at the lower rates, planning, of course, to raise the rates when the initial leases expire. Some of the tenants will renew their leases at the higher rate while many others may not, creating a vacancy problem. If the office building has been presented for your consideration as an investment during this transition period, be wary of the projected income statement based upon the newer, higher rates.

4. *Rapid tenant turnover.* If the office building has a history of tenants continually moving in and out without renewing their short-term leases, an investigation of the reasons behind such a rapid tenant turnover should be made. A detailed inspection of the building and its operation may provide the answers or a chat with a few of the tenants may be enlightening. There is an apparent reason and before investing, the answers should be determined.

5. *Unusually high vacancy factor.* A consistently high vacancy rate is usually indicative of an undesirable location, an unsightly building, poor construction, sloppy maintenance and janitor service, and the lack of other day-to-day necessities which should be provided by the management. *Investigate before you invest. If you feel that you can't remedy the situation, look for another investment.*

6. *Poor construction.* A detailed tour of inspection by the investor and his team of experts will reveal the quality of the construction of the building. All items in need of repair or replacement should be noted and taken into consideration in the evaluation of the building.

7. *Bad management.* If the only risk or problem is bad management, this can be remedied by employing better and more efficient management techniques.

8. *Improperly drawn leases.* Leases with tenants should be read and understood, making certain that items affecting the income of the building are included. Leases which do not provide for tax, insurance and maintenance cost escalation are not adequate. With the rapid rise in these costs, profits can be reduced substantially if such protection is not included in the leases. Also options to renew should be analyzed for their long-range effect on income.

9. *High operating costs.* If the operating costs appear to be unusually high, a comprehensive and detailed study should be made. While your evaluation may take those high costs into consideration, it is good to know that the operating costs may be reduced through more efficient management.

10. *Inadequate parking facilities.* The office building has a real problem if there are not sufficient parking spaces for the tenants and their customers or clients. Additional parking must be provided if the building is to be successful and fully rented. This problem can be solved by acquiring an adjacent or nearby lot. It is always better to have more spaces than too few.

AN OFFICE BUILDING WITH ONLY ONE, SLIGHT AND MANY TIMES OVERLOOKED PROBLEM

A number of years ago, a prominent real estate investor built a new 14,000 square foot office building for his highly successful mortgage company, which he had incorporated previously. Ownership of the building was held by him and his wife and they, in turn, leased it to their mortgage corporation.

The 20 year lease was properly drawn, providing for a rent based upon an acceptable yield at the time. All other expenses of maintenance, operation, insurance and taxes were to be paid by the mortgage company. It was a simple, triple net lease. For some reason, even though he owned both the building and the corporation, he also granted the lessee the right to renew the lease for an additional 20 years on the same terms and conditions—never realizing that this short, concise paragraph would later have such an adverse effect when he decided to sell the building. Some years later, he sold the mortgage business to a large financial corporation but retained ownership of the building.

When he decided to sell the office building, he was convinced that he could get the maximum price based upon its income since it would be an excellent investment for anyone, having a triple net lease with a financially strong corporate tenant. It would have been except for the slight problem of the option to renew the lease.

As each interested investor toured the office building, he was completely satisfied with its appearance, maintenance, and general physical conditions as well as the financial stability of the tenant. After each one read the lease, however, the option to renew on the same terms and conditions for another 20 years was a problem that concerned them.

With growing inflation taking more and more out of every dollar each year and having no provision in the lease for any increase in rent, the investors lost interest in the building.

To conclude the story, the building was finally sold to an investor but at a price substantially lower than the owner anticipated.

OCCUPANCY—KEY TO HIGH YIELDS

To produce the yield expected by the investor, the office building should maintain a high level of occupancy. Naturally, a building completely leased is the desired condition; however, many successfully operated office buildings occasionally will have a vacancy. A 5 percent vacancy factor is not bad, since one tenant moving out and another moving in 30 to 60 days later will create a slight reduction in its 100 percent rental level.

A list of typical tenants for a neighborhood office building are shown below:

1. Accountants
2. Lawyers
3. Real estate brokers
4. Title companies
5. Insurance
6. Mortgage companies
7. Banks
8. Savings and loans
9. Construction firms
10. Stock brokers
11. Engineering firms
12. Architects
13. Employment services
14. Finance companies
15. Public relations
16. Advertising
17. Travel agencies
18. Manufacturer's representatives
19. Food brokers
20. Business consultants

As you can see, very few of the tenants in a neighborhood office building will be nationally rated. However, each tenant should be investigated as to his reputation and conduct of business. An undesirable tenant can make it very unpleasant for the other tenants in the building.

HOW TO ANALYZE AND EVALUATE AN OFFICE BUILDING—WITH GUIDELINES AND CHECKLISTS

In the three preceding chapters we illustrated how to analyze and evaluate an apartment complex, land and a shopping center. Now we will present guidelines and checklists to follow in your analysis and evaluation of a neighborhood office building.

While there is a similarity in the procedure for evaluating any income producing commercial and industrial property, there are slightly different techniques to use for each type being considered as an investment.

The six steps listed below can serve as a guide in your analysis and evaluation procedure for a neighborhood office building.

1. Preparation of a Fact and Information Profile
2. Study of current leases
3. Analysis of income and expense
4. Personal inspection of the property
5. Evaluation
6. Decision

PREPARATION OF A FACT AND INFORMATION PROFILE ON A NEIGHBORHOOD OFFICE BUILDING

Using the Property Check List as a guide, the Profile shown below was prepared by an investor on an office building under consideration as an investment.

COUNTY CLUB OFFICE BUILDING   DATE: 6/30/77
OWNER: A. M. PROPERTIES

1. Price: $750,000.00
2. Description of Property: Office Building
3. Location of Property: 5630 East Indian Road
4. Type of Construction: Masonry
5. Land Area: 36,500 square feet
6. Present Zoning: R-5
7. Size of Building - Rentable Area: 14,200 square feet
8. Number of Units: 12
9. Parking Facilities: 71 spaces
10. Services Provided: Full service
12. Income and Operating Expenses: Income - $105,950.00
    Expenses - 38,809.00
    (For breakdown see attached operating statement)
13. Taxes and Insurance: Taxes - $9,465.00
    Insurance - 1,071.00
14. Encumbrance: $330,000.00
15. Amortization: $2,911.35
16. Tenants—leases—rates: See leases
18. Quality of Area: Medium Income
19. Distances to: City Business Area - 5 miles
    Employment Centers - 4 miles
    Airport—Rail—Bus - 5 miles

20. Public Transportation: Yes
21. Population within: 1 mile - 30,000
    2 miles - 100,000
    3 miles - 200,000

After reviewing the information contained in the above Fact and Information Profile, the investor had completed the first step in his evaluation procedure.

HOW TO ANALYZE CURRENT LEASES

While the leases normally used for apartment tenants are short, concise, standard form documents, the leases used for space in an office building are longer, more descriptive and contain many more provisions, somewhat similar to a shopping center lease.

A lease for office space will usually cover the following items:

1. Description of property and terms
2. Rental
3. Use of premises
4. Services and utilities
5. No representations except as shown
6. Acceptance of premises
7. Destruction of premises
8. Eminent domain
9. Alterations and improvements
10. Taxes
11. Liability
12. Entry by landlord
13. Tenant's fixtures
14. Abandonment
15. Transfer of landlord's interest
16. Assignment and subletting
17. Rules and regulations
18. Signs
19. Building operating costs
20. Default
21. Attorney's fees
22. Holding over
23. Subordination

24. Notices
25. Remedies cumulative
26. Waiver
27. Construction of lease
28. Successors and assigns
29. Reasonable consent

While every item in the lease is there for a specific purpose and reason, those items in which investors should be most interested, contain provisions affecting the income and operation of the building. Special study and emphasis should be given to those paragraphs regarding the following:

1. Description of property and term
2. Rent to be paid
3. Services and utilities provided
4. Tax escalation
5. Tenant's fixtures
6. Escalation for building operating costs
7. Default in payment of rent
8. Attorney's fees
9. Holding over or any options to renew
10. Notices

PROVEN GUIDELINES TO USE IN MAKING A COMPREHENSIVE ANALYSIS OF INCOME AND OPERATING EXPENSES

Every astute investor should receive a current operating statement of the office building—not a pro-forma statement but one which indicates its actual income for the period. It is also wise to have a look at the income and expense for prior years.

While the income and expense figures will be shown on the operating statement, they will probably not be certified as correct by a CPA; therefore such income and expense totals should be verified by the investor.

The income of the building can be verified by the usual practice of checking the accounting records, bank deposits and leases. The leases, of course, will show the amount of rent that should have been paid by each tenant. The accounting records will indicate that such amounts were received each month and the bank deposits will further substantiate their receipt. After the income has been verified and accepted, no further checking should be necessary.

All items of expense in the operation of the building should be thoroughly checked and verified as to amounts and service performed. Such items would normally include the following:

1. Utilities
2. Janitor services
3. Equipment repairs and maintenance
4. Painting and decorating
5. General repair and maintenance
6. Management
7. Accounting
8. Legal

In addition to the charges for the above services and repairs, real property taxes and insurance should be checked and verified as to amounts and coverage.

In the analysis of the income, these three points should be uppermost in your mind:

1. Does the income include additional rent as provided by the escalation clauses in the leases for increases in taxes, insurance and operating costs of the building?
2. How much vacancy actually existed during the year?
3. How much income can be increased by renting the vacant space?

Each item of expense should be analyzed as to whether it is low, normal or high. Every astute investor knows that a decrease in expenses will increase profits, so much thought should be given to those items that are considered excessive. It will probably be in the housekeeping services where savings can be made.

HOW TO CONDUCT YOUR PERSONAL INSPECTION WITH CHECKLISTS

As with the inspection of any type of income producing commercial or industrial property, the purpose of a personal tour of the office building is to determine not only the physical condition of the property but also all other facts relating to the building.

The checklist shown below will serve as a guide in the conduct of you personal inspection.

1. Location
2. Size of land area
3. Zoning
4. Type of construction
5. Size of building
6. Tenants and space occupied
7. Parking—number of spaces
8. Condition of parking area
9. General condition of building—structural
10. Painting and decorating
11. Refrigeration and heating equipment
12. Carpets and drapes
13. Halls and stairs
14. Landscaping and exterior lighting
15. Good features
16. Bad points
17. Quality of area
18. Accessibility

As a general rule, the investor is not knowledgeable enough to properly inspect the mechanical and structural features of the building. Usually he will have qualified specialists to inspect the following:

1. General building structures
2. Roof
3. Windows
4. Electrical facilities
5. Plumbing
6. Refrigeration equipment
7. Heating equipment
8. Painting and decorating
9. Carpets and drapes
10. Elevator

It goes without saying that those items in need of repair or replacement should be itemized and become a condition of purchase, requiring the seller to repair or replace these certain items.

Having followed the first four steps in the analysis of the office building, you are now ready for Step 5—the evaluation of the investment.

PROVEN TECHNIQUES TO USE IN THE EVALUATION OF AN OFFICE BUILDING

A smart investor wants to look beyond the physical condition and appearance of the office building. While some want to enjoy a pride of ownership and only purchase a building that is pleasing to the eye, most investors are interested in the economic factors and the results shown on that bottom line.

In his evaluation, he should determine answers to the following three important questions:

1. Does the investment produce an acceptable yield on the cash invested?
2. Does it provide the tax shelters needed today in every investment program?
3. Will it be a hedge against further inflation in the nation's economy?

Using the information shown in the Fact and Information Profile of the Country Club Office Building, the investor prepared the Income Analysis and Evaluation shown below:

INCOME ANALYSIS AND EVALUATION

Country Club Office Building	Date:	7/15/77	
	Owner:	A. M. Properties	
Total Price	$750,000.00		
Current Mortgage Balance	330,000.00		
8¾% - 2,911.35 Mo. P+I			
Cash Required	$420,000.00		
Total Income	$105,950.00		
Operating Expenses:			
Property Taxes	9,465.00		
Insurance	1,071.00		
Utilities	16,315.00		
Repair & Maintenance	3,780.00		
Janitor & Landscape	8,178.00		
Total Expenses		$38,809.00	
Operating Profit		$67,141.00	
Less Debt Service		34,936.20	
Cash Spendable Income			$32,204.80
Gain In Equity			5,451.93
Total Gain			$37,656.73
Yield—Cash On Cash			7.66%
Total Yield			8.96%

At the conclusion of Step 5, the investor reviewed the Income Analysis and Evaluation of the property and was able to determine the cash yield to expect on the investment based upon the asking price of the owner.

Consulting his table on Acceptable Yields as shown in Chapter 2, the investor found that the yield in office buildings should be from 10 to 13 percent.

Since the foregoing evaluation indicated a cash yield of only 7.66 percent, he realized that the property was over-priced as far as he was concerned. By applying the technique of capitalizing the cash yield, he quickly determined the high and low value of the property by using yields acceptable to him. Those values are shown as follows:

10% -	$652,040.00
13% -	577,723.00

As a result, he decided that he would be willing to purchase the office building at a price from $575,000 to $650,000.

GUIDELINES AND CHECKLISTS FOR PURCHASING AND OFFICE BUILDING WITH MAXIMUM YIELD ON INVESTED CASH

There are times when an investor has two office buildings under consideration at the same time. Naturally, he wants to purchase the one which satisfies his requirements and produces the maximum yield on his invested cash.

The investor shown in the foregoing section had another office building under consideration at the same time he was making his analysis and evaluation of the country club office building.

The other building was much larger, having 44,200 square feet of rentable area. One major nationally rated tenant occupied 29,300 square feet under a 5 year lease with several options. Only 2,100 square feet of the remaining 14,900 were rented to three local tenants, leaving a vacancy of 12,800 square feet. An analysis of the operating statement is shown below:

INCOME ANALYSIS AND EVALUATION

HHK Building — Date: 7/15/77 — Owner: G. M. Inc.

Total Price:	$1,650,000.00
Current Mortgage Balance	1,070,000.00
8½% - 25 yr. - $8,757.00 Mo. P+I	
Cash Required	$ 580,000.00
Total Income	$ 208,808.00

Operating Expenses			
Utilities	$27,490.00		
Repair & Maintenance	8,192.00		
Janitor Service	16,300.00		
Management	2,400.00		
Commissions	8,787.00		
Real Estate Tax	25,401.00		
Insurance	2,888.00		
Miscellaneous	382.00		
Total Operating Expenses		$91,840.00	
Operating Profit			$116,968.00
Less Debt Service			105,084.00
Cash Spendable Income			$ 11,884.00
Gain in Equity			14,898.00
Total Gain			$ 26,782.00
Yield—Cash on Cash			2.04%
Total Yield			4.61%

Needless to say, the results of the above evaluation didn't excite the investor too much. However, as Step 6 in his analysis and evaluation procedure, he continued his decision-making process.

The results of his comparison analysis of the two buildings are shown below:

HHK Building

Good Features	Bad Points
1. 66% leased to Major Tenant	1. 29% vacant
2. Escalation for Taxes, Insurance and Maintenance costs	2. Only 5% rental to local tenants
3. Sufficient parking	3. Poor location
	4. Short lease with major tenant
	5. No rental increase in options
	6. Priced too high

Remarks:

1. Poor location will make leasing to other tenants difficult.
2. Investment would be acceptable if Major Tenant would lease entire building, extend lease and provide for rental increase in the options.
3. A 10 percent cash on cash yield will be required.

CC Office Building

Good Features	Bad Points
1. Fully rented	1. Priced too high
2. Good rental rate	

3. Escalation for Taxes, Insurance
   and Maintenance costs
4. Excellent location
5. Quality construction
6. Financially qualified tenants
7. Adequate lease
8. Sufficient parking

Remarks:
Will make an excellent investment if it can be purchased at a price that will yield from 10 to 13 percent on cash invested.

After completing the comparison analysis of the two office buildings, the investor realized that the larger more expensive building had too many bad points to overcome and decided to make an offer on the smaller building.

Wanting to make the maximum yield on his invested cash, he prepared his offer at the lower price of $575,000, which would provide a yield of 13 percent.

The owner would not accept the offered price but countered back at $650,000. Knowing that the new price would permit a 10 percent yield on the required $320,000 down payment, the investor decided to increase that yield through a proven financing technique. He agreed to pay $650,000 for the building, providing the down payment could be reduced to $160,000 and the remaining balance to be evidenced by an interest-only 7 percent note payable in five years. In this manner, the cash yield would increase from 10 percent back up to the 13 percent he wanted.

In accepting the investor's counter, the owner was satisfied because he had received the price he had set in his mind.

HOW TO MAXIMIZE TAX ADVANTAGES OF OWNERSHIP WITH SHELTERED INCOME

As long as the interest paid on a business encumbrance remains an expense of operation and the tax laws allow the depreciation of a capital asset, the tax shelters available to investors make the ownership of an income producing commercial and industrial property very attractive.

While much is said and has been shown in Chapter 1 about tax shelters, the following example can best explain how it works and how it can be used by an astute real estate investor.

In the foregoing sections, we have seen how the investor followed the 6 steps necessary in the analysis, evaluation and purchase of an office building. The Income Analysis and Evaluation form shows the Cash Spendable Income and the yield on cash that it represents. While all investors are interested in the cash results—that amount of money left over after all expenses and debt service have been paid—the Taxable Income is equally as important since income taxes are calculated from that net amount.

In determining his income tax liability, the investor evaluated the land under the office building at $109,500, representing $3.00 per square foot. Deducting the value of the land from the price paid for the building, he arrived at a value of $540,500 for depreciation. Using established depreciation rates for the various component parts of the building, he determined that his composite rate of depreciation would be 8 percent. Applying the 150 percent depreciation method, the rate of depreciation would be 12 percent each year on the declining value of the building.

Therefore, his operating statement for the building at the end of the first year would be as follows:

CC Office Building
Operating Statement

Total Income		$105,950.00
Expenses:		
Depreciation	$64,860.00	
Interest		
1st Mortgage	29,484.00	
2nd Mortgage	11,200.00	
Property Taxes	9,465.00	
Insurance	1,071.00	
Utilities	16,315.00	
Repair & Maintenance	3,780.00	
Janitor & Landscape	8,178.00	
Total expenses		$144,353.00
Operating loss		- 38,393.00

While the building provided a Cash Spendable Income of $21,004, the actual Profit and Loss Statement showed a loss of $38,393. Naturally, with this loss, no income tax was due from the operation for that year. As interest expense and depreciation decrease, the loss will become less and less until the building will begin to show a taxable profit. At that point, many investors begin to think of selling or trading.

What can be done with the operating loss will be determined by the type of ownership in which the investment is held and applicable tax laws in effect at the time of the loss. It will be wise to consult your accountant and tax consultant at that time.

Even though the foregoing example was shown to illustrate the tax advantages of ownership in an office building, the same procedure and technique can be used in calculating the tax liability on any type of income producing commercial or industrial property.

KEY POINTS

1. Realize the gamble of downtown office buildings
2. Understand the concept of neighborhood office buildings and the profit opportunities available in that type of investment
3. Know the risks involved and investment potential in office buildings
4. Study the story of the office building with an option problem and its effect on a future sale
5. Understand why the level of occupancy and the type of tenants are contributing factors in an investment decision
6. Recognize the importance of the 6 steps necessary in the analysis and evaluation of an office building
7. Learn the importance of the Fact and Information Profile
8. Know what should be in a lease for space in an office building and the key points to check
9. Use guidelines in making an analysis of income and operating expenses
10. Use checklists in conducting your own personal tour of inspection
11. Understand the importance of the Income Analysis and Evaluation Form in calculating the yield on an office building
12. Know how to use the comparison method in your decision making proccss
13. Know how to purchase an office building for maximum yield on invested cash
14. Understand the tax advantages of ownership of an office building

10

Industrial Investments for Secured Income and Profit Growth

The most sought after investment in commercial and industrial real estate is an industrial building under a long-term triple net lease to a nationally-rated tenant producing an excellent yield on cash invested.

This chapter will explain why industrial development is necessary to the growth of every city and will illustrate how the new garden-type industrial park demonstrates the concept of profit and beauty and provides a source of profitable industrial investment as well. The many industrial profit opportunities in single-tenant buildings and multi-tenant facilities will be described and the importance of location and the accessibility of rail and truck routes will be stressed. How one investor capitalized a multi-tenant industrial building with interesting results is also explained. Industrial development in small cities is shown followed by an actual story of how a group of innovative businessmen developed an industrial park in their enterprising little city.

Also discussed will be how to structure financing with a long-term lease showing how to increase profit growth with industrial investments. Procedures to use in analyzing and evaluating an industrial investment with detailed instructions in what to look for are outlined followed by the major points in the analysis of an industrial lease. Proven procedures to use in verifying and analyzing the income and expense of an industrial investment are described followed by practical guidelines for the evaluation of an industrial property. A step-by-step procedure is outlined showing how to purchase an industrial property to provide a secure income. The story of how one astute industrial investor made an investment decision resulting in a tremendous profit is explained. In addition, a number of interesting and informative examples are given, amplifying the many profit opportunities available in industrial investments.

INDUSTRIAL DEVELOPMENT: A BOON TO EVERY CITY

Industrial development is the backbone of developing cities, and each Chamber of Commerce is busy every day of the year trying to entice some factory, manufacturing plant, distribution center or other industrial complex to locate in their city. States and cities pass favorable legislation and grant special incentives to those companies who will move or establish a plant in their areas.

A number of years ago industrial development was confined to those areas adjacent to railroads and usually in very undesirable sections of the cities. Factories were built with satellite businesses serving the needs of industry. Those areas were never known for their beauty.

With the rising growth of the trucking industry, the need for railroad trackage in industrial areas became less important. Cities began to zone other more desirable areas for industrial development so that industrial growth wouldn't be limited to just those areas near the railroad tracks.

When freeways in cities began to take on more importance in the movement of traffic, small industrial tracts began to be developed into warehouses, distribution centers, assembly plants and other such buildings for industrial use. Parcels near or adjacent to freeways proved to be ideal for such developments.

As cities grew, the demand for industrial acreage increased and the industrial developers became more sophisticated in the techniques of providing space for the requirements of clean, light industry. Thus began the development of the garden type industrial park.

THE SPECIALIZED DEVELOPMENT OF THE NEW GARDEN TYPE INDUSTRIAL PARK

This specialized industrial park is designed for beauty and located for profit. The acreage requirement is determined by the size of the projected developments—sometimes requiring 160 acres or more.

The developer in planning his project will subdivide the larger parcel into smaller tracts, varying in size from lots to several acres. A network of streets is designed to service the project. Railroad trackage if available, is also incorporated into the overall plan to achieve maximum use for the larger tracts.

To assure the beauty of the development, all plans for buildings within the project must be approved by the developer, landscaped with grass, trees and shrubs and set back from street lines. In developing the industrial park, improved lots and larger tracts are available for sale to other investors for development or directly to companies desiring a location within the project. In addition, the developer will build certain facilities for lease.

PROFIT OPPORTUNITIES IN GARDEN TYPE INDUSTRIAL PARKS

Such industrial parks provide a tremendous source of profitable opportunities for an astute, industrial investor. There are times when the developer may decide to sell one of the buildings within the project. As a result, the more knowledgeable investors usually keep in close contact with such projects and when an investment is available, they want to know.

One investor purchased an excellent building in a beautiful industrial park. One day in talking to the Vice-President in charge of the development, the investor was told that the corporation would be willing to sell a certain building. When the investor expressed an interest in the building, he received all pertinent information, including selling price, lot dimensions, size of building, tenants and amount of space each occupied along with specific lease data. In addition, all income, operating expenses and debt service were shown.

From the information contained in their letter, the investor prepared the simple Income Analysis and Evaluation Form as shown below:

INCOME ANALYSIS AND EVALUATION

UNIT NO. 20 DATE: 8/20/77

SOUTH INDUSTRIAL PARK OWNER: S. I. B., Inc.

Total Price	$425,000.00
Current Mortgage Balance	None
Cash Required	425,000.00
Total Income	$ 44,650.00
Operating Expenses	None
(Tenants pay all taxes, insurance and maintain building)	
Operating Profit	44,650.00
Cash Spendable Income	44,650.00
Yield—Cash on Cash	10.5%

The investor, consulting the Table on Acceptable Yields, saw that the cash yield on industrial buildings should range from 9 to 12 percent. Since his evaluation indicated the Cash Yield to be 10.5 percent, he realized the building would be a good investment. Not wanting to put that much cash in one investment, he secured a mortgage commitment for $300,000 at 9 percent for 25 years.

His yield on the $125,000 cash he would have invested is calculated below:

Operating Profit	$44,650.00	
Less Debt Service	30,211.20	
Cash Spendable Income		$14,438.80
Gain In Equity		3,400.00
Total Gain		$17,838.80
Yield—Cash on Cash		11.5%
Total Yield		14.2%

Seeing the cash yield increase from 10.5 to 11.5 percent through the technique of long-range financing, the investor lost no time in preparing his offer at the price and on the cash terms the owner had stipulated.

INVESTMENT OPPORTUNITIES IN SINGLE-TENANT AND MULTI-TENANT FACILITIES

Not all industrial buildings are in designed industrial parks. In fact, most of them are situated in industrial areas of a city. Some will be free-standing, single-tenant buildings while others are multi-tenant facilities. Many will be owned by the companies or corporations occuping the building, but most will be occupied by tenants under lease. It is in this second category where investment opportunities can be found.

Industrial buildings occupied by the following or similar businesses make excellent investments, depending, of course, on the income, expense and terms of the lease:

1. Building materials
2. Agricultural chemicals
3. Farm equipment and supplies
4. Air cargo services
5. Heating and air conditioning
6. Appliance distribution
7. Metal building dealers
8. Floor coverings

9. Paints and supplies
10. Protective coatings
11. Concrete and aggregate products
12. Steel fabrication
13. Electrical equipment and supplies
14. Plumbing materials
15. Hardware distribution

Those industrial buildings leased to one tenant are considered the best investment since the lease is usually on a triple net basis with the tenant paying for everything. *As a result, the investor has a secured income for a number of years without the problems of management, vacancy, operations, maintenance or other incidental but time consuming problems.*

Multi-tenant facilities present a slightly different picture. These are generally larger buildings housing a number of different, unrelated businesses. In one respect they are like an industrial shopping center—but in a single building. Since this type of industrial investment has the usual problems of management, vacancies and related expenses, it is not as desirable as the single-tenant building with its triple net lease, but there are more available for the smart investor.

HOW ONE INVESTOR CAPITALIZED THE INCOME ON A MULTI-TENANT INDUSTRIAL BUILDING WITH INTERESTING RESULTS

One such building was purchased by a friend of mine. It was located near the airport on one and one-half acres of land. The building was not too large, having only 22,000 square feet of rentable area. There were three tenants—each with three year leases, expiring at different times.

The owner was asking $542,000 for the building which showed a gross income of $57,525 and chargeable operating expenses of $8,725, leaving an annual net operating income of $48,800. The investor quickly determined that the net income had been capitalized at 9 percent.

Based upon securing a 70 percent mortgage in the amount of $380,000 at 9 percent interest for 25 years, the investor calculated the cash yield after making a down payment of $162,000 as shown below:

Operating Profit	$48,800.00
Less Debt Service	38,268.00
Cash Spendable Income	$10,532.00
Yield—Cash on Cash	6.5%

Realizing that the constant on the mortgage was 10.08 percent and the cash yield on the asking price was only 9 percent, the investor was not surprised when the new cash yield reduced to 6.5%.

Wanting to make at least 10 percent on his cash invested, the investor capitalized the net cash flow of $10,532 at that rate and offered $485,000 for the building. His calculations are shown below:

$10,532.00 ÷ 10%	$105,320.00
New Mortgage	380,000.00
New Valuation	485,320.00

In Salt Lake City another investor doubled his money on a mini-warehouse investment. Also, an investor in St. Louis increased his income tremendously when he remodeled a large industrial warehouse into a combination of offices and smaller storage facilities.

THE IMPORTANCE OF LOCATION AND THE REQUIREMENT OF ACCESSIBILITY TO RAIL AND TRUCK ROUTES

While the location of any business enterprise is relatively important, industrial properties do not need to be near or in the center of a densely populated area, nor do they need to be near shopping, schools, churches or other everyday needs of people. They do need, however, to be accessible to arterial streets, highways, freeways, truck routes and rail, if possible Some industrial businesses deal with the general public, but they are not dependent upon the typical drop-in consumer trade or foot traffic.

In preparing a Fact and Information Profile on an industrial property, it should be noted that seven or eight items on the Property Check List are not required information.

INDUSTRIAL DEVELOPMENT IN SMALL CITIES

The demand for industrial locations and plant sites is far greater in the larger, metropolitan centers than in the smaller cities. This is a natural result of concentrated population, warehousing, distribution, manufacturing, rail and highway networks. The smaller cities have little to offer the big industrial operations in the way of facilities and incentives.

The more aggressive and enterprising small cities do something about such a situation as is described in the following story. This small city is located on the

Interstate Freeway midway between two larger cities. It is the center of a large farming area with a population of about 20,000 people. With the discovery of huge deposits of copper in the mountains to the south of the city a number of years ago, the little city began to change from a quiet farming community to one where industrial businesses began to look for locations and plant sites.

Since the city had not planned for such industrial growth, no facilities were available for those first inquiries. The civic leaders, being an aggressive group, wanted this new industrial opportunity for their city. They organized themselves into a development corporation and immediately began making plans to remedy the situation.

They first acquired 20 acres of land one half mile beyond the city limits adjacent to the railroad tracks. As the next step, the property had to be annexed to the city. Since it was not adjacent to the present city boundary, a narrow strip of land extending along the state highway to the 20 acres was included in the annexation, satisfying the adjacent requirement for annexation.

After annexation the property was zoned industrial, and was planned and designed as an industrial park. Water and sewer lines were extended to the property and arrangements were made with the railroad company to run a spur line along the east edge of the property.

It was not long until this small industrial park was providing sites for a number of industrial facilities. This enterprising venture satisfied not only the needs of the city in its industrial growth but also proved to be an excellent and profitable investment for those aggressive young men who conceived the plan.

INDUSTRIAL FINANCING TECHNIQUES AND THE LONG-TERM LEASE

Many national corporations prefer to lease a building for their operation even though they are finanically capable of constructing and owning the property. This situation presents an excellent investment opportunity for the astute industrial developer and investor.

A long-term lease with a nationally-rated tenant is a very bankable commodity. The more knowledgeable developers and investors use this lease and the credit of the tenant in negotiating the long-term financing necessary to construct the facility.

To illustrate this special financing technique, an industrial developer constructed a 30,000 square foot building on three acres of land for a national tenant under the provisions of a triple net long-term lease. The lease provided a net income to the developer of $105,000 annually. In securing the mortgage commitment, the net income was capitalized at 9 percent, establishing a value of $1,166,666 for the land and building. The lender agreed to loan 70 percent of the value in the amount of $780,000 to be amortized at 8¾ percent over a period of 30 years.

The land was purchased for $100,000 and the building constructed at a cost of $750,000, including all points, fees, plans, etc. As a result the cash investment of the developer was only $70,000.

In analyzing the results of this financing technique, the developer prepared an Income Analysis and Evaluation as shown below:

Total Income	$105,000.00	
Less Debt Service	73,656.00	
Cash Spendable Income		$31,344.00
Gain In Equity		5,600.00
Total Gain		$36,944.00
Yield—Cash On Cash		44.8%
Total Yield		52.8%

In further analyzing his investment potential, the developer projected another evaluation based upon selling the investment at a 9 percent yield—cash on cash:

Cash Flow of $31,344.00 ÷ 9% =	$ 348,266.00
Mortgage Balance	780,000.00
Sales Price	$1,128,266.00
Total Cost	$ 850,000.00
Anticipated Profit	$ 278,266.00

HOW TO INCREASE PROFIT GROWTH WITH INDUSTRIAL INVESTMENTS

As a general rule, leases prepared on industrial buildings do not contain provisions for rental increases through a percentage of sales factors as with shopping center leases. The business is not usually consumer sales oriented. It is customary, however, for the lease to provide for rental increases through regular periodic application of increases in the Economic Indicator Index—a government prepared index which indicates the rise in the economy over an established base period.

At every review period, whether two, three or five year intervals, the rent is increased in proportion to the rise in the Economic Indicator Index. In this manner, profit growth can keep pace with the rise in the nation's economy.

One old time industrial developer made a fortune in an industrial development, using this method. Quite a few years ago, this investor constructed a 20,000 square foot building for a good industrial tenant. At that point costs were low and so were rents. The original 20 year lease provided for a net income of $30,000 a year but with cost of living increases every two years. The building and land cost $280,000 and the investor was able to secure a $185,000 mortgage to be amortized at 6 percent over a 20 year period. As a result, his $95,000 cash investment produced a cash yield of $14,096, representing a yield of 14.8 percent. While this yield would be considered excellent today, it was just fair in those days.

By the time the original 20 year lease was nearing its expiration date, the rent on the building had increased an amazing 80 percent through the application of the cost of living provisions in the lease. This increase in rent and profit growth had been caused by a tremendous rise in the index as a result of growing inflation in the economy of the country.

In Milwaukee another investor increased his profit growth by converting a large factory to accomodate seven small manufacturers. And in Denver, an investor remodeled and enlarged an old 15,000 square foot warehouse into a highly profitable investment. There will be more on this story in Chapter 13.

ANALYZING AND EVALUATING AN INDUSTRIAL INVESTMENT

In previous chapters we have discussed how to analyze and evaluate an apartment complex, a parcel of land, a shopping center and an office building. While the procedures of analysis and evaluation in each type of investment are similar, there is a slightly different technique to use with industrial property.

Again, it is necessary to follow a step-by-step procedure as is outlined below:

Step 1. Using the Property Check List, detailed information on all items in the industrial column is obtained. It should be noted, however, that there are fewer items to check with industrial property. From this factual information, a Fact and Information Profile is prepared as shown below:

Industrial Building — Date: 6/20/77
Owner: J.J., Inc.

1. Price: $490,000.00
2. Description of Property: Garden Industrial Park
3. Location of Property: 2820 Industrial Way
4. Type of Construction: Tilt Slab
5. Land Area: 56,800 square feet
6. Present Zoning: Industrial

7. Size of Building: 14,350 square feet, rentable area
8. Number of Units: 5
9. Parking Spaces: Adequate
10. Services Provided: See leases
11. Income and Operating Expenses: Income - $49,625.00
    Expenses - $ 5,388.00
    (For breakdown see attached operating statement)
13. Taxes and Insurance: Taxes - Tenants pay
    Insurance - $725.00
14. Encumbrance: $315,000.00 - 9¼% - 30 years - 15 year call
15. Amortization: $2,591.50 Mo. P+I
16. Tenants—leases—rates: See Leases
18. Quality of Area: Industrial Park
19. Distances To: City business area - 5 miles
    Employment centers - 1 mile
    Airport - rail - bus - 1 mile
20. Public Transportation: Yes

Step 2. Study and analyze all existing leases with special emphasis on those sections relating to rental, tax, insurance and operating cost escalation. Major points and terms to look for are shown in the following section.

Step 3. The income and expense items of the building should be verified and analyzed as shown in a subsequent section of this chapter.

Step 4. A personal tour of inspection of the property should be made, checking the construction of the building, parking area and lighting, equipment, maintenance of the structure, roof and general condition of the property. Methods prescribed for apartments, shopping centers and office buildings will serve as a guide in conducting your tour of an industrial building.

Step 5. A detailed evaluation of the industrial building should be made using the Income Analysis and Evaluation form as shown with other income producing properties. Other proven techniques to use in evaluating an industrial property will be shown and described in a subsequent section of this chapter.

Step 6. As a result of the five preceding steps, an investment decision can be made. How to make that decision is fully described and explained in a following section of this chapter.

MAJOR POINTS TO LOOK FOR IN THE ANALYSIS OF AN INDUSTRIAL LEASE

A lease on an industrial facility can include as many as thirty or more paragraphs. Each one will be relatively important; however, special emphasis should be given to those paragraphs relating to the following ten important items outlined below:

1. *Term of the lease.* This paragraph should show the commencement date of the lease followed by the date of expiration.

2. *Rent.* The total rent to be paid during the term of the lease will be shown along with the amount to be paid each month. The lease shall also provide that the rent will be increased proportionately with the rise in the Economic Indicator Index or any other business indicator acceptable to the parties. Also this paragraph should stipulate that the lessee will pay applicable city and state sales taxes each month.

3. *Additional rent.* The lease should also provide that any increase in the operating costs of the building over the base month of the lease shall be paid proportionately by the tenants.

4. *Real property taxes.* If the lease does not provide for the tenant to pay the real property taxes, it is absolutely necessary that the lease provide for tax escalation. Any increase in taxes above the base year of the lease should be paid proportionately by each tenant.

5. *Insurance.* Again, if the lease does not provide for the tenant to pay for all insurance, it is necessary that the lease also provide for building insurance escalation above the base year of the lease. In addition, the lease should provide for the tenant carrying the proper and sufficient amount of liability insurance to protect the lessor.

6. *Utilities.* Tenant should be required to pay for all water, gas, heat, electricity and other utilities furnished to or used in or about the premises by the tenant during the term of the lease.

7. *Maintenance of the premises.* In the event the lease does not provide for the tenant to maintain the property, any damage to the interior of the premises shall be repaired by the tenant and at his sole cost and expense. This paragraph will usually stipulate that the landlord will keep the roof and exterior walls in repair, except that tenant shall repair or replace any doors or glass therein broken during the term of the lease.

8. *Option to renew.* The terms and conditions of any option to renew the lease will be given in this paragraph. Special emphasis and study should determine if proper and adequate provisions have been made to provide for economic escalation.

9. *Subletting.* Tenant is usually permitted to assign or sublet the premises; however, tenant shall agree to obtain an experienced and responsible subtenant who is experienced in this type of business and such subtenant be bound by and accept the obligations of the lease. Neither the assignment or subletting of the premises shall relieve the tenant of the obligations or responsibilities of the lease.

10. *Security deposits.* The amount and conditions under which the security deposit is made should be fully described in this paragraph.

PROVEN PROCEDURES TO USE IN VERIFYING AND ANALYZING THE INCOME AND EXPENSE OF AN INDUSTRIAL INVESTMENT

As shown in Step 3, the income and expense of the investment should be verified and analyzed. In the beginning, the investor should have been given a current operating statement by the owner, showing the total income and expense of operating the building. Also, income and expense figures for prior years can be most helpful in determining if the escalation features of the lease are effective.

A thorough analysis of each lease will show the amount of rent and other considerations which should be paid by each tenant. Special emphasis should be given to those features of the lease relating to rent and the application of any economic indicators, additional rent in the form of increases in the costs of operation and the escalation of real property taxes and insurance. Accounting records and bank deposits of the owner can substantiate the amounts paid by each tenant.

In verifying the operating expenses it is again necessary to refer to the leases. In many industrial leases, the tenant will pay all real property taxes, insurance and maintain the property. This type of lease is usually referred to as a triple net lease. In some instances, however, the lease may stipulate that the tenant pay only the real property taxes, the insurance, maintain the property or any combination of the three expenses of operation. In the event the lessor is to pay the operating expenses, then those expenses should be verified as to their amount and accuracy.

PRACTICAL GUIDELINES TO FOLLOW IN EVALUATING AN INDUSTRIAL PROPERTY

The technique of evaluating an income producing industrial investment follows the same procedure as outlined in previous chapters on apartments, shopping centers and office buildings.

Prior to the final evaluation of the property, the investor uses the following proven procedures:

1. Using the Property Check List as a guide, all known facts and information about the property is obtained.
2. From the information in the Property Check List, a Fact and Information Profile is prepared.
3. All leases are studied and analyzed with special emphasis given to those sections relating to rent, tax, insurance and operating cost escalation.

4. A personal tour of inspection is conducted by the investor to determine the physical condition of the property.

5. The income and cost of operating the industrial investment is verified and analyzed.

As a result of the foregoing procedure, the evaluation of the property can be made. As an example and to better explain the process, we will use the building described in a previous section on *Analyzing And Evaluating An Industrial Development*.

Using the information contained in the Fact and Information Profile, the following Income Analysis and Evaluation was made:

INCOME ANALYSIS AND EVALUATION

Industrial Building		Date:	6/20/77
		Owner:	J.J., Inc.
Total Price:	$490,000.00		
Current Mortgage Balance:	315,000.00		
Cash Required:	175,000.00		
Total Income	49,625.00		
Operating Expenses	5,388.00		
Operating Profit		$44,237.00	
Less Debt Service		31,098.00	
Cash Spendable Income			$13,138.00
Gain In Equity			1,980.00
Total Gain			$15,118.00
Yield—Cash On Cash			7.5%
Total Yield			8.6%

A STEP-BY-STEP PROCEDURE SHOWING HOW TO PURCHASE AN INDUSTRIAL PROPERTY TO PROVIDE A SECURE INCOME

After following the guidelines in evaluating the industrial property shown in the preceding section, the investor made plans to purchase the property using the step-by-step procedure outlined below:

Step 1. Determine the purchase price. Wanting to make at least 9 percent on his invested cash, the investor capitalized the Cash Spendable Income at 9 percent and added the mortgage balance to reach an offer price of $460,977 which he rounded off to $460,000.

Step 2. Decide upon a plan of purchase. His purchase plan followed the cash to mortgage technique, making a down payment of $145,000 with an earnest money deposit of $10,000 and assuming the mortgage in the amount of $315,000. The escrow was to be opened upon acceptance of his offer and to close 30 days thereafter.

Step 3. Special terms and conditions. The following were included as special conditions to the offer:

1. Approval of the Preliminary Title Report
2. Approval of the leases with tenants
3. Approval of the assumed mortgage

Step 4. Prepare the offer. Using escrow instructions as the purchase agreement as shown in Chapter 8 on shopping centers, the offer of purchase is prepared by the investor.

The front side of the escrow instructions are prepared in the normal and customary manner wherein both the seller and the buyer are identified along with the legal description of the property and the close of escrow date.

The price and terms are then shown. In this purchase all of the cash was paid at the close of escrow, followed by the assumption of the existing mortgage. If there had been a balance due the seller at the close of escrow, the amount would have been shown in the space provided. All of the proper boxes are then checked showing how various fees and charges are to be paid. Items to be prorated are shown.

On the back side of the instructions and below the fine print, there is a space provided for additional instructions. In this space the "Binding Agreement" paragraph is written and numbered consecutively from the last numbered paragraph of the escrow instructions. This paragraph is necessary to make the instructions a binding agreement between the parties, and without it, the escrow instructions are only instructions to the escrow agent—not enforceable as a contract. This paragraph should read as follows:

> "These Escrow Instructions, in addition to being instructions to the Escrow Agent, shall when executed constitute a binding agreement between the parties relating to the sale and purchase of the within described real property subject, however, to the conditions herein provided."

Following the "Binding Agreement" paragraph, those special conditions as shown in Step 3 are itemized as contingencies to the purchase using the format as shown in Chapter 8. The concluding paragraph, also numbered consecutively, states that the escrow will be opened upon the execution of the agreement by the parties and shall close upon a certain specified date.

Step 5. Presentation and acceptance by the seller. The offer of purchase is then presented to the seller for his acceptance.

Step 6. Open and close the escrow. In accordance with the provisions of the escrow instructions, the escrow is opened at the agreed-upon title company. During the escrow period, those special conditions of the escrow are either satisfied or waived and the escrow closed upon the date specified.

HOW ONE ASTUTE INDUSTRIAL INVESTOR MADE AN INVESTMENT DECISION RESULTING IN A TREMENDOUS PROFIT

A very knowledgeable investor recognized the profit opportunity in his industrial investment. The following story relates to the analysis, evaluation and investment decision regarding his building described in the section of this chapter on Profit Growth.

His 20,000 square foot industrial building was originally leased to a national tenant for a net income of $30,000 a year. During the term of the lease and through the application of the rental escalation features of the lease, the net rental income increased to $54,000 a year.

At the time of this evaluation, the original lease had expired and a new lease was entered into with the same tenant at a net rent of $60,000 a year, but again with the same rent escalation features. The original mortgage had been paid out, and the building had used up all of its depreciation.

The new simple Income Analysis and Evaluation of the building is shown below:

INCOME ANALYSIS AND EVALUATION

Total Value—Capitalized at 9%		$666,667.00
Current Mortgage Balance		None
Cash Required		666,667.00
Total Income	$60,000.00	
Operating Expenses	None	
Operating Profit		$ 60,000.00
Less Debt Service		None
Cash Spendable Income		$ 60,000.00
Yield—Cash on Cash		9%

Seeing the results of the above income analysis and evaluation, the owner/developer had a decision to make. As he saw it, he had four options available to him in his decision.

1. Retain the investment—as is.
2. Retain the investment and refinance.
3. Sell the investment.
4. Trade the investment.

In further analyzing the four options, the investor gave thought to his investment position as a result of each option.

Option No. 1. Retain the investment—as is. He realized that he would be receiving the maximum income, but his tax shelters had disappeared with the building depreciation gone and the mortgage paid off. Paying a large tax on the income did not appeal to him.

Option No. 2. Retain the investment and refinance. By refinancing, he would be able to have a sizeable amount of cash, and the interest on the new mortgage would be deductible but without depreciation. His income would still be highly taxable.

Option No. 3. Sell the investment. This decision would produce a lot of cash for another investment but the amount of gain would be subject to a combination of capital gain tax and ordinary income due to the amount of depreciation taken over the years.

Option No. 4. Trade the investment. By trading his building into a much larger industrial investment, the investor realized that he could not only retain the same income but also could offset that income with tax shelters available in the new larger investment. Also he would be able to defer any taxable liability in the transaction by trading instead of selling. In addition, the free and clear value of his building would make a down payment on an industrial property valued in excess of $3,000,000. Not bad, considering the fact that his building and land only cost $280,000 with a cash investment of $95,000. The many other advantages of trading will be further described and explained in a subsequent chapter of this book.

KEY POINTS

1. Know the importance of industrial growth to every city
2. Appreciate the garden type industrial park as a source of profitable industrial investments
3. Investigate the many profit opportunities in single tenant and multi-tenant industrial buildings
4. Understand and be able to capitalize the income from an industrial investment
5. Realize the importance of location and the accessibility to rail and truck routes
6. Recognize the profit opportunities available in small city industrial growth
7. Understand how to use a long-term lease in financing
8. Use guidelines to greater profit growth in industrial investments
9. Know procedures to use in analyzing and evaluating an industrial property
10. Learn to recognize the major points in an industrial lease

11. Understand how to verify and analyze the income and expense of an industrial investment
12. Use practical guidelines to follow in evaluating an industrial property
13. Understand the step-by-step procedure in purchasing industrial investments
14. Recognize the investment options available as shown by one astute investor who made a tremendous profit

11

Carefree Profit Opportunities with Shops, Stores, Service and Medical Buildings

Scattered throughout every city are numerous strip commercial centers with stores, shops and service facilities as tenants. Also many free-standing commercial buildings can be found on well-located lots. In addition, medical buildings are situated in neighborhoods where doctors can adequately and properly administer to people. Such commercial facilities provide a never ending stream of profit opportunities to the knowledgeable investor.

In this chapter, we will see the phenomenal growth of the neighborhood convenience markets and understand how one investor was able to make a fantastic cash yield of over 73 percent. We will also discuss how another investor, on a small cash investment, increased his cash yield from an excellent 30 percent to an amazing 49 percent through the use of an innovative financing technique and planning in a free-standing service building. In addition, we will see how an astute investor made an excellent investment in a medical building through the use of the purchase/leaseback technique.

There are other informative sections showing the many profit opportunities in free-standing stores and service buildings followed by dependable techniques to use in analyzing a medical center with guidelines and checklists, special paragraphs to check and study in medical center leases, simple procedures to use in verifying the income and expense of a medical facility along with procedures and guidelines to follow in purchasing a medical center.

HOW TO MAKE MONEY IN STRIP COMMERCIAL CENTERS

Strip shopping centers were the first type of shopping facility built in the neighborhoods. They were located along major arterials, usually on corners. Due to the size and shape of the land, stores were often constructed with common walls in a strip facing the street. Parking was generally in a single or double line in front of the stores with a limited number of spaces provided because of the lack of depth to the property.

Even with the building of neighborhood shopping centers on larger parcels of land with more convenient parking, strip centers continued to be built where the size and shape of the land dictated this type of construction. Since they were not as large or as costly, the profit opportunities available from this type of specialized shopping were recognized by many astute investors. With the growth and financial strength of the large chains of convenience markets, such as Circle K, U-Totem and 7/Eleven, strip centers can now be anchored with a nationally-rated tenant.

In making your investment decision on a strip center, the following major points should be considered:

1. Location
2. Construction
3. Parking
4. Financial strength of tenants
5. Leases
6. Financing
7. Income
8. Expense
9. Real property taxes and insurance
10. Yield

THE IMPORTANCE OF LOCATION AND THE PHENOMENAL GROWTH OF THE CONVENIENCE MARKET

As has been said in previous chapters, location is the most important factor to consider in any retail, income producing investment. Strip shopping centers aren't any different. They must be accessible and convenient to the retail buying consumer, preferably located on a heavily traveled arterial street but not necessarily on a corner. The phenomenal growth of the convenience market, either as a free-standing building or as a part of a strip center, is a classic example of this fact.

A number of years ago, when the convenience market first appeared, the initial consideration was finding an investor who would construct a building for them under a long-term lease. They were interested only in prime, retail locations but were willing to pay a guaranteed minimum rent which would yield an excellent return to the investors. In addition, they would agree to increase the rent to an amount equivalent to 2 percent of their gross sales. Since they only required from 2,000 to 2,400 square feet of space, the cost of the building and land was relatively inexpensive. With mortgage financing the cash requirement of the investor was minimal.

Many investors recognized the investment potential, so convenience markets began to appear in cities all over the country. Today, there are thousands situated in prime locations paying an excellent yield to investors.

PRACTICAL PROCEDURES TO FOLLOW IN EVALUATING A STRIP CENTER

Following the procedures outlined in determining the profit opportunities in other income producing commercial investments, the steps shown below should also be used in evaluating a strip center:

1. Property Check List
2. Fact and Information Profile
3. Physical inspection of the property
4. Study of leases
5. Verification of income and expense
6. Income analysis and evaluation

Since a commercial strip center is actually a small shopping center, the procedures outlined and described in Chapter 8 on shopping centers should be followed for the first five steps shown above. As Step 6, the center should be analyzed and evaluated using the Income Analysis and Evaluation form as shown for other income producing properties.

The information contained in the following form is taken from a strip center currently under consideration by an investor. A digest of the Fact and Information Profile shows the following information:

The center has 12,300 square feet of rentable space with nine tenants and a net income of $63,500. All leases provide that each tenant pay his prorata share of all real estate taxes, all insurance and all maintenance expense including exterior walls and roof. All leases are for a term of five years with three leases, providing those tenants with one 5-year option at an increased rental based upon a Consumer Price Index cost of living adjustment. In addition, four leases have percentage clauses for increased rents based upon 6 percent of gross sales. The owner was asking $643,000 for the center with an encumbrance of $315,000, payable at 9⅞ percent interest over a period of 25 years with annual payments of $34,020.

As a result of the foregoing information, the Income Analysis and Evaluation form was prepared by the investor as shown below:

INCOME ANALYSIS AND EVALUATION

Total Price	$643,000.00	
Current Mortgage Balance	315,000.00	
9⅞% - $2,835.00 Mo. P+I		
Cash Required	$328,000.00	
Total Income	$ 63,500.00	
Operating Expenses	None	
Operating Profit	$ 63,500.00	
Less Debt Service	34,020.00	
Cash Spendable Income		$29,480.00
Gain in Equity		3,000.00
Total Gain		$32,480.00
Yield—Cash on Cash		8.98%
Total Yield		9.9%

The investor, after checking his table of acceptable yields, found that the cash yield on a strip center should range from 13 to 15 percent. Seeing that the center under consideration produced only a 9 percent yield at the seller's asking price, he decided to make an offer based upon a cash yield of 15 percent.

Capitalizing the Cash Spendable Income at 15 percent and adding back the mortgage balance, he determined that the purchase price should be $511,533. Rounding off that price, he made an offer of $510,000 for the property. The seller didn't accept the offer but countered back at $600,000, a price that would yield 10.34 percent to the investor.

The investor, after analyzing the property again, decided the quality of the tenants and the remote possibility of excess rentals bringing the cash flow to the amount he expected, was not sufficient to warrant the higher price. He did say, however, that he would have accepted a lower cash yield if the center had a nationally-rated convenience market which could have reached excess rentals quickly.

PROFIT OPPORTUNITIES IN FREE-STANDING STORES AND SERVICE BUILDINGS

Free-standing stores and service buildings offer many profit opportunities to the knowledgeable investor. In most investments the buildings are leased on a triple net basis, providing a carefree yield to the investor without the problems of management, increased taxes and insurance, maintenance and other operating expenses.

A number of typical free-standing stores and service buildings found in every city are listed below:

1. Convenience markets
2. Laundry and cleaning facilities
3. Liquor stores
4. Furniture stores
5. Service stations
6. Air conditioning
7. Plumbing
8. Floor covering
9. Business equipment
10. Theatres
11. Garages
12. Television sales
13. Audio equipment
14. Building materials
15. Appliance stores

In analyzing and evaluating the profit opportunity in this type of investment, the investor must follow the same procedures as outlined in previous chapters on other income producing commercial properties.

To further amplify these procedures, we will see how two investors made profitable investments: one, in a free-standing store, and the other, in a service-type building.

How to get a 77 percent yield

One investor owned an excellent neighborhood corner at the intersection of two heavily traveled arterials. Since his location was excellent for a commercial development, he was contacted by a national convenience market chain.

During the process of negotiations, he was able to obtain a 20 year lease at a rental figure (if he paid cash for everything) which would represent a cash yield of 15 percent. The 2,400 square foot building cost $48,000 to construct and his 20,000 square foot lot represented an investment of $40,000. In addition to the $1,100 per month rent, the lease also provided that the rent would be increased to an amount equivalent to 2 percent of their gross sales.

Not wanting to invest that much cash in one investment and knowing that he could increase the yield through financing, the investor secured a loan in the amount of $65,000, amortized over twenty years at 9 percent interest. His initial operating statement is shown below:

Total Income	$13,200.00	
Operating Expenses	None	
Operating Profit	$13,200.00	
Less Debt Service	7,017.96	
Cash Spendable Income		$6,182.04
Gain in Equity		720.00
Total Gain		$6,902.04
Yield—Cash on Cash		26.8%
Total Yield		30%

Even at the minimum rent, the investment showed an excellent yield. After two years of operation, the gross sales of the market increased to $1,200,000, thereby increasing the rent through the escalation portion of the lease to $24,000 a year. His later operating statement is shown below:

Guaranteed Minimum Rent	$13,200.00	
Excess Rental	10,800.00	
Total Income	$24,000.00	
Operating Expenses	None	
Operating Profit	$24,000.00	
Less Debt Service	7,017.96	
Cash Spendable Income		$16,982.04
Gain in Equity		770.00
Total Gain		$17,752.04
Yield—Cash on Cash		73.8%
Total Yield		77.1%

Needless to say, this investor is not interested in selling his convenience market investment!

How to get a 55 percent yield

The other investor became interested in a service-store building on a well-traveled arterial street. The lot was large and deep, being nearly an acre in size with a 4,500 square foot building on the front of the lot and a smaller 2,000 square foot building on the rear of the lot. The larger building on the street was leased to an air conditioning company at a very low rental rate but the lease was about to expire. The smaller building on the back was vacant. The owner of the property had been having difficulty in selling the property because both buildings were in pretty bad shape. The investor, however, immediately recognized the excellence of the location and the commercial value of the large lot. Checking further with the owner, the investor learned that the property had been appraised for $115,000. During his tour of inspection, he determined that he could paint and remodel both buildings at a cost of $10,000.

In projecting his anticipated income from the investment, he knew that he would be able to lease the larger building on the street at $3.50 per square foot on a triple net basis. By dividing the property with the larger portion in the rear, he would be able to lease the smaller building to a builder who could use the large area for equipment parking and storage for $3.00 per square foot also on a net basis.

In checking with a mortgage company, he found that he would be able to borrow 75 percent of the appraised value on a 20 year 9½ percent loan which would be at least $85,000. With the $10,000 he intended to spend in renovating the buildings, his invested cash would total $40,000.

With this information, he prepared his first pro-forma operating statement as shown below:

Total Income	$21,750.00	
Expenses	None	
Operating Profit	$21,750.00	
Less Debt Service	9,508.80	
Cash Spendable Income		$12,241.20
Gain in Equity		1,500.00
Total Gain		$13,741.20
Yield—Cash on Cash		30.6%
Total Yield		34.3%

In evaluating the above statement, the investor immediately recognized the tremendous profit opportunity in the investment. Knowing that the owner had been having difficulty in selling the property, the investor further improved his profit potential by offering the seller $100,000 for the property, to be paid in full at the close of escrow.

The cash offer was the right move. The seller accepted the offer as written. The investor secured his $85,000 loan, adding his $15,000 at the close of escrow. Now he had only $25,000 invested in the property after remodeling, instead of the $40,000 originally planned. By reducing his cash investment, the cash yield jumped to 48.9 percent and the total yield reached 54.9 percent!

MEDICAL BUILDINGS AND MEDICAL CENTERS, THOUGH COSTLY, CAN BE PROFITABLE

As cities grew and the need for medical services increased, medical centers began to be built. Doctors, who were able to lease space in the planning stages or even during construction of the center, had their offices designed to their specifications. Other doctors, recognizing the convenience of a complete medical center with its pharmacy, laboratory, and other technical facilities, began to lease space until the center was filled with many types of physicians and surgeons. In time, smaller, medical buildings were constructed for different specialists—dentists, ophthalmologists, OB and gynecologists, pediatricians plus numerous others.

Many of the medical centers were built by the doctors themselves, each one participating in the ownership of the property and renting space in the center. Also, the smaller buildings were constructed and owned by the specialists who occupied nearly all of the space in the small medical building.

In nearly every situation, the doctors decided to sell. To them, the problems of management, income, maintenance, taxes and other personal matters were more than they had anticipated. Thus, the door was opened for an excellent profit opportunity for smart investors.

In some situations, two doctors formed a partnership for the purpose of owning their small medical building. Often later and for personal reasons, they decided to dissolve their partnership by selling the building. Even though medical centers and medical buildings are costly to construct due to the heavy demand for electricity and plumbing, the rents paid by the specialized tenants are in proportion to those costs, permitting an excellent yield to a knowledgeable investor.

Cash yields on this type of investment should range from 10 to 13 percent. While doctors are not nationally rated such as some shopping center tenants, they are usually well-qualified to pay the rent required for their space.

ANALYZING A MEDICAL CENTER—WITH GUIDELINES AND CHECKLISTS

Even though the cost per square foot is greater in a medical center than in apartments, shopping centers or office buildings due to the increased cost of construction, the income is proportionately higher. As in every specialized, single-purpose structure, the occupancy of leased space is limited to medical tenants. However, since there are many physicians requiring more space each year, the vacancy rate in medical centers is very low.

In analyzing and evaluating a medical center as an investment, the astute investor will always make certain of the numbers in this day of rents, yields, expenses, leases, taxes, amortization, interest and depreciation. To him it's the bottom line that counts. To arrive at that bottom line, certain dependable techniques should be followed.

As in every income producing commercial or industrial property, the investor should follow these same proven six steps as shown below:

1. Property Check List
2. Fact and Information Profile
3. Physical inspection of the property
4. Study of leases
5. Verification of income and expense
6. Income analysis and evaluation

Using the Property Check List, all necessary information is obtained and a Fact and Information Profile is prepared on the medical facility as outlined and described for other income producing properties.

As part of the analysis and evaluation procedure, an inspection tour of the property is made to determine not only the physical condition of the medical center but also to verify other pertinent and necessary information. Those items to check and verify are outlined below:

1. Location
2. Size of land area
3. Zoning
4. Type of construction
5. Size of building
6. Tenants and space occupied

7. Parking—number of spaces
8. Condition of parking lot
9. General condition of the building—structural
10. Painting and decorating
11. Landscaping
12. Good features
13. Bad points
14. Quality of area
15. Accessibility

In making the tour, the investor should inspect the property thoroughly. Every item on the foregoing checklist should be checked and verified regardless of how long it takes. A smart investor will look at everything, using the services of specialists to determine the condition of the following items:

1. General building structures
2. Roof
3. Plate glass
4. Electrical facilities
5. Plumbing
6. Refrigeration equipment
7. Heating equipment
8. Painting and decorating
9. Landscaping
10. Parking

Any item in need of repair or replacement should be noted and must become a condition of the purchase, requiring the seller to repair or replace those specified items.

WHAT TO CHECK AND EXAMINE IN A MEDICAL CENTER LEASE

Each lease for space in a medical center should be studied and checked thoroughly with special emphasis given to the following sections:

1. *Term of lease.* Make certain that this section properly states the commencement of the lease and the expiration date.

2. *Rent.* The total rent to be paid during the term of the lease should be shown along with the amount to be paid each month. In addition to the rent, this

section should show that applicable city and state sales taxes should be paid by the tenant.

3. *Additional Rent.* The escalation of rent through the application of an acceptable cost of living index should be fully described in this section.

4. *Real Property Taxes.* It is absolutely necessary that the leases provide for tax escalation with any increase in taxes above the base year of the lease paid proportionately by every tenant.

5. *Insurance.* Each lease should provide for the tenant carrying the proper and sufficient amount of personal liability insurance to protect the lessor. In addition, this section should also provide for escalation in the cost of the building and common area insurance provided by the lessor.

6. *Utilities.* Tenant should be required to pay for all water, gas, heat, electricity and other utilities furnished to or used in or about the premises by the tenant during the term of the lease.

7. *Taxes.* Tenant should pay all taxes levied upon fixtures, furnishings, equipment and other personal property belonging to the tenant contained on the premises.

8. *Building maintenance costs.* This section usually stipulates that the lessor will keep the roof and outside walls in repair while any damage to the interior of the premises shall be repaired by the tenant.

9. *Building operating costs.* Any increase in the cost of the janitor service and other related building operating costs above the base year of the lease should be paid proportionately by each tenant.

10. *Options to renew.* The terms and conditions of any option to renew the lease should be fully described in this section.

SIMPLE PROCEDURES TO USE IN ANALYZING AND VERIFYING THE INCOME AND OPERATING EXPENSES OF A MEDICAL CENTER

When a medical center is under consideration as an investment, the first item usually checked by the investor is the operating statement of the building which shows the income actually received and the operating expenses paid along with debt service payments.

This statement is normally prepared by the owner or his accountant and as a general rule will not be certified as to its accuracy. Therefore, the total income and all items of expense should be analyzed and verified by the investor. The income can be verified by the usual practices prescribed for other income producing properties in checking accounting records, bank deposits and leases.

All items of expense should be thoroughly checked as to amounts and services performed. Those items would normally include the following:

1. Janitor services
2. Equipment repairs and maintenance
3. Painting and decorating
4. General building repairs
5. Accounting

In addition to the charges for the above services and repairs, real property taxes and insurance should be checked and verified as to amounts and coverage.

HOW TO EVALUATE THE PROFIT OPPORTUNITIES IN MEDICAL BUILDINGS

As the final step in the analysis and evaluation process of a medical center, all of the pertinent information is studied, analyzed and evaluated. As a result, an Income Analysis and Evaluation form on the property under consideration is prepared.

One investor, not long ago, was interested in a 22,000 square foot medical center. In obtaining all of the information on the property, the investor learned that the building was five years old, had an annual rental income of $165,000 and was completely leased. In checking the operating statement as provided by the owner, the operating expenses including real property taxes and insurance totaled $32,175. There was a 25 year 8¾ percent encumbrance on the property, amortized at $7,811 a month with a current mortgage balance of approximately $895,000. The owner was asking $1,350,000 for the property.

Following the established procedure of evaluating the property, the investor prepared an Income Analysis and Evaluation form from the above information. A copy of his evaluation is shown below:

INCOME ANALYSIS AND EVALUATION

Total Price	$1,350,000.00
Current Mortgage Balance	895,000.00
8¾% - $7,811.00 Mo. - P+I	
Cash Required	$ 455,000.00
Total Income	$ 165,000.00
Operating Expenses	$ 32,175.00
Operating Profit	$ 132,825.00
Less Debt Service	93,732.00

Cash Spendable Income	$ 39,093.00
Gain in Equity	15,750.00
Total Gain	$ 54,843.00
Yield—Cash on Cash	8.6%
Total Yield	12%

The foregoing income analysis and evaluation indicated the yields available in the medical center, based upon the asking price of the owner. Since the investor was further interested in acquiring the center, he decided to make an offer on the property.

PROCEDURES TO USE AND GUIDELINES TO FOLLOW IN PURCHASING A MEDICAL CENTER

Before making any purchase of an income producing property, whether it be an apartment complex, a shopping center, an office building, an industrial facility or a medical center as described in this chapter, an investor should follow proven techniques and procedures in analyzing and evaluating the property.

During that process, he should have referred to the Property Check List to obtain all of the necessary information applicable to the property as shown in his Fact and Information Profile. After reading and thoroughly understanding the contents of each lease, he should have inspected the property and verified all items of income and expense. Only after analyzing the income and evaluating the property as presented by the owner, should he prepare his own evaluation as a guide in the preparation of the offer to purchase.

The technique of purchasing a medical center should follow the established and proven procedure as outlined below:

1. Determine the purchase price
2. Decide upon a plan of purchase
3. Specify the most advantageous terms and conditions
4. Prepare the offer
5. Present the offer for acceptance by the owner
6. Open and close the escrow

Continuing with the investor who was interested in the medical center described in the preceding section, he was ready to prepare an offer of purchase, using the technique shown above.

In determining a purchase price, he had decided upon a cash yield of 10 percent, this being the low range of acceptable yields for medical centers.

Capitalizing the cash spendable income at 10 percent and adding back the current mortgage balance, his offer was for a price of $1,285,000.

His plan of purchase included a down payment of $390,000 with an appropriate earnest money deposit and the assumption of the existing note and mortgage in the approximate amount of $895,000. Any difference in the mortgage balance was to be adjusted in the down payment. The escrow was to be opened immediately after acceptance and closed 60 days later.

As special conditions of purchase, the offer was subject to the approval of the Preliminary Title Report by the buyer. In addition, all leases were to be assigned to the buyer at the close of escrow.

Using escrow instructions as the "Binding Agreement" between the parties and following the technique described in the preceding chapter, the offer was prepared by the investor and presented to the owner for his acceptance. After the acceptance of the offer by the owner, the escrow was opened and later closed as specified.

HOW TO USE THE TECHNIQUE OF PURCHASE AND LEASEBACK FOR MORE PROFIT OPPORTUNITIES

As pointed out in a preceding section, many small medical buildings have been constructed by specialists in the various fields of medicine. In some instances there could be only one occupant in the small medical building. In others there would be two or maybe three specialists occupying space—each participating in the ownership of the property. Generally, there are two specialists—each occupying one-half of the rentable space.

Many times these doctors decide to sell their building but want to remain as tenants, having established their medical practice at that particular location. This situation presents an excellent profit opportunity to a knowledgeable investor.

In discussing the purchase and subsequent leases with the doctor/owners, the investor informs them that everything in a purchase/leaseback situation is relative. The rent to be paid by the doctors should be consistent with the price paid for the building—all related to the cash yield he expects from his investment.

In further discussions regarding the property, the investor decided that he wanted a cash yield of 12 percent, and the doctors decided that they would be willing to pay $7.50 per square foot as an annual rent with all services to be provided by the lessor. The building contained 3,600 square feet of rentable area with each physician occupying one-third of the building.

Having available all current building operating costs, real property tax and insurance amounts, the investor was able to accurately prepare a pro-forma operating statement for the building as shown below:

Total Income		$27,000.00
Operating Expenses		
Real Estate Taxes	$3,825.00	
Insurance	550.00	
Janitor	1,800.00	
Utilities	3,545.00	
Total Expenses		9,720.00
Operating Profit		$17,280.00

Capitalizing the operating profit at 12 percent, the investor arrived at a price of $144,000 for the property.

In preparing a lease for each doctor, the investor included all of the necessary paragraphs plus escalation of rents through the periodic application of a cost of living index. Also, escalation of real property taxes, insurance, building maintenance and operating costs were included with each tenant paying his proportionate share of all such increases.

The investor then prepared his offer in the purchase amount of $144,000, contingent upon his approval of the Preliminary Title Report and the execution of the leases by the doctors for their respective spaces. When the escrow closed, everyone was satisfied. The investor obtained the cash yield he wanted. The doctors were paying a rent which they considered fair with a resultant sales price which they considered to be acceptable.

KEY POINTS

1. Understand the major points to consider in making an investment decision in the acquisition of a strip center
2. Realize the importance of location
3. Follow the practical procedures shown in evaluating a strip center
4. Study the profit opportunities in free-standing stores and service buildings
5. Understand that medical buildings and medical centers, though costly, can be very profitable
6. Know how to use dependable techniques in analyzing a medical center
7. Recognize those special sections to check and study in medical center leases
8. Learn the simple procedures to follow in verifying the income and operating expenses of a medical center
9. Understand how to evaluate the profit opportunities in medical buildings
10. Know the procedures to use and the guidelines to follow in purchasing a medical center
11. Study the technique of purchase and leaseback
12. Understand how to increase cash yield through innovative financing techniques for more and greater profits

12

Proven Development Procedures for Greater Profits

Profit opportunities in the development of commercial and industrial property are everywhere. Many knowledgeable investor/developers know of the tremendous profits available in the development and sale of shopping centers, apartments, office buildings, industrial warehouses and distribution centers, stores, shops, and service buildings, plus, the market in the ''build-to-suit'' projects. Those successful investor/developers follow proven procedures in their specialized fields of real estate.

In this chapter, we will discuss how any smart investor can develop commercial and industrial real estate for profit. The step-by-step process in developing a shopping center from site selection to completion of the center is explained in detail, followed by the profit opportunities in building apartments with proven procedures and guidelines. In addition, the technique of assuring success with ''build-to-suit'' projects will be described. Successful strategies and methods to minimize the risks in office building development will be outlined and illustrated.

Also, we will explain the new concept of the condominium approach to commercial and industrial development along with the technique of financing a commercial or industrial development for maximum profits. The chapter concludes with an analysis of the tremendous profit potential in this type of commercial and industrial real estate development.

DEVELOPING COMMERCIAL AND INDUSTRIAL PROPERTY FOR PROFIT

There are many profit opportunities in existing commercial and industrial properties and large profits can be made by knowledgeable investors who *develop* such properties.

This very profitable field of real estate includes the development of the following types of commercial and industrial property:

1. Shopping centers
2. Apartments
3. Office buildings
4. Industrial warehouses
5. Medical centers
6. Stores, shops and service buildings
7. Plus, packaging zoned land for other developers

It is not necessary for the investor to be a contractor or builder in developing commercial and industrial property. As long as he can employ the services of an architect to design the project and award the construction contract to a reputable builder, he can develop any project within his financial capabilities.

Many investors, however, are builders whose real estate program is aimed at building apartments, shopping centers, office buildings and other commercial and industrial facilities for immediate sale upon completion. To them a fast nickle is much better than a slow dime. Often, it is not unusual for the project to be sold before completion.

DEVELOPING SHOPPING CENTERS: A STEP-BY-STEP PROCESS FROM SITE SELECTION TO COMPLETION

The more experienced investor/developers follow a certain step-by-step procedure in the development of a shopping center. These steps are shown below and are followed by a descriptive explanation of how each step is implemented:

1. Site selection
2. Availability of the property
3. Initial preliminary plot plan
4. Tenant interest
5. Feasibility of the project
6. Purchase of the property

7. Securing tenants and finalizing leases
8. Securing mortgage commitment
9. Final planning and design
10. Construction and completion of the shopping center

This section will outline the steps required in developing a neighborhood shopping center.

Step 1. Site selection

Through the use of the Property Check List and the Fact and Information Profile as shown in Chapter 2, each potential location should be analyzed as to its suitability for a shopping center. Additionally, a demographic study of each area should be made, providing such information as population, number of households, price of homes, income, buying habits, age of occupants, number of children, rate of growth, new construction and other such information as may be necessary to interest prospective tenants. Such information can be obtained from the local Chamber of Commerce. After a thorough study of each location and its adjacent surroundings, the investor should grade each such location, 1-2-3. If by chance the first choice is not available or priced too high, the second choice can be selected or the third.

Step 2. Availability of the property

In determining the availability of each location, the owner of the property should be contacted to obtain not only the price, terms and conditions under which he would be willing to sell, but also those items necessary and required in the building of a shopping center. Such additional information should include current zoning, whether the owner would permit rezoning if required, releases, subordination, topographic and engineering studies, soil tests and feasibility studies.

After determining the availability of each location, a small amount of money should enable the investor to secure a short-term option on the best of the three properties under consideration. The term of the option should be for a period of six months enabling the investor to accomplish what has yet to be done before the property is purchased.

Step 3. Initial preliminary plot plan

The next step is to see an architect, preferably one who has designed neighborhood shopping centers. He can prepare an initial, simple plot plan showing a typical, small shopping center with a supermarket, drug, variety, and a number of other stores situated on the proposed location. This plot plan need not be in too much detail, other than identifying its location and size of the parcel because the principal tenants have a lot to say about how the shopping center will finally be constructed.

Step 4. Tenant interest

Now that the property is under a six months option and a preliminary plot plan, the next step is to talk to potential tenants. Since the primary tenant in the shopping center is to be a supermarket, the local supermarket chains should be contacted first. They all have a real estate department and are always interested in a good location. If one of them can be interested in the site, their market will become the ''bell cow'' of the new shopping center.

During the presentation of the shopping center site to the supermarket chain, the head of their real estate department will want detailed information relative to its location. You will be able to provide this information from the Fact and Information Profile plus the statistics from the demographic study. When the supermarket decides the location is desirable, they will prepare a Letter of Intent evidencing their interest and stating the conditions under which they would become a tenant. One of their conditions is usually a co-tenancy requirement for a drug store.

Now it becomes necessary to present your site to other tenants. To assist in this process, there is a Directory of Leading Chain Stores in the United States published by Chain Store Business Guide, Inc., 2 Park Avenue, New York City, New York, 10016.

Since your Letter of Intent from the supermarket requires a drug store, the site must be presented to the drug chains in your local area. This time the process is much easier. Usually with a Letter of Intent from the supermarket chain, the interest for a drug store increases immensely and a letter from them is not difficult to obtain.

At this point, you can be certain that the shopping center will be developed at your location. However, to add a little ''frosting on the cake,'' it is best to secure one more Letter of Intent—from the chain operating variety stores in the area. This is a simple maneuver with the other two letters.

Step 5. Feasibility of the shopping center

With Letters of Intent evidencing the interest of strong national tenants who will occupy approximately 50,000 square feet of an 80,000 square foot neighborhood shopping center, the feasibility of your project is evident.

Step 6. Securing other tenants and finalizing leases

Now thought should be given to securing other tenants for the center. With several Letters of Intent already obtained, you have an excellent start in renting space in the shopping center. By special advertising, a large sign on the property and by personal contact, you will be able to rent the remaining space. After construction actually commences, leasing space becomes easier and usually by the time the center nears completion all of the space will have been rented. Also during the option period, your attorney can prepare leases for those tenants who initially signed Letters of Intent.

Step 7. Securing mortgage commitment

The mortgage commitment can be obtained prior to the purchase of the property or the completion of the final working plans from the architect. With firm Letters of Intent or finalized leases, a pro-forma operating statement can be prepared showing the total anticipated income of the proposed shopping center. After deducting all operating expenses plus real property taxes and insurance, an operating profit before debt service can be determined. By capitalizing the operating profit at a predetermined yield, a value of the shopping center can be calculated. The amount of the mortgage commitment will be a negotiated percentage of the valuation.

In many instances, the income from the national tenants will pay the expenses of operation, insurance, real property taxes and service the debt, while the smaller, local tenants will provide the profit to the developer. In these situations, the securing of a mortgage commitment is a simple process. After obtaining the commitment for the permanent mortgage, the developer can go to his bank and obtain an interim mortgage loan which will provide the funds needed to construct the shopping center.

Step 8. Purchase the property

During the option period, the developer should have completed all of the foregoing necessary steps. Now, he is ready to conclude the purchase of the property in accordance with the terms provided in the option.

In the event the developer had decided to make a contingent purchase of the property instead of being granted an option, he should include as contingencies the following items:

1. A feasibility study
2. Engineering studies
3. Soil tests
4. Rezoning, if required
5. Obtaining certain leases
6. Securing an acceptable mortgage commitment

By completing the foregoing steps, all contingencies are satisfied and the escrow is ready to close.

Step 9. Final planning and design

The design, plans and working drawings for the shopping center will be prepared by the architect. Knowing the requirements of each tenant by the terms of their lease and other special instructions, the architect can now complete the final plans for the shopping center. Each major tenant usually has his own planning department where the completed plans from the architect are checked, verified and approved.

Step 10. Construction and completion of shopping center

During the construction period, the remaining space in the shopping center can be leased. A well-planned and successful shopping center will have approximately 65 percent of its space leased to national tenants and 35 percent to local and regional tenants. This ratio will provide an acceptable income for the center.

HOW ONE DEVELOPER MADE A HUGE PROFIT IN THE SALE OF A NEW SHOPPING CENTER

Many developers like to build shopping centers and then sell them when construction has been finished. They know that the best time to sell a shopping center is immediately upon completion. At that time, buyer interest is at its highest peak because he can realize the tax advantages available to a first user, the principal one being accelerated depreciation.

One developer built an excellent neighborhood shopping center with approximately 80,000 square feet of rentable space on 8 acres of land. His tenants included a national supermarket, drug and variety store plus 20,000 square feet of strong local and regional tenants.

Its annual income totaled \$290,000 with operating expenses of \$57,000 including property taxes, leaving an operating profit of \$233,000. Having secured a mortgage commitment in the amount of $1,500,000 to be amortized over 25 years at 9 percent interest, the developer prepared his pro-forma operating statement on the nearly completed shopping center as shown below:

Total Income	$290,000.00	
Operating Expenses	57,000.00	
Operating Profit	$233,000.00	
Less Debt Service	151,056.00	
Cash Spendable Income		$81,944.00

Capitalizing the cash flow at 8 percent and adding the mortgage, the developer calculated that his new shopping center should be valued at $2,525,000. Since his total cost in the project was only $1,760,000, this figure represented a huge profit of $765,000! Also the developer knew that he had saved nearly $300,000 in leasing and sales commissions by being able to lease the space and sell the center himself.

PROFIT OPPORTUNITIES IN BUILDING APARTMENTS

As the demand for apartments increases and the vacancy factor diminishes, knowledgeable apartment developers begin to look for suitable locations. Following proven procedures as outlined below, the apartment developer begins his plan of development:

1. *Site selection.* As we pointed out in Chapter 6, a good apartment location should be on or near major arterial streets with easy access to all points in the city. In addition, the location should be near schools, churches, shopping and employment centers. Also public transportation, while not mandatory, is helpful. Certain recreational facilities can be included within the new apartment complex, but it is advisable for the location to be near or within a reasonable distance to public recreational facilities.

2. *Preliminary plans.* After the dimensions of the property have been determined, a preliminary plot plan and floor plan should be prepared by an architect. Detailed drawings and specifications can be completed as soon as the mortgage commitment has been obtained and the property purchased.

3. *Mortgage commitment.* When the location has been selected but not purchased, it is wise to have a preliminary meeting with the mortgage company to determine if mortgage money is available at that location for apartments. Upon completion of the preliminary plans by the architect, the developer should prepare a pro-forma operating statement, showing the projected income and expense of the proposed apartment development.

Based upon an acceptable operating statement, a mortgage commitment can be given for the project. The amount of the commitment is determined by an agreed upon percentage of the total value of the completed project. The terms and conditions of the commitment are negotiable items between the mortgage company and the developer.

4. *Purchase property.* Usually property purchased for the construction of new apartments are cash transactions since sellers are unwilling to subordinate their interest in the property to a mortgage on an apartment project. Therefore, when purchasing property for an apartment complex, be prepared to pay cash—either from your own account or from construction draws paid as acquisition money from interim mortgage funds.

5. *Completion of plans and specifications.* The architect can now finish the plans and specifications in accordance with the preliminary plot plan and floor plan as submitted to the mortgage company. When the plans are completed, the mortgage company will require that a final set be submitted to them as part of their loan package.

6. *Commencement of construction.* With a mortgage commitment, the developer can go to his bank and secure an interim mortgage loan for funds to build the apartment complex. As soon as the financing is arranged, the developer can award the contract for the construction or can commence building the project himself if he so desires.

7. *Leasing.* A good time to begin leasing apartments in the project is during construction. If a small rental office can be included in the construction program, many apartments can be rented on the site as construction progresses.

8. *Completion of construction.* As the apartment complex nears completion, the developer will begin to receive offers from investors who want to buy the apartment building as soon as construction is completed. Usually by the time construction is finished, at least 60 percent of the apartments will have been leased, so it is wise not to be too hasty in taking the first profitable offer that is presented. After the permanent mortgage has been recorded and construction officially completed, the developer will consider selling the complex.

THE APARTMENT DEVELOPER WITH AN EYE FOR BIG PROFITS

At the time of writing this book, a prominent apartment developer is building a large 200-unit apartment complex in one of the faster growing cities in his state. He selected this city because there were no vacancies and the demand for apartments was high. Following the procedures outlined in the foregoing section, he was able to secure a mortgage commitment of $2,000,000 and commence construction. By the time the foundations had been poured, he had leased 40 apartments and knew that when the buildings were completed all of the apartments would be leased.

When I asked how much he intended to make on the project, he said—"$800,000." He explained that there would be 128 one-bedroom unfurnished units which would rent for $189, 72 two-bedroom units which would rent for $198 unfurnished and $220 furnished. He then handed me his pro-forma operating statement shown below:

Rental Income		
128 units @ $189.00	$290,304.00	
36 units @ $198.00	85,536.00	
36 units @ $220.00	95,040.00	
Total rental income		$470,880.00
Operating Expenses		145,972.00
Operating Profit		324,908.00
Less Debt Service		
$2,000,000.00-9% - 25 years		$201,408.00
Cash Spendable Income		$123,500.00

He explained that he would offer the complex for sale at a price of $3,235,000, yielding an investor 10 percent on cash. He said that he would take $3,000,000 for the facility which would be a 12 percent yield on cash for a sophisticated investor. He further explained that he could build the project for $11,000 per unit including everything. His cost would be $2,200,000, leaving him an $800,000 profit.

THE TECHNIQUE OF ASSURING SUCCESS WITH "BUILD-TO-SUIT" PROJECTS

Another field of commercial or industrial development that produces many profitable investments is in "build-to-suit" projects for a specific, predetermined tenant. This type of development requires the purchase of a specific parcel of land, construction of the building in accordance with the requirements of the tenant and then leasing the completed facility to that specific tenant. All of this is usually accomplished in accordance with the procedure outlined below:

1. *Financial study and business experience of proposed tenant.* The investor is only interested in building a facility for a specific tenant if he is sound financially and his background in the business indicates a capability of operating a

successful business. If the results of this investigation are satisfactory, the investor will proceed to the next step in the process.

2. *Site selection.* Following the desires and recommendation of the tenant, the site for the proposed development is selected and analyzed by the investor.

3. *Estimated cost of construction.* After the location of the building has been determined, the investor will meet with his architect who will prepare a preliminary plot plan and give an estimated cost of construction based upon the size of the building, floor plan and other related features required by the tenant.

4. *Mortgage commitment.* At this point in the procedure, the investor knows the cost of the land and the estimated cost of the building. Now he wants to know the cost of money. With the proposed lease as security along with the financial strength of the tenant and the investor, a satisfactory mortgage commitment can be obtained.

5. *Preparation and execution of the lease.* The investor can now determine the total cost of the building, including land, construction and financing. After adding the additional amount to provide the required yield for the investor, the lease can be prepared and executed.

6. *Purchase of property.* The investor usually does not purchase the property until the foregoing five steps have been completed to his satisfaction.

7. *Construction.* As the final step in this procedure, construction of the building is commenced and completed in accordance with the terms of the approved plans and specifications.

By following this simple technique, the investor knows at all times not only where he stands in the development process but also he can feel that the success of his investment will be virtually assured. The transaction described in Chapter 1 is an example of how this "build-to-suit" technique works and should be reviewed after the completion of this section.

PROVEN STRATEGIES AND METHODS TO USE TO MINIMIZE THE RISK IN OFFICE BUILDING DEVELOPMENT

In Chapter 9, *Profitable Investments in Neighborhood Office Buildings*, it was explained how certain risks are ever-present in office building investments and how to overcome or minimize those risks was illustrated.

At least in analyzing and evaluating an existing office building, the investor has available to him all current information on the property, including total income, operating expenses, property taxes, insurance, and an amortization schedule. In addition, he can inspect the building to determine its condition.

A smart office building developer will avoid those known risks and pitfalls by taking care of such situations before they happen as outlined below:

1. *Suitable location.* The developer will make certain that the location is on a highly traveled and well known arterial street, providing access to all points of the city.

2. *Costly financing.* In negotiating the terms of a mortgage commitment, the investor must obtain the best rate of interest available, keeping in mind that the lower the cost, the higher the cash spendable income will be. If the cost of financing is too high, then the rental rates of the building may be too high.

3. *Low rental rates.* While low rental rates will rent space in the building, they may not necessarily provide sufficient income to operate the office building profitably. Rates consistent with other comparable office buildings should be considered in preparing leases.

4. *Rapid tenant turnover.* It is costly to the owner of an office building to have tenants continually moving in and out. An astute office building developer will eliminate this risk by establishing an acceptable rental rate and by providing good management which will adequately service the needs of the tenants.

5. *Unusually high vacancy factor.* A consistently high vacancy rate is usually indicative of an undesirable location, an unsightly building, poor construction, sloppy maintenance and janitor service, and the lack of the other day-to-day necessities which should be provided by the management. In offsetting this risk, the developer will make certain that these conditions do not exist by providing a clean, pleasant building climate and will use efficient management techniques.

6. *Poor construction.* Knowing that a poorly constructed building will be costly to maintain, the developer should avoid this problem at all costs. A few bucks saved in cheating on construction can be very costly in operation.

7. *Bad management.* This is one risk that can be avoided by employing better and more efficient management techniques.

8. *Improperly drawn leases.* An astute office building developer will prepare leases for space in his building, covering those paragraphs itemized in Chapter 9, *Profitable Investments in Neighborhood Office Buildings.* In addition, the lease should provide for tax, insurance and maintenance cost escalation above the base year of the lease. If options to renew are to be granted to certain tenants, each should be analyzed for its long-range effect on the income of the building.

9. *High operating costs.* Operating costs directly affect the cash spendable income of the building. Any reduction in those costs will increase the operating profit by that same amount. Therefore, the costs of operating the building should be controlled through the use of efficient management techniques.

10. *Inadequate parking facilities.* Any office building that does not provide

sufficient parking spaces for the tenants and their clients or customers has a real problem. Every developer should make certain that adequate parking facilities are available even if additional property has to be purchased.

A NEW CONCEPT: THE CONDOMINIUM APPROACH TO COMMERCIAL AND INDUSTRIAL DEVELOPMENT

Since the condominium concept in residential housing has proven to be so very successful, commercial and industrial developers have tried that approach in the development of shopping centers, office buildings and industrial space.

In the development of a condominium shopping center, the center is designed and built in the usual manner with each occupant willing to purchase his portion of the premises instead of leasing the required space. The parking lot and loading area along with all sidewalks become common areas and are owned jointly with the cost of operation and maintenance paid proratably by all occupants.

Condominium office and industrial buildings can be developed in somewhat the same manner. It is necessary, however, to study the requirements of each state regarding the ownership of property in this manner. Following the same procedure as used in the development of condominium apartments, the developer can design an office building patterned to the concept of selling space instead of leasing. All common areas such as halls, rest rooms, utility rooms, etc., will be owned jointly with the cost of maintenance paid on a prorata basis by all occupants. While this type of commercial or industrial development and ownership is in the early stages of experimentation, it can become more popular and accepted in later years.

FINANCING COMMERCIAL OR INDUSTRIAL DEVELOPMENTS TO PROVIDE MAXIMUM PROFITS

Mortgage companies, in analyzing an application for a loan commitment on a commercial or industrial development, are most interested in the planned occupancy and the quality of the leases. When leases with financially strong national tenants can be assigned to service the debt, an advantageous mortgage commitment can be obtained. It must be remembered that the lower the rate of interest and the longer term will reduce the applicable constant. Therefore, reducing the cost of money is an important factor in the overall cost of the development.

The financing technique used by many successful commercial and industrial developers follows the simple procedure outlined below:

1. *Pro-forma operating statement.* The developer prepares a pro-forma operating statement of his projected development, using income information contained in the executed leases. Projected operating expenses are determined and shown along with real property taxes and insurance.

2. *Evaluation.* The mortgage company can then determine the value of the development by capitalizing the operating profit at a percentage factor, based upon the type of development and the quality of the leases.

3. *Terms of commitment.* After the value of the development has been determined by the mortgage company, the amount of the mortgage commitment will be a percentage of that value. It can vary from 50 to maybe 75 percent depending upon the type of development and the security of the loan. The rate of interest and term of the loan are usually dictated again by the type and quality of the development. In other words, these factors are negotiable. An astute developer will negotiate the best interest rate available on the longest terms possible to lower the constant to a point where the maximum amount of spendable income can be shown.

4. *Interim financing.* Based upon the terms and conditions of the permanent mortgage commitment, the developer can secure an Interim Mortgage loan from his bank to furnish the necessary funds to construct the development. Again, the rate of interest to be paid on the interim construction loan is negotiable. This type of financing is very attractive to local banks since their funds are secured by a firm take-out commitment from the lending institution.

This technique of financing used by the more sophisticated developers is based entirely upon the quality and security of the leases. While the cost of construction, including land, is important and is taken into consideration, the maximum loan can be obtained for the project as determined by the secured income of the development.

AN ANALYSIS OF PROFIT POTENTIAL

Making big profits in commercial and industrial investments through the development of various types of real estate has been outlined and explained in detail. Those developers who specialize in shopping centers have been known to realize tremendous profits. Other developers have used their knowledge and expertise to develop large apartment projects for huge profits. Builders and investors who specialize in the "build-to-suit" market have also made profits in this tailor-made facet of real estate. While the risks of office building development are many, the developers who avoid these pitfalls have found success and profit in that type of development.

Every real estate development whether it is a shopping center, an apartment complex, office building, industrial warehouse or distribution center, medical center or just stores, shops and service buildings, is conceived, planned, built and either operated or sold by some astute and innovative investor. The tremendous profit opportunities in this field of real estate are real, ready and available for the innovative investor who can recognize the potential of developing commercial and industrial real estate for profit.

KEY POINTS

1. It is not necessary for an investor to be a builder or contractor to develop commercial and industrial property for profit
2. Study the proven procedures in developing a shopping center with its ten required steps
3. Understand how one developer made a huge profit in the development and sale of a shopping center
4. Recognize the profit opportunities in building apartments with the eight steps to success
5. Review how one apartment developer had an eye for a big profit
6. Know how to assure success with "build-to-suit" developments
7. Study the ten pitfalls of office building development
8. Evaluate the condominium approach to commercial and industrial development as a new concept for the future
9. Review the technique of financing for maximum profit
10. Understand the tremendous profits available in developing commercial and industrial property

13

Redevelopment: Converting Problems to Profits

Someone else's problem can become an excellent profit opportunity for the creative and innovative investor who knows what to do and how to do it. For example, in this chapter, we will see how an old free-standing Safeway supermarket was converted into a successful Food Bazaar serving all kinds of exotic foods. Also, we will discuss how a theatre owner changed a losing operation into a men's clothing store in Albuquerque. In addition, it will be interesting to know how an old lumber yard in Fort Worth is being redeveloped into a large business plaza and to study how drive-in theatres in a number of cities are being converted into shopping centers.

As the chapter unfolds, we will discuss how problem properties and areas exist in every city, but we will evaluate the many profit opportunities in this field of redevelopment by explaining what to look for and how to proceed. Also, we will see how greater profits can be made by following the technique of remodeling and changing use. When to tear down and rebuild is fully explained along with how to remodel and upgrade a commercial investment property to increase income. In addition, the procedure of adding additional rental space for more income is described, followed by an example of how an investor used this technique with fantastic results. Advanced financing techniques that lead to greater profits in your redevelopment program are also explained. To answer the question of whether to hold for income or sell for profit, we will illustrate how two astute investors made their decisions.

PROBLEM PROPERTIES AND AREAS EXIST IN EVERY CITY

As times change and cities continually expand their boundaries to meet the demands of progress with new development, the older inner-city areas become less and less desirable. Investment properties in these depressed areas no longer provide the income or stability needed in today's economy.

The more progressive cities plan and initiate redevelopment projects requiring acquisition and demolition of certain areas. Many astute investors experienced in governmental redevelopment programs find an abundance of profit opportunities in this field of real estate—from low-income apartment buildings to commercial business structures.

The development of neighborhood shopping centers practically eliminated the old free-standing supermarket, drug store and variety store. The oil embargo and subsequent shortage of gasoline closed many service stations throughout the country. Also, the downturn in our economy caused many businesses to close.

All of the properties affected by change in one way or another became a problem to the owner. But to the innovative and creative investor, these properties presented many profit opportunities. Knowing that it would be necessary to change the present operation to another more productive use, the problems became a challenge.

PROFIT OPPORTUNITIES FOR THE CREATIVE AND INNOVATIVE INVESTOR

As has been proven in the past and will continue to be evident in the future, the best buys in commercial and industrial property can be made during periods of a downturn in business, in depressed areas of a city or when the property is no longer useful for its intended purpose.

The creative and innovative investor who can look at an old building and know what should be done can find many profit opportunities at bargain prices. As a general rule, the owner has lost his interest in the property when his last tenant moved out. Not wanting to remodel for another use and having recaptured his investment many times through profits and depreciation, the owner will probably accept any reasonable offer on the property.

An astute investor, with the ability to visualize changes in the use of a commercial or industrial property, coupled with his knowledge of how to increase income through the implementation of his preconceived plan, can find an abundance of profit opportunities in this particular field of real estate.

PROBLEM BUILDINGS: WHAT TO LOOK FOR AND WHAT TO DO

Owners of free-standing commercial and industrial buildings situated on major streets throughout every city in the country have lost good tenants to the newer, more convenient shopping centers. What to do with those large, vacant buildings was a problem confronting many owners. Those owners who did not have the time, patience or money to remodel and lease to another tenant decided to sell the property.

The creative investor with the ability to convert someone else's problems to his gain can find profit opportunities in many types of commercial and industrial buildings. A few of those commercial buildings are listed below:

1. Free-standing supermarkets
2. Service stations
3. Covered theatres
4. Lumber yards
5. Drive-in theatres
6. Restaurants
7. Furniture stores
8. Depressed commercial areas
9. Single-purpose buildings
10. Garages

After finding a good investment property for redevelopment, the investor will usually follow one of the plans outlined below:

1. Remodel and change the present operation to another more productive use.
2. Demolish and rebuild into a new development.
3. Remodel and upgrade the property so that rents can be raised.
4. Enlarge the building to accomodate more rental area.

THE TECHNIQUE OF REMODELING AND CHANGING USE FOR GREATER PROFITS

Often a building becomes a problem when one or more of the following situations occur:

1. *Its use is no longer desirable or profitable.* This situation can happen in owner-occupied properties. When the business ceases to be profitable, the owner usually decides to remedy the situation by either selling the property or remodeling and leasing for another use and purpose.
2. *Tenants move out at the expiration of their leases.* When a tenant of many years moves out at the termination of his lease because of the lack of business at that location, the owner should either sell or plan to remodel and change the use of the building.
3. *Unable to lease to other tenants for the current use.* Usually, if a building is no longer desirable to a reputable tenant for his business, other tenants of similar operations will be reluctant to lease the premises for the same purpose.
4. *A change in economic conditions and consumer buying habits.* A downturn in business or a change in consumer buying habits can make a specific location outdated and no longer desirable for the present operation.

The innovative investor who can determine a profitable and desirable use for a problem commercial property will find greater profits in his remodeled investment.

Free-standing supermarkets have been converted into office buildings, service facilities, restaurants, government centers and even discount sales operations. Service stations with the shortage of gasoline have been changed into fast-food outlets, convenience markets, dress shops, small offices such as real estate, legal and accounting, donut shops and other similar small businesses. Covered theatres due to their locations in heavily populated areas have been remodeled into retail consumer sales such as clothing stores, shoe stores and discount operations.

Remodeling a supermarket

A classic example of changing the operation to something else to make a better income producing commercial property was the remodeling of a free-standing Safeway market. The Safeway operation had moved out of the building into one of the new shopping centers. This particular market was not an old building and was well-constructed, containing about 20,000 square feet. It was in an excellent location situated in the mid-town section of the city. After the Safeway lease expired, the owner decided to sell the property. The price was realistic, but no one wanted the property as another supermarket. The question then was what to do with it. An enterprising investor knew the answer.

In his analysis of the property, he determined that the location was excellent for a restaurant. Since the building was too large for one restaurant, a Food

Bazaar—having a number of distinctive individual restaurants, each serving different types of food—was planned.

After purchasing the property, the investor remodeled the building in accordance with the plans and specifications of the master tenant who had leased the entire building. The tenant then subleased space to each food operation. Tables and chairs were in the center of the building and around the walls were places to buy all sorts of food—Mexican, Chinese, Italian, Bavarian, Kosher, and plain old everyday American dishes—along with various places to buy beer, pop and tea. At one end was a cocktail lounge for those who wanted something stronger to drink. It was a very popular place to eat, and after ten years it is still doing a good business. A good use for a problem building was the end result.

In another situation, a man in Albuquerque owns a number of theatres throughout the state and had one operation that was losing money. Deciding to close the theatre, he remodeled the building into a men's clothing store because of its location in the downtown area. Now, instead of losing money in a marginal theatre operation, he collects a sizeable rent check each month.

Another investor in San Diego purchased a number of well-located corners throughout that city and converted the closed gas stations into a chain of fast-food operations. It was a wise choice since his business has been tremendous from the beginning of his new venture.

DEMOLITION AND HOW NEW DEVELOPMENTS ARE PLANNED

Many times an investor is unable to remodel or change the present structure to another use. In such situations demolition is the answer. Tear it down and build from the ground up. Old, dilapidated houses have been torn down to make room for new apartments or office buildings. Lumber yards have been changed into business complexes, having an office building, industrial warehousing and distribution center. Drive-in theatres have become shopping centers. Their large ground area, strategic locations and inexpensive improvements make them a prime investment opportunity for a creative and innovative investor.

In planning the new development, consideration should be given to the type of development best suited for the property. All information contained on the Fact and Information Profile should be studied and analyzed.

As a general rule such property can be redeveloped into one of the following commercial or industrial categories:

1. Apartments
2. Shopping centers

3. Industrial warehouses
4. Office buildings
5. Distribution centers
6. Mini-storage facilities
7. Medical centers
8. Stores, shops and service buildings
9. Manufacturing
10. A combination complex having several different categories

If a depressed area is in need of low-cost housing, an apartment complex can be constructed under one of the current government programs. By following the development procedures for apartments as outlined in the preceding chapter and using the guidelines set forth in Washington, an investor can successfully develop that much needed low-cost housing.

A 12 acre site in Fort Worth which was the location of an old lumber yard is presently being redeveloped into a large business plaza. The development program includes a large office building and showroom space along with a distribution center of nearly 75,000 square feet. The program is in keeping with the city of Fort Worth's inner-city studies that concern urban design projects in small, older commercial areas.

One of the largest shopping center developers in the country with over 25 million square feet of shopping space under his control could see the profit opportunities in old drive-in theatre locations as sites for new shopping centers. By purchasing five old theatres situated in prime locations in Little Rock, Riverside, Tulsa, Atlanta and St. Louis, he added another half million square feet of shopping centers.

HOW TO REMODEL AND UPGRADE COMMERCIAL PROPERTY TO INCREASE INCOME

That old saying—"A little paint will make the old girl look like what she ain't"—is equally true in real estate. Those investors who purchase the older, run-down commercial or industrial properties, find many profit opportunities in this field of real estate.

In analyzing this type of commercial and industrial property, the investor must consider not only the purchase price but also must determine the cost of remodeling, renovating, painting and replacing old, worn-out equipment. If the income can be increased and the cost of acquisition and remodeling kept considerably lower than building a new facility, this type of redevelopment can be very profitable.

Many investors make a business of buying old apartment buildings where rents are low because of the condition of the apartment units. By purchasing the building based upon its current low-income and run-down condition, the investor can remodel the old building, raise the rents and then sell the completely renovated apartment building at a price based upon its new higher income. In this manner, big profits can be made in old apartments.

Renovating an apartment building

One investor purchased an older 16-unit apartment building in a good rental area. Due to its age and run-down condition, the current annual income was only $19,200 with several vacancies. After paying maintenance costs, operating expenses, insurance and taxes, the operating profit reduced to $12,288. The owner was asking only $125,000 but the investor made an offer of $115,000 which was accepted.

After remodeling, repainting and renovating the building and all apartment units at a cost of $32,000, the investor began renting units at newer, higher rates. In less than three months, all apartments had been rented at rates that produced an annual income of $39,840. After deducting total expenses of $11,752, his new operating profit was $28,088. Securing a new mortgage in the amount of $175,000, he prepared the following evaluation of the newly modernized apartments:

Total Income	$39,840.00	
Operating Expenses	11,752.00	
Operating Profit	$28,088.00	
Less Debt Service 9¼% - 25 year	17,984.00	
Cash Spendable Income		$10,104.00

Capitalizing the cash flow at 12 percent and adding the new mortgage, the investor could see that the property was now worth $260,000 as shown in the calculations below:

$10,104.00 ÷ 12% =	$ 84,200.00
New Mortgage Amount	$175,000.00
Total Evaluation	$259,200.00

Since he had been able to purchase the old apartment building for only $115,000 and spent an additional $32,000 in remodeling, he knew that his total cost had been $147,000. By selling the property for $260,000 to another apartment investor, he was now able to make a very nice profit of $113,000.

This same redevelopment procedure can be followed in remodeling and reconditioning old office buildings, industrial warehouses, stores, shops and service buildings, providing the location is good and the shell of the old building is structurally sound.

ADDING MORE RENTAL AREA FOR GREATER INCOME

Another proven procedure followed by many investors in the redevelopment of older commercial and industrial property is remodeling and adding more rental space to increase income. Providing the size of the lot is large enough to accomodate more rental area, this procedure can greatly increase income at a minimum of cost. Since no additional land is needed, that cost is eliminated.

In evaluating this type of industrial property, the investor should carefully plan his redevelopment program. By purchasing the property based upon its current low income and general condition, an astute investor should be able to make a good investment. Checking into the cost of remodeling the present structure and the construction of additional rental space, the investor should analyze all costs in relation to the new rental income provided. If the profit potential is there, the redevelopment program should be undertaken.

One of the most profitable investments of this type occurred in Denver. An investor was considering the purchase of an old 15,000 square foot industrial warehouse on about one and a half acres of land. The building was currently being leased at $1.50 per square foot; however, the lease was about to expire and would not be renewed.

Knowing that it would cost $40,000 to remodel and recondition the old building, the investor offered $150,000 for the property. After the escrow closed, plans were completed for the remodeling of the existing structure and for the construction of a 15,000 square foot addition, doubling the size of the building.

By the time his redevelopment program was completed, his investment totaled $415,000 but he had leased the 30,000 square foot warehouse to a nationally-rated tenant at 20¢ per square foot per month on a triple net lease. Submitting the executed 20 year lease and his own strong financial statement, the investor negotiated an excellent $500,000 mortgage at 8¾ percent interest to be amortized over 25 years.

In evaluating his redevelopment investment, the investor prepared the Income Analysis and Evaluation form shown below:

Total Income	$72,000.00
Operating Expenses	None
Operating Profit	$72,000.00

Less Debt Service	49,330.00	
Cash Spendable Income		$ 22,670.00
Cash Spendable Income ÷ 9% yield		$251,888.00
Current Mortgage Balance		$500,000.00
Total Valuation		$751,888.00

With his total cost being only $415,000, the above valuation shows a gain in value of $336,888. Also, since he had recaptured his total cash invested in the new mortgage funds, his investment can only be described as terrific.

ADVANCED TECHNIQUES IN FINANCING THE REDEVELOPED PROJECT FOR GREATER PROFITS

As a general rule, the older commercial or industrial properties, whether an apartment building, a shopping center, an office building or an industrial warehouse, will have only a small mortgage balance or no encumbrance at all. In such situations, refinancing is a necessary procedure. In negotiating a new mortgage commitment, all costs must be taken into consideration: acquisition and remodeling and/or additions to be added to the present structure. The loan officer will require that complete plans for remodeling and/or additions be submitted with the loan application. In addition, a new pro-forma operating statement must be prepared and included in the commitment package.

To assure the most advantageous terms in the new mortgage commitment, the investor should have an executed lease with a strong tenant to occupy the redeveloped building. With an executed lease coupled with the financial strength of both the tenant and the investor, the advanced technique of financing the lease instead of evaluating the building can be followed as was shown in the preceding section on the redeveloped warehouse.

In that situation, the net income from the lease determined the value of the investment. Also, the security of the mortgage was assured and the mortgage company issued a commitment which provided not only sufficient funds to recapture the entire initial investment costs but also provided a most advantageous rate of interest, thereby resulting in greater profits to the investor.

REDEVELOPED PROPERTY: WHETHER TO KEEP FOR INCOME OR SELL FOR PROFIT

As with every other commercial or industrial property which has been purchased as an investment, redeveloped property should also be analyzed and evaluated as to whether the property should be held for income or sold for profit.

Usually the determining factors in making the decision are taxes, economic conditions and the financial needs of the investor.

Federal Taxes. Many investors who redevelop commercial and industrial property will hold the investment for income until such a time as their tax advantages are no longer applicable. Usually when the depreciation has been reduced and the investment begins to show a sizeable book profit, the investor decides to sell.

Economic conditions. With a general slowdown in the economy and when resulting vacancies begin to affect the income, an investor may consider selling while there's still time to make a profit.

Financial need. There are times when an investor needs to sell for financial reasons. While he may be happy with the income produced by the investment, other financial obligations may determine his need to sell.

One of the foregoing factors may be the reason many investors use to determine whether to hold an investment for income or sell for a profit. Other investors, however, purchase or redevelop property for the income it produces, having no plans or desire to sell until a much later date. They are not influenced by tax implications, economic conditions or financial need while others develop or redevelop property with the intent to immediately sell for a profit.

The investor in Denver who remodeled and enlarged the old warehouse as described in a previous section decided to retain the redeveloped property as an investment. The long-term 25 year lease with a national concern on a triple net $72,000 a year was too good to sell. The secure Cash Spendable Income of $22,670 coupled with the tax advantages available to him was better than he could find in another investment. Also, since the new $500,000 mortgage recaptured more than his costs, he really had no cash invested in the property. Therefore, he decided to retain the property as an investment until such a time tax implications determined that he should sell.

PROVEN METHODS AND STRATEGIES TO USE IN SELLING A REDEVELOPED COMMERCIAL AND INDUSTRIAL PROPERTY

Proven methods and strategies to use in selling all types of commercial and industrial property have been outlined and described in preceding chapters of this book relating to the sale of apartments, shopping centers, office buildings, industrial warehouses, stores, shops and service buildings. While the procedures are similar in the sale of all types of commercial and industrial property, each can be distinctively different in certain aspects of the sale.

In other words, the procedures used in the sale of an apartment complex are similar to those used in the sale of a shopping center to a point. From that point, the distinctive differences of the two investments prevail. Apartment investors can see the advantages of owning an apartment complex while a shopping center investor wouldn't be interested in buying an apartment building. Those differences should be amplified as they appeal to the individual investor.

The sale of redeveloped commercial and industrial property isn't any different. Proven procedures used in the sale of existing or newly-constructed income producing property can be followed in the sale of redeveloped property to a point. That point of fact is that the property has been completely remodeled, renovated, or reconditioned.

The most successful strategy to use in selling redeveloped property is to let the investment speak for itself and try not to hide or circumvent the fact that the property has been completely remodeled and renovated. If the redevelopment has been done with proper care and consideration, the building will pass the physical inspection of an interested investor. As a general rule, a few construction problems can be overcome with a good operating statement and a bottom line that shows the value of the investment.

A good example of this strategy occurred in the sale of the old 16-unit redeveloped apartment building described in a previous section of this chapter. The older building was purchased for $115,000 and the investor spent $32,000 remodeling and reconditioning the building and apartment units. As a result, the income increased from $19,200 a year to $39,840. After expenses and servicing the new $175,000 mortgage, the investment showed a cash spendable income of $10,104.

In showing the apartments, it was explained that the building had been completely remodeled and the extent of the improvements was shown to the buyer. While the buyer was interested in what had been done to the building, he was satisfied with its general condition, but was more interested in the operating statement. The property had been priced at $260,000 which would return a 12 percent cash yield to the buyer. Explaining that he would require at least a 15 percent cash return, the buyer offered $240,000 for the apartments, cash to the mortgage.

Deciding that a profit of $100,000 on his redeveloped apartments would be an excellent return, the investor countered back at $250,000, splitting the difference between his asking price and the offered amount. The buyer then approved the price and the sale was closed. As in other situations, the strategy of fully disclosing everything that had been done to the old building proved to be an asset to the sale rather than a hinderance.

KEY POINTS

1. Realize that problem properties and problem areas exist in every city
2. Understand how the creative and innovative investor who can visualize a new

use for a problem building can find an abundance of profit opportunities in this field of real estate

3. Know what to look for in locating problem buildings and what to do about them when you find one
4. Find how greater profits can be made by following the technique of remodeling and changing use
5. Follow the transformation of an old Safeway supermarket into a successful Food Bazaar
6. Know when to tear down and build from the ground up
7. Understand how to remodel and upgrade a commercial property to increase income
8. See how one investor made a big profit remodeling a small apartment building
9. Understand how to use the procedure of adding more rental space for greater income by following the redevelopment of an old warehouse in Denver
10. Know how to use advanced financing techniques in redevelopment for big profits
11. Understand the decision-making process in determining whether to hold a redeveloped property for income or sell for a profit
12. Know how to apply proven methods and strategies in selling a redeveloped commercial or industrial property

14

Leases and Leaseholds for Profit and Growth

In the development of commercial and industrial property, the land will either be owned or come under a long-term lease. Each of these situations permits the developer to exercise complete control of the property. If there is a choice, the developer will probably choose the method which produces the greater profit with the least initial expense, weighing of course the advantages and disadvantages of ownership or leasing.

For those investors who have given little or no thought to leasing land for development, this chapter should be informative, instructive and interesting. In this chapter we will see the many advantages of leasing land for development along with a proven financing technique in securing a mortgage loan for a leasehold improvement. An interesting comparison of a leasehold development with the ownership of land is also shown. In addition, successful procedures to use in securing subordination are explained followed by a study of the different types of subordination. Whether to buy or lease land or whether to sell or lease, are two important questions with the right decision resulting in greater profits. Also, proven methods and techniques to use in structuring a sale and leaseback are outlined and described.

It should also be interesting to read how one investor decided to sell a parcel of land and then changed his mind—too late—and to see why another investor who wanted to lease decided to sell. In addition, we will discuss how one sale and leaseback was negotiated and consummated with interesting results.

THE ADVANTAGES OF LEASING LAND FOR DEVELOPMENT

Very few investors know or understand the technique of leasing land for development especially in areas where such practice is not prevalent. Their first thought is to purchase and own the land, not giving any consideration to leasing the fee. In other areas, such as Honolulu, leasing the land is the way of doing business.

There are times when an advantageous long-term land lease is better than owning the property. To some investors this may sound strange, but the advantages listed below will explain the reasoning for this type of land control:

1. Frees capital for other improvements
2. Less expensive
3. Expense of operation
4. Leasehold improvement fully depreciable
5. Subordination to mortgage for leasehold improvements
6. Options to renew
7. Options to purchase
8. Advantages of ownership without owning
9. Greater profit potential
10. Easily saleable

Each of the foregoing advantages is more fully explained in the following descriptive outline:

Frees capital for other improvements. The funds necessary to acquire the land can be used for leasehold improvements or to reduce the mortgage loan required in the construction of the development.

Less expensive. A long-term land lease calculated at 8 to 10 percent of value is like owning the land and paying interest except that the principal is never paid off. Since the investment will produce a higher cash yield, the lease is less expensive.

Expense of operation. As has been explained in a previous chapter, land is not depreciable, so this does not offer any tax advantage to the owner. The rent paid on leased land, however, is fully deductible as an operating expense, thereby creating a tax advantage equivalent or better than depreciation.

Leasehold improvements fully depreciable. Buildings or other improvements placed on leased land are fully depreciable as if the land were owned. The rate of depreciation is often determined by not only the type of construction and use but also by the term of the land lease.

Subordination to mortgage for leasehold improvements. Since investors very seldom build leasehold improvements with their own funds, the lessor will subordinate his interest in the land to a mortgage loan for the purpose of constructing improvements on the land. Successful procedures to use in obtaining such subordination is fully explained in a subsequent section of this chapter.

Options to renew. Usually it is simple to include options to renew the leases on terms and conditions mutually agreed between the parties.

Options to purchase. If the investor initially wants to lease the land but purchase later at a specific price on a predetermined date, the option to purchase can be included in the terms of the lease.

Advantages of ownership without owning. An investor doesn't have to own the land to have complete control of its use. Through the terms of a long-term ground lease, this control can be exercised and maintained with all the benefits of owning but with the tax advantages of leasing.

Greater profit potential. With less cash being invested, the cash yield should be at a higher percentage. This, coupled with land rent being an expense of operation, the bottom line figure after taxes is greater, thereby resulting in greater profits to the investor.

Easily saleable. When a potential buyer has been conditioned to the advantages of leased land, the leasehold improvements can be more easily sold since less cash would be received to purchase the property.

FINANCING TECHNIQUES FOR LEASEHOLD IMPROVEMENTS

The technique used in financing improvements placed upon leased land follows the same procedures as if the land had been purchased, providing the lessor subordinates his interest in the land to a mortgage loan for construction purposes. For purposes of explanation, we will use the development of an 80,000 square foot neighborhood shopping center on 10 acres of subordinated leased land.

In accordance with the provisions of leases with nationally-rated tenants for over 60,000 square feet of space, the investor prepared and submitted the following pro-forma operating statement for consideration by the mortgage company:

Rental Income		
25,000 sq. ft.—Supermarket @ 3.50	$ 87,500.00	
15,000 sq. ft.—Drug Store @ 3.00	45,000.00	
10,000 sq. ft.—Variety Store @ 3.00	30,000.00	
30,000 sq. ft.—Local Tenants @ 4.50	135,000.00	
Total Rental Income		$297,500.00
Operating Expenses		59,500.00
Balance		$238,000.00
Land Lease @ 10%		40,000.00
Operating Profit		$198,000.00

The leases and tenants were acceptable to the lending institution, so the operating profit was capitalized at 9 percent, resulting in a valuation of $2,200,000 on the leasehold improvements. The mortgage company then agreed to loan almost 75 percent of that value or a total of $1,600,000 to be amortized over 25 years at 9¼ percent interest. Since the cost of construction was $1,760,000, the investor was required to make a cash investment of $160,000.

In further calculating the yield on his leasehold investment, the investor prepared the following evaluation:

Operating Profit as shown above	$198,000.00	
Less Debt Service	164,436.00	
Cash Spendable Income		$33,564.00
Gain in Equity		17,600.00
Total Gain		$51,164.00
Yield—Cash on Cash		20.9%
Total Yield		31.9%

As you can see, this leasehold development produced an excellent yield. Now let's compare this type of leasehold financing with the same development but on land that was purchased for the leased value of $400,000.

COMPARING A LEASEHOLD DEVELOPMENT WITH OWNERSHIP OF LAND

By referring to the above operating statement, the Operating Profit becomes $238,000 without the deduction of land rent. Capitalizing the Operating Profit at the same Cap Rate the new valuation was $2,600,000 and the new mortgage amount was $1,900,000, also amortized at 9¼ percent for 25 years. The new evaluation is shown below:

Cost of Improvements	$1,760,000.00	
Land	400,000.00	
Total Cost	$2,160,000.00	
New Mortgage Amount	1,900,000.00	
Cash required		$260,000.00
Operating Profit as shown above	$238,000.00	
Less Debt Service	195,264.00	
Cash Spendable Income	42,736,000	
Gain in Equity	20,900.00	
Total Gain	$ 63,636.00	
Yield—Cash on Cash	16.4%	
Total Yield	24.4%	

By comparison, you will notice that the cash yield on the leasehold plan is 4.5 percent higher than owning—an increase of 27 percent—while the total yield is 7½ percent higher, an increase of 30 percent. As to which is better—that's a matter of choice. About 50 percent of shopping centers are built on leased land, so each method has its following. If, however, leasing is the only way a good location can be obtained, don't be afraid of the results.

SUCCESSFUL PROCEDURES IN SECURING SUBORDINATION FOR LEASEHOLD IMPROVEMENTS

There was a time not too long ago when SUBORDINATION was a "dirty word." Very few owners would even consider discussing the subject let alone do anything about it. They had been led to believe that through default of the buyer on the mortgage they could lose their land. Through the years, as both buyers and sellers became more sophisticated and knowledgeable in their financing techniques, the practice of financing subordinated land became more widely used.

Owners became more receptive to the practice when it was explained to them that they were actually subordinating their interest in the land to the lease of a very strong nationally-rated tenant or tenants and not necessarily to the buyer. Also, explaining that the lending institution who will supply the mortgage funds must approve the leases before a loan will be granted made a difference.

In preparing a lease where subordination is to be granted, the following paragraph has proven to be understood and acceptable to many owners:

> "Lessor shall agree to subordinate his interest in the property for on-site and off-site improvements when the Lessee shall have produced

satisfactory leases or letters of intent manifesting a firm commitment by the tenants, which said leases will produce sufficient annual income to properly and adequately service the mortgage or mortgages to which the position of the Lessor is being subordinated, including principal, interest and other related or standard costs. (The determination as to whether or not such leases are satisfactory to permit subordination to the Lessor's interest to the lien or mortgage or mortgages for construction purposes shall be the acceptance of said lease by a recognized lending institution as a condition of their making the mortgage loan or loans.)''

A STUDY OF THE DIFFERENT TYPES OF SUBORDINATION

When the owner decides that subordination is possible, it then becomes a matter of negotiation to determine the amount and degree of subordination.

The two types of subordination an owner will grant are shown below:

1. Full subordination
2. Limited subordination

By granting full subordination, the developer will have the right to obtain the maximum loan available, regardless of the cost of construction or other related costs.

Limited subordination is as the name implies. The right of subordination can be limited in certain areas as further described below:

1. *Total value of completed project.* The owner may stipulate that the subordination will not exceed a designated percentage of the total value of the completed project, including land. This percentage factor can range from 50 to 75 percent.

2. *Total value of cost of improvements.* Again, the owner may be willing to subordinate his interest in the land but only to the amount of the construction costs of the improvements.

3. *An amount less than the cost of improvements.* Wanting the developer to have some of his own money in the project, the owner may subordinate to a percentage of the cost of improvements. Again, this percentage factor can range from 50 to 75 percent.

4. *A specified amount.* The owner may decide that he is willing only to subordinate to a specified amount. In this situation, it can be an amount less than the 50 percent shown above.

As you can see, the type, amount and degree of subordination is variable and negotiable. After the lessor has agreed to subordinate, the investor must then negotiate the best terms and conditions obtainable.

WHETHER TO BUY OR LEASE LAND: THE RIGHT DECISION CAN RESULT IN GREATER PROFITS

As a general rule, most investors think of buying or selling land for development and give very little consideration to leasing. Of course, there are advantages in both and the astute investor will weigh those advantages to him in each situation. In considering a parcel of land for development, the investor has certain questions regarding whether to purchase or lease the land.

1. *Which method produces the greater profit.* In analyzing and evaluating the development profit potential, the investor should prepare two pro-forma operating statements: one with the purchase of land and the other with a land lease, deducting the land rent from the operating profit. Whichever method produces the greater profit should be given consideration.

2. *Long-range potential.* Looking beyond the immediate results, the investor should project the income into the future to determine the long-range effect each method will have on his investment. Again, the method producing the greater long-range potential should be given due consideration.

3. *Cash investment.* In most situations, the amount of cash required to complete the development is less in land leasing, providing a satisfactory subordination agreement can be obtained from the lessor. Whether this question is important to the investor can only be determined by the financial condition of the investor and his willingness to invest more cash in purchasing the land.

4. *Greater yield.* As has been explained and shown in a preceding section of this chapter, a development placed on subordinated leased land will produce a greater cash yield to the investor because of the smaller amount of capital required in the initial investment.

5. *Ease in development.* It is easier to develop a property when the land has been purchased than when subordination has been granted on leased land. No matter how neat and clean the subordination agreement appears to be, there seem to always be problems, disputes and renegotiations with some lessors—not that those problems can't be resolved but it is sometimes aggravating to have the lessor continually investigating to determine if the terms and conditions of the subordination agreement have been met.

6. *Tax advantages in leasing.* There is a distinct tax advantage in leasing land for development, this being the deduction of land rent as an expense of operation, whereas land owned is not depreciable.

7. *Saleability*. Since more investors will prefer to own the property and not a leasehold improvement subject to the terms of a land lease, the saleability of the development should be greater if the land is included in the sale. However, those investors who can recognize the advantages of leasing in their investment program will be willing to purchase the leasehold improvements. Therefore, only a slight edge can be given to owning the land.

8. *Investment program*. Many astute investors have a definite investment program which determines their methods and procedures in acquiring commercial and industrial property as an investment. If their program has been to own and not lease, they will want to purchase the land. If, however, they have open minds, then consideration will be given to both sides of the question.

WHETHER TO SELL OR LEASE LAND: THAT IS THE QUESTION

On the other side of the coin, one investor owns a parcel of land which he is considering to either sell or lease to another investor for development. He, too, has certain questions that will determine his decision.

1. *Financial need*. The need for immediate cash can sometimes influence the decision as to whether to sell or lease. Since a sale will produce more immediate cash, this decision is usually made. However, a knowledgeable investor/owner can have his cake and eat it too, if he knows how to do it. The technique of a mortgage loan on the leased property is fully explained and described in the following section.

2. *Yield*. The rent on a ground lease is usually calculated as a percentage of the valuation of the land. This percentage factor can vary from 8 to 12 percent per year with the lessee paying all real property taxes and assessments. In addition, an astute owner will want a stipulated percentage of the excess rentals received as income from the development. Therefore, the cash yield will be the amount of percentage used in calculating the rent. If the owner wants a 12 percent yield, the rent will be 12 percent of the value of the land.

3. *Subordination*. Since subordination of the owner's interest in the land will be required by the developers, the owner/investor must be willing to grant such subordination. If the owner is adverse to this requirement, then the property should be sold instead of leased.

4. *Long-term profit*. The long-term profit in a 50 year ground lease is far greater than selling, especially when the rent can be increased through a share of excess rentals paid by tenants.

5. *Capital gain versus ordinary income.* Generally, the profit made from the sale of a parcel of land can be treated as a Capital Gain, whereas rental income is taxed as ordinary income. To many investors, this fact has a bearing on the ultimate decision.

6. *Tax implications.* Since land is not depreciable, the rental income has no off-setting expenses to use as a tax advantage.

7. *Saleability.* A parcel of land, subject to the terms of a ground lease is saleable; however, its value is determined by the income it produces. Since many investors are interested only in tax-sheltered income, the sale of leased land will be limited to only those investors who want straight, ordinary income.

8. *Investment program.* Many investors have an investment program which influences their decision on whether to lease or sell. Those who prefer the long-range profit potential without regard for tax shelters or other sales incentives will retain the property under a long-term ground lease. Those that want the quick, capital gain profit will sell. Again, it's a question of whether they want a fast nickel or a slow dime.

HOW ONE INVESTOR FIRST DECIDED TO SELL AND THEN CHANGED HIS MIND—TOO LATE

An investor was developing a neighborhood shopping center. His plan was to sell two corner parcels as the center was being constructed. During this construction period, I was able to sell the two parcels. One was more or less routine—the sale of one corner to an oil company for $100,000. The other sale was more interesting and provides a good lesson.

I knew that a savings and loan had been granted a certificate to operate in the area of the new shopping center. The remaining corner was then presented to the president of that savings and loan. After pointing out the advantages of locating at the shopping center corner, he agreed to lease the parcel of land for 50 years. A Letter of Intent was then prepared in his office and signed by him.

Later that afternoon, the Letter of Intent was presented to the developer. He would not approve the letter, stating that he needed cash at this time and wanted to sell. In further discussing the lease proposal, I tried to point out the advantages of the lease and what could be done with it, but my friend wouldn't listen. He then asked if I would go back to the savings and loan to see if I could get the president to buy instead of lease.

I then discussed with the president why he should buy instead of lease. I had previously pointed out to the developer that the savings and loan intended to construct a $200,000 building on their property which would certainly be adequate security on the ground lease. In talking with the president, I explained that if he planned to construct a $200,000 building on the property, he should certainly buy the land instead of leasing. I finally convinced him, and he agreed to pay the purchase price of $75,000. Escrow instructions were then prepared with the total purchase price to be paid at the close of a 30 day escrow.

I now returned to the developer with the signed escrow instructions, wherein the property was sold for the $75,000 he had instructed me to get. When I presented those instructions, I thought that I would be congratulated for a job well done. Instead, I was told that he now wanted to lease. I asked what had changed his mind. His reply was that he had discussed the 50 year leased property with his banker, and had been told that he could borrow $75,000 against the lease. The proceeds of the ground lease would amortize the mortgage over a 20 year period and the remaining 30 years would be all profit. So now he wanted to lease.

I told him that I had said the same thing when I presented the lease, but he had been so busy talking about selling that he failed to grasp what I had said. I further stated that I had done too good a selling job this time—the savings and loan would not be interested further in leasing the property. If he wanted to sell the property, he should sign the escrow instructions. He reluctantly signed the instructions, mumbling to himself while doing so.

WHY ANOTHER INVESTOR WHO WANTED TO LEASE DECIDED TO SELL

This investor had purchased a large parcel of land a number of years ago. During the following years, he had rezoned the corner 40 acres to commercial as a large shopping center site and had sold the remaining residential acreages to other developers and builders.

In the beginning, he had intended to sell the commercial corner; however, as the last remaining residential acreage was sold, he decided that he wanted to ground lease the commercial acreage instead of sell. As the location became more desirable as a site for a large shopping center, he received an offer to purchase the 40 acres.

It was a good offer with a purchase price of $1,600,000, payable $475,000 at the close of escrow and $1,125,000 in five equal annual payments bearing interest at the rate of 9 percent per annum. A release schedule was included in the terms of the Trust Agreement which would permit a phase type of development. Since his base cost in the land was only $150,000, the fantastic $1,450,000 profit from the sale caused him to reassess his position and intentions.

After several sleepless nights, he decided to try to convert the purchase to a ground lease. Without accepting or rejecting the offer, he countered with a lease proposal. Not wanting to lease, the buyer rejected his proposal but added another $50,000 to the purchase price, increasing the down payment $15,000 and spreading the balance over the term of the Trust Agreement.

Knowing that a bird in the hand is worth two in the bush, my investor friend wasn't a big enough gambler to turn down $490,000 in cash at the close of escrow with a total profit of $1,500,000 and then wait for someone to come along and lease the 40 acres. He accepted the offer at $1,650,000.

PROVEN METHODS AND TECHNIQUES IN STRUCTURING A SALE AND LEASEBACK

There are times when the owner of a building wants to sell for various reasons but would like to retain the location for the continued operation of his business. The sale and leaseback technique is the method whereby this can be accomplished.

The term in itself can be explained as being two-sided—either a purchase/leaseback or a sale/leaseback. The only difference between the two expressions is who is doing what to whom. In a purchase/leaseback, the buyer usually says that he will purchase the property if the seller will lease it back. In the the sale/leaseback, the owner/seller agrees to sell if he can lease the property back for his continued operation.

In these situations everything is relative—sales price, rent and yield. The owner who is selling wants as much money for the property as he can get but doesn't want to pay any more rent than he has to. On the other hand, the buyer doesn't want to pay any more for the property than he has to but wants as much rent as he can get. Somewhere in these figures a deal is made. Normally the process starts with the amount of rent the seller wants to pay on his leaseback. The rent is then capitalized at the yield the buyer wants to make on his investment.

Let's say that the rent is $1,200 per month with the lessee paying all taxes, insurance and maintaining the building. This totals $14,400 annually. Then let's assume the buyer wants to make 12 percent on his investment. By capitalizing the annual rent at 12 percent, the value of the property will be $120,000. If you don't remember, divide $14,400 by .12 and you will have capitalized the annual rent.

Other terms and conditions of the leaseback can then be discussed and negotiated, including the length of lease and rent escalation. When this has been done, the property can be sold—subject to the execution of the lease between the parties.

HOW ONE SALE AND LEASEBACK WAS NEGOTIATED AND CONSUMMATED

An appliance distributor had been operating his business for many years in the same building. The building was still in good condition, but his depreciation was beginning to run out and the mortgage was low. Needing additional capital to expand his business, he decided to either sell the building and lease it back or secure a new mortgage loan.

The building appraised at $225,000 but the mortgage company would only loan 60 percent or $135,000 to be amortized over 20 years at 9¾ percent interest. Realizing that the high rate of interest and other costs in making a new mortgage loan were too expensive, he decided to consider selling the property and then leasing it back from the new owner.

Knowing that comparable space would rent for at least .15¢ per square foot per month or an annual rent of $27,000, he didn't want to pay that much in rent. He would, however, be willing to pay .10¢ per foot or a total of $18,000 triple net per year. At a meeting with an investor who was interested in his proposal, he was told that his building would have to be priced to yield at least 10 percent. This would place its value at $180,000.

After some negotiating, the seller agreed to increase his monthly rent to $1,687.50 or $20,250 per year, and the buyer agreed to accept a 9 percent yield. Based upon those figures, the sale price of the building was calculated to be $225,000—its appraised value.

KEY POINTS

1. Understand the advantages of a ground lease
2. Study the 10 reasons why many developers consider leasing instead of owning land
3. Follow the financing techniques used in financing a leasehold improvement
4. Compare the financing of a leasehold improvement with the ownership of land
5. Know when land expense can be a deduction
6. Realize the advantages of subordination
7. Study the successful procedures used in obtaining the right of subordination
8. Know the difference between full subordination and limited subordination
9. Follow the decision process in determining whether to lease or buy or sell
10. Understand the eight questions on both sides of the coin

11. Remember how one investor first wanted to sell then changed his mind—too late
12. Review why another investor wanted to lease but decided to sell
13. Study the proven methods and techniques used in structuring a purchase and leaseback
14. Know how to plan a sale and leaseback

15

Trading Strategies that Can Bring Big Profits in Commercial and Industrial Investments

Trading has become an established method of handling certain real estate transactions because there are a number of tax advantages available and other factors which make trading an attractive alternative to the normal sale or purchase. There are investors who own property and are interested only in a trade transaction. In fact, trading has become so widespread that trading clubs made up of people in the real estate business have been formed all over the country. The most sophisticated organization is the Society of Exchange Counselors with approximately 135 members from all over the country. The headquarters of this organization is in San Jose, California and meetings are held every four to six months. At these meetings, information is exchanged between members and often trades are consummated. Various other states and cities also have trader's clubs which meet periodically. Those of you who are interested in trading as a part of your commercial and industrial investment program should investigate and join your local organization.

In this chapter, we will see not only what can be traded but also the advantages of trading commercial and industrial property. When and how to use the technique of trading ''up'' for greater profits will be fully explained along with a most informative example of how this is done. Requirements and guidelines for a successful tax-free exchange are given. Also, we will discuss how to use a trade as a down payment with another descriptive example included. How to dispose of undesirable property in a trade transaction is fully explained along with the reasons why trading is sometimes necessary and how it can help you. In addition, the strategy of a purchase and trade through the use of a third party will be described and explained in a classic example of how one developer did it. The technique of trading during periods of tight money and tactics to use in trading unusual and difficult property should be most interesting and informative. Understanding the taxable implications of trading and how the IRS looks at trading should be helpful. All of this is followed by a special paragraph to insert in a contract when a trade is contemplated, along with a trade agreement form to use in trade transactions.

WHAT CAN BE TRADED

To some, trading comes naturally. As has been said, there are those who prefer trading to selling. Those who may consider trading for the first time should know what can be traded.

Many years ago, it was necessary to trade ''like for like'' to make a tax-free exchange, keeping in mind that it also had to be ''value for value''. In other words, a trade had to be a house for a house, an apartment for an apartment, a farm for a farm, etc. Through the years, the tax regulations have been changed so that now real property may be exchanged for real property without regard for quality or value. For example, an apartment building can be traded for a farm, vacant land for income property etc., *provided that the property being traded has been held for investment.* Later in this chapter, certain guidelines and requirements will be explained having to do with the tax implications of trading.

THE ADVANTAGES OF TRADING COMMERCIAL AND INDUSTRIAL PROPERTY

The advantages of trading are many, but the most important are shown below:

1. Trading ''up'' for increased tax benefits
2. Deferment of tax liability

3. Tax-free exchange
4. Using a trade as a down payment
5. Illustrating a method whereby undesirable property may be included in a transaction at a negotiated value.

In subsequent sections of this chapter, we will see how all of the foregoing situations were resolved through the use of trade techniques that were most successful.

TRADING FOR GREATER PROFITS: THE TECHNIQUE OF TRADING "UP"

It is true that taxes can be a determining factor in why, when and how an investor sells a commercial or industrial property. This section will explain how a tax situation was improved through trading.

The buyer or seller or both may have a tax problem which could preclude a normal sale/purchase transaction. The solution to the problem is an exchange of properties. A description of an actual trade transaction will amplify the foregoing Situation No. 1.

An investor friend owned an industrial warehouse of approximately 16,000 square feet, valued at $225,000 and having a net income of $15,000 after debt service. His depreciated base had been reduced to $75,000 and his mortgage balance was approximately the same amount. He wanted to trade for a larger building, gaining a tax advantage in the exchange.

His interest centered on a new, larger building having a sale price of $900,000 with an existing mortgage balance of $600,000. The net income of the newer building was $90,000 less a debt service of $60,000, leaving a cash spendable income of $30,000.

In working out the terms of the trade, the investor agreed to trade his building, valued at $225,000 less its existing mortgage balance, pay $150,000 in cash and assume the existing mortgage on the new, larger building.

By trading "up," my friend did not incur any tax liability at this time and the new building had a new tax base totaling $825,000. This represented the $600,000 mortgage assumed, the $150,000 cash paid and the transfer of the old base from his traded building of $75,000. The cash spendable income from his new investment was equivalent to the net income from his old building plus a solid 10 percent yield on his cash invested. But now he has greater depreciation and more interest expense to charge against the total income, resulting in more spendable dollars to him. Similar trades can be negotiated to resolve Situation No. 2 whenever one party wants to *defer* his tax liability.

REQUIREMENTS AND GUIDELINES FOR A SUCCESSFUL TAX-FREE EXCHANGE

The Internal Revenue Service has set certain requirements and guidelines regarding the tax implications in trade transactions. In the beginning of this chapter, the different types of property that may be traded to have the tax advantage of a trade were shown. To be able to structure a tax-free exchange within the guidelines of the Internal Revenue Service, the following must be determined.

1. The properties should be "like for like" as defined by the IRS
2. The values should be equal
3. If there are mortgages due on each property, such mortgages should also be equal

If these basic requirements have been met, the transaction can be structured as a tax-free exchange. If the values are not equal and a cash consideration must be paid by one party, the party receiving the cash (which is referred to as "boot") will be liable to taxation. If some other consideration is given in lieu of cash, it is evaluated the same as cash. If the mortgages are not equal, a taxable liability results with the party transferring the larger mortgage to the amount of the differences.

We frequently refer to the "even trade" of properties as a "tax-free" exchange. This reference is not completely accurate; the taxes are just *deferred* to a later date when the property received in trade is sold. At that time taxes must be paid. One main point to remember is the party trading "up" does not incur any taxable liability at the time of the trade. They party trading down usually incurs a tax liability.

Since the IRS regulations change from time to time, it is always best to consult with an accountant regarding the latest rulings for the exchange of properties.

THE TECHNIQUE OF USING A TRADE AS A DOWN PAYMENT IN A LARGE TRANSACTION

One of the financing methods available in purchasing commercial and industrial property is the using of a trade as a down payment. In these situations, the value of the traded property is determined either by an appraisal or by negotiation. The purchase is then structured with the trade property being accepted in lieu of cash with the balance payable either by an assumption of an existing encumbrance or the creation of a new one.

A good case in point is a transaction wherein a property in California was traded for a shopping center in another state. The California property was a parcel of real property on which an office building had been constructed. There was a 99 year lease on the parcel which was also subject to a First Deed of Trust in the approximate amount of $1,000,000 which was subordinate to the land owner's interest in the parcel of land.

The shopping center was owned by a corporation and included a parcel of land of approximately eight acres. The center was subject to a mortgage in the amount of $1,025,000. The valuation agreed upon by the parties was $300,000 for the parcel of land in California, excluding the improvements and $1,425,000 for the shopping center.

The terms of the trade were for the owners of the California property in consideration of the conveyance to them of the shopping center property, conveying their interest in the California property, paying $100,000 in cash at the close of escrow and assuming the existing mortgage in the amount of $1,025,000.

In addition to these considerations, the owners of the shopping center agreed to leaseback the center for $120,000 per year, payable monthly for a period of ten years. The lessee would pay all operating costs, real property taxes, insurance and would maintain the property. To the lessor, this represented a triple net lease. The amount of the annual rent would service the mortgage and give a 10 percent return on the traded property and the cash consideration.

INCLUDING UNDESIRABLE PROPERTY IN A TRADE TRANSACTION

There are times when an investor wants to dispose of an undesirable parcel of land which he had been unable to sell. This can be done by trading the parcel in on a larger transaction and letting the seller absorb the trade. If the seller wants to know what the property would be good for—tell him that it's good for "tradin'."

In one such situation, an investor owned 320 acres of mountainous New Mexico land. He wanted to buy a neighborhood shopping center. In the negotiations, the investor simply insisted that the land be accepted in trade at a value of $30,000 as part of a much larger down payment. The seller accepted the trade because he knew that he could absorb the trade in his price on the shopping center.

What did the seller do with the 320 acres of mountainous New Mexico land he received in trade? He traded it to someone else on his next purchase.

WHY TRADING IS SOMETIMES NECESSARY AND HOW IT CAN HELP YOU

Under certain circumstances, trading can become necessary and very useful. A few typical examples of such situations are listed below:

1. One party wants to buy but the other party will only trade
2. During periods of tight money
3. Unusual or difficult property to sell

We will see in the following sections of this chapter how each of the foregoing situations was resolved by astute investors using proven trade techniques.

THE STRATEGY OF A PURCHASE AND TRADE THROUGH THE USE OF A THIRD PARTY

This situation develops when one party wants to buy but the other will only trade. The only solution to this problem is bringing into the transaction a third party. To fully explain this situation, the sequence of events as they actually occurred during the purchase and trades involved will be related.

This particular purchase involving a trade was built around an investor/developer who wanted to purchase a farm on the edge of the city for subdividing and other development. The farmer who owned the property did not want to sell, but would trade for another farm farther out from the city.

As in all trades, the investor knew his real problem in negotiating this transaction was getting agreement on acceptable values by each party. It is difficult to get two parties to agree, but now he had a third party—the owner of the farm that was to be traded. To take first things first, he was able to negotiate a value on the 160 acre farm that he wanted to develop. He had to know this amount to know what could be available in the trade of the other farm. They finally agreed upon a price of $8,000 per acre for a total price of $1,280,000. Now he had to find another farm where the owner was willing to sell. He certainly didn't need another trading farmer. He also knew that the new farm should not be too far distant and that it should be at least twice as large as the original farm. This meant the new farm should be at least 320 acres at a value of $4,000 per acre. It would have to be well-located and in the path of future development because he could see his trading farmer trading again when values got high enough.

He finally found a farm that was acceptable for the trade. It was 320 acres at $4,000. All he had to do now was tie everything together, working out all of the terms of the purchase and trade, all to close concurrently in simultaneous escrows. The farmer with the 320 acres had agreed to sell for 20 percent down and the balance in 10 years at 9 percent interest, so this format became the basis of his purchase of the 160 acre farm. The trade agreement between the farmers was prepared, along with the necessary escrow instructions wherein the farms were exchanged on an even trade basis with no consideration being paid by either party. This was subject, however, to the concurrent closing of a companion escrow covering the purchase of the 160 acre farm to the investor/developer.

Another set of escrow instructions was now prepared, covering the purchase of the 160 acre farm. The terms of the purchase were 20 percent down with the balance payable by Trust Agreement over a 10 year period, bearing interest on the unpaid balance at 9 percent per annum. The Trust Agreement was the standard subdivision trust agreement wherein release provisions were provided along with other necessary items included for development purposes, including the right to plat and subdivide, subordination for off-site improvements, dedication of streets, deed out and back for financing purposes and the right to rezone the property. All documents were then signed by all of the parties, and the escrows opened and closed on time. In this trade transaction you can readily see how Situation No. 1 became apparent and the steps taken to complete the purchase and trade.

THE TECHNIQUE OF TRADING DURING PERIODS OF TIGHT MONEY

During periods of tight money there is usually a general downturn in business. Real estate sales become less frequent and very difficult to make. Buyers are short on cash and sellers are hard pressed to make payments on their property. All of this makes trading more prevalent and a natural solution to the problem.

There are four important questions which must be considered when trading in tight money situations:

1. How can you find prospects for a trade?
2. How can you find a seller?
3. How can you find a buyer?
4. How can you convince the other party that a trade will help or solve his problem?

Before answering these questions, you must first understand the problem—the shortage of money. In these situations the trade of property is used in lieu of the cash requirements of either a purchase or a sale or as part of the down payment.

Where are your prospects? You must remember that your purpose is to buy or sell a property through the use of a trade—not to make a trade of properties. Therefore, follow the customary procedures in locating prospects under normal conditions.

How can you find a seller? Your tactics now change to meet the situation. In discussing the purchase of his property, simply ask the owner if he would consider a trade. If his answer is "No," then ask if he would consider a trade as part of the purchase price. If he again answers negatively, ask if he would consider a small trade as part of the down payment. Usually in periods of tight money and if the owner really wants to sell, the answer will be "Maybe" to one of those questions. Now, you have your foot in the door. You can move in and structure the purchase accordingly.

How can you find a buyer? Finding the buyer in this situation is the easiest part of the process. All you have to do is let it be known that you will consider a trade in the sale of your property or, better still, run an ad in the trading column of the classified ads stating that you would consider a trade. You will be amazed at how many offers you will receive from other traders. After you have found a buyer, your technique should change to meet the requirements of the trade.

How can you convince the other party that a trade will help or solve his problem? If you will follow the tactics and techniques shown in the foregoing sections of the chapter, the other party to the trade will realize the advantages of the trade transaction. Once you have crossed that bridge, their problem and yours will be solved.

TACTICS TO USE IN TRADING UNUSUAL OR DIFFICULT PROPERTY

There are times when a sale is difficult to make because of the nation-wide economic situation, the lack of buyer interest, or the location and general condition of the property. All these point to the trade tactic as the solution. A list of several difficult situations is itemized below:

1. Non-depreciable income property
2. Disposing of a problem property
3. Property with poor development possibilities
4. Property in run-down condition

The most difficult trade to make is the exchange of non-depreciable land for depreciable income property. Just about the only way to conclude this type of exchange is when the land will appreciate in value either in time or by rezoning and intelligent planning. On this basis, the owner of the income property might be interested in trading.

My recommendations in resolving the other itemized difficult situations is to keep the trade small and let the seller absorb the trade in the sale of his property.

TAX IMPLICATIONS AND INCENTIVES FOR TRADING: HOW THE IRS LOOKS AT TRADING

The taxable implications of a sales transaction can be one of the most important incentives in determining whether a seller should sell or trade his property. The most important of these are listed below:

1. Unusually high profit
2. Other profitable sales in that taxable year
3. Desire to defer taxes
4. Desire to trade "up" for better tax position

When the first three of the above situations influence a seller's decisions, he will most generally decide that trading is his solution.

Since the exchange of real estate has become an established method of handling certain real estate transactions, the Internal Revenue Service is receptive to the concept of trading. Providing the transaction meets all guidelines and requirements of the IRS, the trade will be permitted. The resultant taxable implications will be governed by their rules and regulations. These rules and regulations continually change. Therefore, it is always wise to consult with your accountant in determining your taxable position.

WHAT TO DO WHEN A TRADE IS CONTEMPLATED IN A SALE OF PROPERTY

Occasionally during the sale of a commercial or industrial property, the seller may consider that he might be interested in acquiring another property through a trade. This would require the buyer of his property to acquire the other property and then trade that property to him. To be able to accomplish this so that it meets the requirements of the IRS, a certain paragraph must be inserted in the original sales agreement. This paragraph reads as follows:

"Notwithstanding any provision herein to the contrary, prior to the closing of this Escrow, Seller may direct Buyer forthwith to acquire title to a parcel or parcels of property located in the state of Arizona for the uses and purposes of Seller for such purchase price as Seller shall determine, and to convey said property to Seller in exchange for said property hereinbefore referred to and particularly described; however, that in the event the purchase price for said parcel or parcels of property which Seller shall direct Buyer to purchase, as herein provided, shall exceed the sum of ONE MILLION EIGHT HUNDRED FIFTY THOUSAND ($1,850,000.00) DOLLARS, Seller shall pay to Buyer the difference between the purchase price of said parcel or parcels of property to be acquired by Buyer and said sum of ONE MILLION EIGHT HUNDRED FIFTY THOUSAND ($1,850,000.00) DOLLARS. In the event Seller shall direct Buyer to acquire title to a parcel or parcels of property for exchange as herein provided, then and in such event, amended Escrow Instructions shall be executed by the parties hereto, which such Escrow Instructions shall provide for the exchange by Seller of such property to be obtained by said Buyer for the property hereinbefore referred to and particularly described, and any adjustment required to be made by and between Seller and Buyer by reason of the difference in the sum of ONE MILLION EIGHT HUNDRED FIFTY THOUSAND ($1,850,000.00) DOLLARS and the purchase price of said parcel or parcels of property which Seller shall direct Buyer to purchase, shall be provided for in this Escrow for the purpose of carrying out the exchange of said properties. The Buyer shall have no liability or obligation for any additional cost or expense which may be incurred by virture of the transaction herein contemplated being modified from an outright sale to an exchange of properties. Seller hereby agrees to indemnify and hold harmless Buyer from any obligation, liability, cost or expense which Buyer may incur by reason of Seller exercising his rights under the provisions of this paragraph. Buyer shall have the right in connection with the acquisition of the parcel or parcels of property to be exchanged for said property hereinbefore referred to and particularly described, to condition its acquisition upon the close of this Escrow and upon such other conditions and provisions as it shall, in its sole discretion, determine necessary and required to fully protect its interests."

This particular special paragraph has proven most beneficial in the sale of property where the seller contemplates possible or future trade during the escrow period. It precludes a lot of explaining to the Internal Revenue Service that the sale was intended to be a trade. Such a "sale and trade" is more fully described in the following section.

HOW THE SPECIAL TRADE PARAGRAPH WAS USED IN A "SALE AND TRADE" TRANSACTION

Not long ago a very astute investor received an offer of $1,850,000 on a large parcel of land. Since his base cost in the land was low, the profit from the sale would be unusually high. Also, he had made other large sales that year and was concerned with the additional taxes that would have to be paid on this latest sale. Knowing that by trading he would be able to defer his tax liabilities, he gave thought to injecting a trade into the transaction.

Not knowing what he would want in a trade property but realizing that something acceptable could be found before the close of escrow, he accepted the offer after inserting the special trade paragraph shown in the preceding section. In this manner, he alerted the buyer, the IRS and everyone else that a trade was contemplated.

During the escrow period, the investor located a ranch in California that he wanted. In accordance with the provisions of the special trade paragraph, he notified the buyer of the trade property which was acceptable to him.

After amending the basic sales escrow to provide for the trade of the California ranch, the buyer entered into a companion escrow wherein he was to acquire the California property. Each escrow was contingent on the simultaneous closing of the other. At the time of closing, the buyer acquired the California ranch and simultaneously traded it for the property in the original sale. In the end everyone was happy. The buyer was conveyed the property he wanted, and the seller was conveyed the ranch in California without incurring any taxable liability at the time of closing.

A TRADE AGREEMENT FORM TO USE IN DOCUMENTING A TRADE TRANSACTION

The standard form Trade Agreement as used by many traders was not complete enough to document adequately a trade transaction. In working with attorneys on various trades, we were able to come up with an exchange agreement that seemed to fit almost every situation. A copy of that agreement is shown below in its entirety.

AGREEMENT
FOR
EXCHANGE OF REAL PROPERTY

This agreement made and entered into this day of 19xx, by and between XYZ Corporation, an Arizona corporation, hereinafter sometimes referred to as "XYZ", and John Q. Public and Mary M. Public, his wife, hereinafter sometimes referred to as "Public".

W I T N E S S E T H

WHEREAS, XYZ owns certain parcels of real property in the county of Maricopa, State of Arizona, legally described as follows:
Lots 2, 7, 11, and 15 NORTHSIDE:

upon which has been constructed 24 apartments, which real property and improvements thereon and appurtenances thereto are subject to a mortgage in favor of Western Savings and Loan Association in the approximate amount of $140,000.00 and are hereinafter sometimes referred to as the "Apartments."

WHEREAS, Public owns a certain parcel of land legally described as Lot 23, GRANDVIEW upon which has been constructed an Office Building, which real property and improvements thereon and appurtenances thereto are subject to a mortgage in favor of First Federal Savings and Loan Association in the approximate amount of $275,000.00 and are hereinafter sometimes referred to as the "Building."

NOW THEREFORE, the parties mutually agree as follows:

1. EXCHANGE: XYZ shall deliver to Public a Warranty Deed to the Apartments warranting title to be free and clear of all liens and encumbrances except the aforementioned mortgage and current taxes. As an additional consideration XYZ shall pay to Public, in escrow, the sum of $55,000.00. Public shall deliver to XYZ a Warranty Deed to the Building warranting title to be free and clear of all liens and encumbrances except the aforementioned mortgage and current taxes.

   XYZ shall furnish Public with a Preliminary Title Report on the Apartments and Public shall furnish XYZ with a Preliminary Title Report on the Building within 15 days following the execution of this agreement. Any objections to the condition of title as disclosed by the Preliminary Title Reports issued on the respective properties must be in writing within 15 days after issuance or failing such objections, the conditions of title shall be deemed conclusively approved. In the event such objections are made and are not resolved within 15 days following the receipt thereof, this agreement shall terminate, each party to bear its own costs. Each party at its own expense shall furnish the other party with a title insurance policy on the property being conveyed insuring title subject only to the matters herein specified.
2. PRORATIONS: Items customarily prorated between the parties shall be prorated at the close of escrow.
3. ASSUMPTION OF EXISTING MORTGAGES: XYZ shall assume and agree to pay the mortgage on the Building in favor of First Federal Savings and Loan Association in the approximate amount of $275,000.00.

   Public shall asssume and agree to pay the mortgage on the Apartments in favor of Western Savings and Loan Association in the approximate amount of $140,000.00.

   Any variation in the amounts of mortgages assumed shall be adjusted in the cash payments at the close of escrow.
4. RENTS AND DEPOSITS: Each party will furnish the other party a statement of rents and deposits relative to their respective properties. Said rents and deposits shall be adjusted to the close of escrow.

5. BROKERAGE COMMISSIONS: XYZ agrees to pay a real estate commission to Weldon Girard Realty, 2920 North 7th Street, Phoenix, Arizona 85014 in the amount of $21,600.00 representing a 6% commission on the value of the Apartments as and for the consummation of this exchange of properties. Said commission shall be payable at the close of escrow. Public agrees to pay a real estate commission to Weldon Girard Realty, 2920 North 7th Street, Phoenix, Arizona 85014 in the amount of $33,000.00 representing a 6% commission on the value of the Buildings as and for the consummation of this exchange of properties. Said commission shall be payable at the close of escrow.
6. ESCROW: The parties agree to enter into escrows with Blank Title Insurance and Trust Company as Escrow Agent for the purpose of consummating this exchange of real properties. Said escrows shall be opened upon the execution of this agreement by the parties and shall close upon a date 30 days following the approval of the Preliminary Title Reports as shown in Paragraph 1 herein.

ACCEPTED and APPROVED:

____
John Q. Public

____
Mary M. Public

Date: ________________

XYZ Corporation
By ____________________
John Jones, PRESIDENT
Date: __________________

WELDON GIRARD REALTY

By ____________________
Weldon Girard, BROKER

Date: __________________

The foregoing Exchange Agreement form was not taken from any particular transaction, so figures used are only for the purposes of exhibit. By additions and deletions, the form can be adapted to fit any particular trade transaction.

KEY POINTS

1. Understand what can be traded
2. Realize the five important advantages in trading
3. Understand that trading can produce greater profit through the technique of trading "up"
4. Know the three basic requirements in a tax-free exchange

5. Learn how to use a trade as a down payment in a large transaction
6. Know how to dispose of undesirable property in a trade transaction
7. Understand why trading is sometimes necessary and how it can help you
8. Know how to bring in a third party in a purchase and trade transaction
9. Realize that in periods of tight money trading is possible
10. Know the answers to the four tight money questions
11. Learn how to trade unusual or difficult property
12. Understand the tax implications of trading and how the IRS looks at trading
13. Realize the importance and use of the special trade paragraph when a trade is contemplated
14. Know how to use the trade agreement form

Index